SAINT MARY OF EGYPT

An Icon Painter's Notebook:

The Bolshakov Edition

(An Anthology of Source Materials)

Translated and Edited by

Gregory Melnick

Originally Published in Slavonic under the title:
Iconographic Patternbook
by S.T. Bolshakov, 1903
Society of the Lovers of Spiritual Enlightenment
Moscow

Copyright © 1995
Oakwood Publications
3827 Bluff St.
Torrance, California 90505-6359

ISBN No. 1-879038-19-6

Typesetting: **Gregory Melnick**
                 Mary Ann Dibs
                 Orthodox Information Data Associates
Slavonic Type: **O.I.D.A.**
Cover: **Mary Ann Dibs**

Serge Bolshakov dedicated the original 1903 edition of the *Iconographic Patternbook* to the Emperor of Russia, Nicholas II. Since the Tsar was very interested in icons and spoke English very well, it is appropriate to dedicate the English translation to the king who will be known as the "Holy Orthodox Tsar Martyr Nicholas" to future iconographers. The inscription on his scroll says, "For a righteous and blameless man became a subject for mockery, for it had been ordained that he should fall under others at the appointed time, and that his house should be laid waste by the lawless. Job 12:4" (Septuagint) Photograph courtesy of Holy Trinity Russian Orthodox Monastery, Jordanville, NY.

—Gregory Melnick, translator.

TABLE OF CONTENTS

Dedication   iii

Foreword   ix

Publisher's Preface   x

Geneology   xi

Translator's Introduction   1

Glossary   7

Symbols and Abbreviations   13

✝ ✝ ✝ ✝ ✝ ✝ ✝ ✝ ✝ ✝

Start of Bolshakov text

From the Publisher, Serge Bolshakov   15

ANTHOLOGY

1	Description of Jesus Christ	18
	Description of the Most Holy Mother of God	
2	No Improper Murals to be Painted	18
3	Icons must be Painted according to the Rules	19
4	No Novelties may be Painted on Icons	20
5	Icons should be Painted according to the Ancient Prototypes	20
6	"The Seven Ages of Man"	21
7	Description of the Three Magi	22
8	Inscription on the Icon of the Protection	23
9	Description of Jesus Christ	23
	Description of the Most Holy Mother of God	
10	Description of Sts. Athanasius and Cyril	24
	Description of the Three Hierarchs	
	Description of St. Euthymius	
11	Description of the Icon of the Church of the Holy Sepulchre	25
12	Descriptions of the Prophets	26
13	Descriptions of the Holy Forefathers	26
14	Descriptions of the Prophets	27
15	Names of the Prophetesses	29
16	Description of the Most Holy Mother of God	29
17	The Crucifixion of Christ	30
18	Praises of the Cross	30
19	The Icon of the Divine Wisdom	32
20	The Icon of the Descent of the Holy Spirit	34

Section 21 The Icons on the Royal Doors   35
            The Icons on the Posts next to the Royal Doors
Section 22 Concerning the Veneration of Icons   35
Section 23 A Decree of the Council of the 100 Chapters on Iconographers   37
Section 24 From the *"Kormchaya Kniga"*   39
            Another Decree on Iconographers
            Another Decree on Iconographers
            Another Decree on Iconographers
            Icons are not to be Sold to Heretics
            No Icons on Glass
            No Prices on Icons
            Financial Support of Iconographers
Section 25 The Lettering on the Gospel Book of the Savior   44
            The Lettering on the Gospel Book of St. Nicholas
            The Lettering on the Halo of the Savior

✝ ✝ ✝ ✝ ✝ ✝ ✝ ✝ ✝ ✝

DESCRIPTIONS OF ICONS IN THE ORDER OF THE CHURCH YEAR

September   46
October   61
November   76
December   89
January   101
February   113
March   123
April   136
May   148
June   162
July   174
August   192

✝ ✝ ✝ ✝ ✝ ✝ ✝ ✝ ✝ ✝

APPENDIX

Set of 8 Drawings
1   The Ladder of Divine Ascent   206
2   Judas takes the money from the Sanhedrin   207
3   The Mystical Supper   208
4   Jesus before Pilate   209
5   Jesus before Herod   210
6   Pilate washes his hands   211
7   Simon of Cyrene carries Christ's cross   212
8   Joseph asking for the Body of Christ   213

Set of 23 Drawings

1   Three saints   215
2   Scene from St. Elias' Life: the priests of Baal pray   216
3   Scene from St. Elias' Life: Elias kills the priests of Baal   217
4   Scene from St. Elias' Life: Elias prays to God   218
5   Exile to Babylon   219
6   Scene from Genesis: The Creation of Light   220
7   Scene from Genesis: Noah summons the animals   221
8   Scene from Genesis: The Angel leads Lot away from Sodom   222
9   Scene from Genesis: Sara sends away Hagar   223
10   Scene from Genesis: Creation of animals   224
11   Scene from Gospel: Paralytic let down through roof   225
12   Scene from Genesis: Sarah and Abraham prepare food for the three young men   226
13   Scene from Matthew: two demoniacs at Gadara   227
14   Scene from Gospel: Jesus cures cripple   228
15   Scene from Luke: The Prodigal Son   229
16   Scene from Genesis: Adam and Eve bury Abel   230
17   Scene from John: Jesus heals the Blind man   231
18   Scene from Gospel: Jesus heals the man with palsy   232
19   Scene from Luke: Jesus raise the Widow's son   233
20   Scene from John: Jesus cures the man born blind   234
21   Scene from John: The wedding at Cana   235
22   Scene from Luke: Jesus raises the daughter of Jaoirus   236
23   Jesus calms the storm   237

End of Bolshakov complete text   238

Plates: A LA VIELLE RUSSIE CALENDAR ICONS   240

Bibliography   243

Index   245

FOREWORD

Another valuable resource from OAKWOOD PUBLICATIONS is the publication of *The Icon Painter's Notebook: The Bolshakov Edition (An Anothology of Source Material)*, commonly referred to as the "Bolshakov Patternbook" (after the late nineteenth-century editor who published a collection of ancient Russian patternbooks), which augments and suppplements the "Stroganov Patternbook," (published by Oakwood in 1992) and likewise serves as an invaluable resource book for both the iconographer's studio and the scholar's library.

The "Bolshakov Patternbook" is itself an anthology and compilation of material from many patternbooks and other references available at the time (from the 16th-17th centuries and earlier), much of which would have been lost to the modern scholar and painter, had it not been for this collection. The Anthology is a type of "hermeneia," as is the earlier Byzantine edition of *The Painter's Manual of Dionysius of Fourna* (Oakwood, 1990), but much more complete in its calendar of saints. With extended literary descriptions, it is the perfect mate to the Stroganov, which is largely pictorial. And with convenient page numbers providing cross-references to the Stroganov, it is remarkably (almost perfectly) consistent with the latter, but includes many additional saints. Just as a festal liturgical hymn defines and describes its corresponding icon of the feast, the Bolshakov Anthology describes the sketches in the Stroganov Podlinnik, but offers many more details and descriptions which fill in missing gaps of information in the headnotes to the sketches (such as text of scrolls), never before available in English. The wealth of new material takes away a lot of the "guesswork" in painting icons. The Anthology includes a helpful glossary of terms, especially those concerning colors and items of liturgical vestments.

This latest publication will answer many questions posed by those practicing the art of icon-painting, and should stimulate new questions from those studying icon history and development. Significantly, the translator is also a much accomplished writer of icons himself, and thus is quite sensitive to the practical needs of those who paint the holy images; his notes often explain technical or obscure (or even missing) references in the text. Gregory Melnick is more than adequately trained in iconography and theology to undertake and successfully complete such an ambitious task as this. As a dedicated master of Slavonic, iconography, and theology, he has provided us with a painter's manual "par excellence."

Dennis G. Bell, President
St. John of Damascus Iconographers Association

PUBLISHER'S PREFACE

Continuing its mission of making known the classics of traditional iconography and icon theology, Oakwood Publications is pleased to offer this Bolshakov Edition: An Anthology of Source Materials. This book offers much in the way of authentic and inspiring information, designed to enlighten any level of learner or practitioner, as well as the faithful who wish to read it for edification and personal understanding. Most especially, we hope this Edition enlightens the novice and journeyperson to understand the context of the saints and events depicted. This Edition brings to bear information from many ancient sources.

This Edition's translator, Reader Gregory Melnick, is himself an iconographer (since 1961) and a student of Orthodoxy and the pillars of Orthodox Tradition. Icons painted by him are found in many churches. Mr. Melnick is not only a worthy translator, but his interpretive and explanatory notes add significantly and fill in gaps left by Bolshakov. Melnick has added the proper year of commemoration of most of the saints not found in the original. He is a graduate of St. Basil's College Seminary and received his Master of Sacred Theology from the University of Innsbruck (Austria). A convert to the Orthodox faith in 1962, he is also actively involved with the Orthodox Christian Education Commission and with 'Tradition Today' a cable TV Orthodox outreach series in upstate New York.

We have included on the following page the Bibliographic Geneology written for our companion volume, *An Iconographer's Patternbook: The Stroganov Tradition* (Fr. Christopher Kelley), since it incorporated the development of these particular patternbooks. As noted there, Bolshakov included an almost-complete copy of the Stroganov Patternbook in his Edition, although copied in a much less detailed manner than the original 1869 Patternbook from which our edition was taken. Accordingly, we have not duplicated it again here.

Much of Bolshakov's Church Calendar and Anthology sections have never appeared in English before. The translation of scrolls carried by many saints adds to the wealth of information not previously available. With well over 1,000 entries in the Calendar section alone, much never-before available information is included. The Anthology section contains not merely historical data, but information valuable for all those interested in applying traditional rules of icon painting to their contemporary work and understanding and faith. Hopefully this work does advance our personal mission of providing important information about authentic iconography, as well as in the publishing of significant works about Orthodox spirituality, personalities, unavailable elsewhere.

Thanks also to friends who provided encouragement and help in various aspects of this translation: Karyl Knee who located library copies of the Edition and other patternbooks; Elena Silk, Librarian of St. Vladimir's Orthodox Theological Seminary Library for the comparison copy of a Bolshakov original; and to Fr. Basil Parent, Fr. Christopher Kelley, Charles Kovacs, John Barns, Dennis Bell, Mary Ann Dibs and others for their assistance.

Philip Tamoush
Publisher

BIBLIOGRAPHIC GENEALOGY

of the

S T R O G A N O V   P O D L I N N I K

THE STROGANOV PODLINNIK, the original studio manuscript, now lost.
Original Manuscript drawn by several hands, late 1500s;
several additional notations over the centuries.

"ZAGORSK CALENDAR"
12 Painted Panels

A La Vieille Russie Calendar
Icons (16th century)

СТРОГАНОВСКІЙ ИКОНОПИСНЫЙ ЛИЦЕВОЙ ПОДЛИННИКЪ:
Facsimile lithographed in Moscow, 1869, in two tones, from Museum copy,
by the Moscow Theological Academy Press,
from a copy missing 5 pages (10 drawings):
under the direction of Archpriest Philaret Sergievsky.

IKONENMALERHANDBUCH der FAMILIE STROGANOW
The Same reproduced in Munich, 1965, in black and white,
by the Slavisches Institut, Günzerburg (Donau),
with translation of saints' names (usually accurately).
Notice taken of some, but not all, missing pages.

ICONPAINTERS HANDBOOK of the Stroganov School of Iconpainting
German Ed. reproduced in Willits, CA, c. 1973?, from xerox,
by Eastern Orthodox Books, two pages together on one,
with translation of German Preface and saints' names
from the German edition, some left incorrect; a few
efforts at answering textual questions.

Sergei T. Bolshakov's *PODLINNIK*, Moscow, 1903, for Church Archaeological
(=Historical) Dept, Soc. of Lovers of Spiritual Englihtenment
A.N. Uspensky, editor, A.I. Snegirevoy & Co., printers
228 plates, 189 pages of text: black and white:
a redrawn copy of original Stroganov, somewhat crude,
often backwards; headnotes hasty and less complete;
includes two of the ten drawings missing from 1869 edition,
+ a (composite?) written Podlinnik independent of
Stroganov, including many more saints, and lengthy
descriptions of some saints and festal scenes, and
texts to be put on saints' scrolls in many instances.

Oakwood Edition (Melnick) 1994

Oakwood Edition (Kelley), 1991
Torrance, California

TRANSLATOR'S INTRODUCTION

An Icon Painter's Notebook: The Bolshakov Edition is the companion to *An Iconographer's Patternbook: The Stroganov Tradition* published by Oakwood Publications. These together are included in the complete *The Iconographic Patternbook* published in Moscow in 1903 by S. T. Bolshakov and edited by A. I. Uspensky from which this current translation is taken. While *An Iconographer's Patternbook* is a book of illustrations with very little text, *An Icon Painter' Notebook* is a book of narrative descriptions of icons, which will be most useful when used with the Oakwood edition of *The Stroganov Tradition,* which page numbers facing the illustrations have been added here in italics (as *"S. 123,"* for example). Both books can help an iconographer to produce an authentic icon of a saint whose "likeness" is otherwise not available. In this way new icons can be painted "according to the prototypes" in the words of writers long ago. Both books compliment and complete each other. At the same time each book is an independent witness to the Orthodox tradition of iconography. Many of the icons described in this present book are illustrated in *The Stroganov Tradition* but one should not look for contradictions among parallel traditions, or judge legitimate variations "un-Orthodox." Three hundred years ago the figurative patternbooks or drawing collections were used to produce sets of twelve calendar icons; while the books of narrative descriptions were probably used to make sets of "weekly" icons and altar screens, both the large church iconostases and portable ones. The original compilers of this volume included miscellaneous information as an "Anthology." Please refer to the Glossary for more information on patternbooks.

The original 1903 *Iconographic Patternbook* was published with the permission of the Ecclesiastical-Archaeological Department of the Society of the Lovers of Spiritual Enlightenment, whose president, Archpriest N. Izeyekov, was also the theological censor of the Society's publications. Except for the section republished as *An Iconographer's Patternbook: The Stroganov Tradition,* this present *Icon Painter's Notebook* contains the entire text of the 1903 edition. This edition also contains a sample of the remarkable "A La Vieille Russie" Calendar Icons. Additional drawings from the 1903 *Iconographic Patternbook* are in the Appendix. All of the words, dates, and comments in brackets, the notes, the color plates, glossary and index have been added to make this edition more accessible than the original edition. A few descriptions of saints have been transferred to the dates where they are found on contemporary church calendars, or to assemble all the data on one saint within one entry. The Index should locate those saints who were assigned to another day in the manuscript tradition.

The text is divided into two very unequal parts: the "Anthology" of materials from various sources; and the calendar descriptions for the twelve months. The latest text in the "Anthology" is dated 1690. The main body of the text is divided into the twelve months of the ecclesiastical year which begins with September. The latest saint entered appears to be St. Damian, also known as St. Diodorus of George Hill, who died in 1633 and was honored as a saint locally in the very northernmost part of Russia. Although it seems he was never formally or officially glorified, he is found in complete Russian church calendars on November 27.

The word "anthology" translates the words *"kniga sobornik"* in Slavonic, the language of the *Iconographic Patternbook* edited by A. I. Uspensky. The 1903 edition does not give any information on the origins or sources of this "Anthology" and so it is not known whether it was copied intact from one manuscript, edited from several manuscripts, or compiled by the editor A. I. Uspensky himself. In any case the excerpts will be treated as selections from the anonymous collections of canon law, pious practices, icon painters' lore and miscellaneous information current in Russia at the time the original patternbook was being compiled. The "Notes" following some of the sections were compiled from standard reference books and literature. According to the scholar George Fedotov:

> The *Isborniki* or collections of short "articles" and excerpts of various content, constituted at all times a favorite reading of ancient Russia. Satisfying the practical religious needs of the readers, they served more for edification than for theoretical knowledge. Their content was not fixed; their authorship uncertain. Most of the articles were ascribed to great church fathers—John Chrysostom, Basil, Gregory, and others. In many cases these venerable names were but a covering for unknown Slavic or Russian compilers. The delimitation of Greek, Slavonic (Old Bulgarian or Moravian), and Russian contributions is a difficult, though very important, task. Only in rare cases can the Greek originals be determined. As a rule, even this part belongs either to the anonymous or to the *spuria* department of the Patrology. Very often this literature was inspired by the great authors or represented popular restatements of their work. The exposition is usually sustained at such a low level that it is impossible to distinguish Greek translations from Russian originals by their contents, especially if the third element, the Old Bulgarian, is a possible source. After a century of philological research very little progress has been made in the distinction between Greek, Bulgarian, and Russian contributions within this anonymous literature.[1]

It is possible some of the selections are from the *Domostroy* written by Archpriest Sylvester, the advisor and educator of Tsar Ivan the Terrible, one of the most representative and widely read books in Russia at the time the patternbooks were compiled. According to descriptions of this work in popular literature, the *Domostroy* contains extensive details on every aspect of everyday life, exactly like   some of the excerpts in this Anthology.[2] Intrepid scholars can research the original texts in Archangelski, *(The Works of the Church Fathers in Ancient Russian Writing: Extracts from Manuscripts and Essays in Historical-Literary Studies)* 4 vols., Kazan, 1889 - 1890 [in Russian] and A. I. Ponomarev, ed., *(Monuments of Ancient Russian Ecclesiastical Literature)*, 4 vols., St. Petersburg, 1894 - 1898 [in Russian].[3]

The Anthology, as well as the rest of the book, assumes an Orthodox context; that is, the writers assumed their readers would be serious Orthodox Christians. The beginning of the seventeenth century was a time of troubles in Russia, an Orthodox society. The Russians considered the Renaissance in Europe a rebirth of paganism; influences from the Protestant Reformation and Catholic Counter-reformation nothing but threats to the Orthodox Faith. The literature of the time was not written to convert non-Orthodox, but was intended to explain the Orthodox Faith to those living within an Orthodox culture besieged by western, non-Orthodox (and therefore heretical) ideas and life style. The principle underlying the Anthology is that the Orthodox Church is the True Church which will last until the end of time according to our Savior's promise in the Gospel despite the turmoil of history and the weakness of individuals. Nothing has been deleted from *The Iconographic Patternbook*. Some will be stunned by the content of a few of the selections; others will discover they have not been faithful to the teachings of the Church by permitting non-Orthodox paintings instead of traditional icons in their churches. Since the selections were addressed to Orthodox Christians being tempted to betray their Faith, no one should be offended personally by the passages which do not compromise the unchanging teaching of the Church about herself in the Creed, "I believe in One, Holy, Catholic and Apostolic Church."

The 1903 "Publisher's Forward," says the text was transcribed and combined from several different sources without mentioning that most of the work was done in the seventeenth century. Thus, there is inconsistent terminology and ambiguity since the same words can have different meanings in the Russian and Church Slavonic languages. Actually the language used is similar to the captions in *An Iconographer's Patternbook: The Stroganov Tradition*. It is the shorthand of a person writing notes for his own use, in his own words, using the framework of the Orthodox Church's *Typicon*. The original manuscripts were personal aids to memory. The text of the book is written partly in the solemn language of a liturgical book and partly like telegrams describing specific icons the writers had before them. It seems that the 1903 *Iconographic Patternbook* is not quoted in popular literature on icons because it is so hard to use. There are no references, footnotes, explanations, definitions or captions on the original drawings to aid the reader. When published, the Bolshakov *Iconographic Patternbook* must have been exceedingly difficult for Russian iconographers to use because of its intentionally archaic typeface, the abundance of obscure and obsolete technical terms; unfamiliar abbreviations, numerals, spellings and misspellings; verbosity, run-on sentences, proper names spelled without capital letters, and the countless idiosyncrasies of several different manuscripts combined. All of these difficulties have been kept to a minimum in this translation. A few words have been added for English usage and flow. For all its complexity, this text is a valuable resource precisely because of its variety of sources and descriptions. In the calendar section alone, there are over 1,200 descriptions of saints and feast days compared to the approximately 700 figurative descriptions in *An Iconographer's Patternbook*.

In the practical sphere there are some limitations of English usage that made a few of the phrases in *An Icon Painter's Notebook* translation obscure, and not always because the original was ambiguous. This does not matter to the practicing iconographer because the meaning and content have been preserved. For example, when the text says, "a green cloak with white" or "a green with white tunic," this is to be understood as follows: there is a green (or any other color) garment, on which lines are drawn in a dark shade of green, perhaps mixed with black or umber, and then the garment is lightened with a mixture of the same green and white, and again with a lighter shade; and finally with pure white highlights. Some iconographers do not mix colors at all, but apply thinly diluted colors that are transparent, even black and white, so that the basic color always shows through successive layers. Either way the painting has perceptible "terraces;" the shades are not blended into each other. Scarlet garments are often lightened with ocher, so the robe is painted in the same manner, but using ocher instead of white. And so any color is lightened with the prescribed color in the text. Sometimes there are colors listed after each other, "greenish brown, reddish brown, purple." This means that different areas of one garment have different base colors; perhaps greenish brown on the folds about the waist, reddish brown on the thigh going into purple at the lower hem and towards the shoulders. The reader's personal study of classic icons will clarify the meaning of the text.

The icon patternbooks are witnesses to the Orthodox Tradition, even if the books all vary in details from each other. Perhaps the writers and illustrators in seventeenth century Russia were aware their era was coming to an end (as, in fact, it did) and they had to preserve the tradition as they knew it as best as they could from the onslaught of the Renaissance, Reformation and westernization. The following is a personal insight having worked on the translation of *An Icon Painter's Notebook* and thus having been immersed in the original words in Slavonic. It is very difficult to relate the thoughts that passed through my mind at different times, not because of language as such, but because the ideas expressed created mental pictures rather than words. On the surface, many of the descriptions in the *Notebook* seem the same and some of them are identical. But while translating, one must ponder and consider every word and its meaning. And after reading and rereading the same passages again, there comes an understanding of the mind of the author that can not be expressed in words. Knowing what I know now after several years of study of this text, I would never attempt to take this book, read the description of a particular saint and then expect to paint an icon on the basis of that description without knowing the totality of this *Notebook* and *The Patternbook*. Therefore I recommend that iconographers do not consider this book as a reference volume to be used only in time of need, but as a book to be read as a part of one's devotions and preparation for painting other icons. It is for this reason that I tried to make the text as readable as possible. Knowledge of the underlying logic and familiarity with *The Bolshakov Edition* will make *The Stroganov Tradition* illustrations come to life. The terse and laconic descriptions will suddenly be full of meaning, independent of the language and vocabulary. The rigidity of the line drawings will melt into flowing graceful images. The clutter of conflicting traditions of colors and details will vanish. Icons based on these patternbooks then will not be obviously dependent on the words and drawings, but will reflect their heavenly prototypes, and thus be genuine icons. Therefore, it is essential that a true iconographer be devout because painting icons is a spiritual and liturgical activity assuming a life style of prayer and fasting.

A translation always strives to give the reader the content and intent of the original. Everyone must always remember the warning of the humble and prudent Priest John, a copyist or editor of the original text sometime after the year 1630, who inserted this comment after the month of May: "It is necessary for iconographers to distinguish and find out for certain what is genuine among these accounts and other sources, and what is true in the lives of the saints, and to ask good, skillful and knowledgeable people, who are artist painters and readers of books, so that it [the iconographers' work] will be without error [literally "sin"], because I, the sinful Priest John, discovered that the patternbooks together with the "Lives of the Saints," *The Prologue, The Monthly Reader* and the "Kievan printed pages" do not agree in many passages, and for this reason one ought to do research in them with great discretion."

I thank my brother Raymond Melnick for making it possible for me to complete this *Icon Painter's Notebook* with the convenience of a personal computer; Mrs. Susan Price and the reference desk staff at Syracuse University Library; the Fathers of Holy Trinity Monastery in Jordanville, New York for their patience. But without the interest and constant encouragement by Philip Tamoush, to whom special thanks is due, the translation of an important traditional text of iconography would never have been completed.

Gregory Melnick
Syracuse, New York
June, 1994.

GLOSSARY

The Glossary was placed near the beginning of the book to help avoid any confusion that might be caused by a few conventions that had to be retained in this translation in order to be faithful to the original text. The entries are intended to clarify some special usages and to help the reader visualize the original icons the original authors were describing. There are alternative translations for many of the Slavonic words transliterated into italics within quotation marks. In the seventeenth century the iconographer's palette was limited. Some of what are considered common pigments often were not available at all three hundred years ago. For this reason the translator chose common words for colors or pigments which are widely available so that an icon painter can buy or mix the prescribed colors as seems best. In this way one will stay within the guidelines of the Orthodox tradition and at the same time avoid rare or toxic pigments. The saints who are named as models in the text may be found in *An Iconographer's Patternbook*, the "A La Vieille Russie" Calendar Icon, or various books of Orthodox icons. *The Icon: Image of the Invisible* by Egon Sendler, S.J., translated by Fr. Steven Bigham, published by Oakwood Publications (1988) is recommended to those readers and iconographers who need more detailed information on specific topics.

Abyss—A black crevasse or cave in an icon that may denote a hole in the ground or the underworld; i.e., hell or Hades.

Anna—This saint is a model for a saint who is an old woman.

Apostles' robes—the technical term for the cloak (which appears more like a toga) and the tunic as worn by the Savior and the Apostles. Their tunics very often have a golden ornamental stripe on the right shoulder down to the right ankle which distinguishes it from a martyr's tunic. One should remember that the Seventy-two Disciples are called "Apostles" in Orthodox texts. Almost always the Disciples are distinguished from the Twelve Apostles by the omophorion prescribed to be worn on their shoulders.

Basil of Caesarea—or St. Basil the Great, is a model for his hair and beard.

Bishops' cap—This is not the high bulging miter of modern times, but a flat topped cloth hat with several sections sometimes ornamented with small icons. At times it is a triangular hat.

Blaise—This saint typifies a middle aged man with the hair and beard one expects to see in an icon. His beard is the average, and other beards are longer or shorter; wider or narrower as specified.

Blessed—Translates *"blazheny"* which generally denotes a saint who is not assigned to a certain category, e.g. "martyr." Thus in the Slavonic church books "Saint" Olga is literally "Blessed" Olga, but this does not diminish her sainthood in any way. (The term should not be confused with a stage of the canonization procedure in the Roman Catholic church.) More often it is the title for a "fool for Christ's sake," i.e., the saint feigned insanity and literally lived the words of the Gospel ignoring the opinions and sensitivities of society around him.

Blue—Translates *"lazor,"* an indigo dye corresponding perhaps to the dark blue color of denim material.

Brocade—Translates *"kamka,"* the silk material with floral designs.

Brown hair—Translates *"rus,"* which means "fair" as opposed to "black." It describes young men with hair that appears to be a brown color, perhaps umber that is lightened with a reddish color such as burnt sienna or mars yellow. Certain saints are described as having "red" hair or a "red" beard; some others as having light or bright brown hair.

Cloak—Translates *"verkhaya riza."* This outer or upper garment has various forms depending on the life circumstances of a saint. It can resemble a toga, but it also can be a cape, especially as "martyrs' robes". The same word is used for a priest's or bishop's phelonion as well as a monastic mantle. The material piled up on a deacon's shoulder over the orarion is a cloak.

Confessor—A person who witnesses for Christ but is not killed.

Cosmas—This saint is a model for a young man distinguished by his thin, straggling beard and hair. He is generally in martyrs' robes.

Crimson—Translates *"bakan"* and might correspond to the modern alizarin crimson pigment.

Cross patterned—Describes the "polystaurion" or "many crosses" pattern (which may include circles, squares or angles) and is reserved to bishops. It may be painted on either a saccos or cloak.

Dark gray—Translates *"reft"* and might correspond to the modern payne's gray, which is a mixture of ultramarine blue, black and yellow ocher.

Demetrius—This saint is a model for a young man who is clean shaven but with hair sort of wavy and parted. Generally depicted as a soldier.

Elizabeth—This saint is a model for a saint who is an old woman.

Eudokia—This saint is a model for a saint who is a nun.

Field—This refers to one of several areas or separate "scenes" in an icon; it is not necessarily separated by lines. Sometimes the fields or scenes overlap or "flow into one another."

Florus—This saint is a model for a young man with a shaggy beard and curly hair that does not go down much below his ears. He is generally in martyr's robes.

Fountains—The alternating three sets of white red white stripes found on bishops' mantles. Some writers call them "rivers."

Gospel—The book held by many saints usually in the left hand.

Gregory the Theologian—This saint is marked by his hair and beard.

Green—Translates *"prazelen"* and might be "terre verte," which can be approximated by a mixture of ultramarine blue and yellow ocher.

Greenish brown—Translates *"sankir,"* the mixture used for the basic flesh tone.

Hieromartyr—A martyr who is ordained, usually a bishop.

Highlights—Sometimes a red garment is lightened with light blue instead of red mixed with white, etc.

Holy—Used somewhere before a proper name is equal to "saint."

John the Theologian—This saint is marked by his hair and beard.

Kamilavka—The high monastic head covering that does not conform to the curve of the skull.

"Kievan printed pages"—Perhaps this is another name for the "Sophian" patternbook mentioned in S. Bolshakov's Introduction..

Klobuk—The soft round monastic headgear with two strips of cloth coming down the shoulders. Not to be confused with the schema worn on the head, which is pointed. Some bishop saints have white klobuks.

Light blue—Translates the color called *"golubets,"* or "little dove."

Light gray—Translates *"dimchat"* or "smoky colored."

Martyrs' robes—The technical term for the tunic and cloak worn by the holy martyrs. Many martyrs wear a short or half tunic over the long tunic. The tunic worn with a breastplate is always a short tunic. The cloak is usually not worn like a toga.

Monastic robes—The technical term for the cloak and tunic worn by monastic saints as the cassock and mantle, which in iconography usually are not black as in earthly life. In the text "schema" is specified in additional to these garments. See "schema."

Monastic saint—Translates *"prepodobny,"* which literally means "most like [the ideal, Christ]", and which can refer to any holy person as a saint in general. More specifically it denotes a monk or nun saint. In this book it is translated also by the phrase "our holy father or mother . . . in monastic robes." It can be used together with "martyr."

Mountains—The technical term for the fanciful landscape of hills and rugged te rain in icons and may have unusual trees, caves, ravines, crevices, etc.

Nicholas—This saint, the Miracle Worker of Myra in Lycia, is distinguished by his hair and beard.

Ocher—Translates *"vokhra,"* a dull, earthy yellow pigment corresponding to the modern pigment.

Omophorion—The "Y" shaped vestment reserved to bishops worn over the shoulders and hangs down in the front and back. In icons it is always white with three crosses, and perhaps three dots and horizontal stripes, unless specified otherwise, as in the icon of the Protection of the Mother of God, October 1.

Palaces—The technical term for the fanciful exteriors of buildings before which events occur in iconography. They may be adorned with drapes, grills, canopies, etc.

Parasceva—this saint is a model for a saint who is a young woman.

Patternbook—Translates the Slavonic word *"podlinnik"* and the Greek word *"hermeneia."* These are the traditional and anonymous iconographers' guides and handbooks. They are of two types: representational or figurative, that is, drawings of icons, (e.g. *An Iconographer's Patternbook: The Stroganov Tradition)*; or prose descriptions of icons, recipes for artist materials, directions or procedures to execute an icon or decorate a church, and miscellaneous information. The Slavonic text of this *Icon Painter's Notebook* was compiled from translations into Slavonic from the Greek combined with traditional Slavonic material in the seventeenth century. Like the icons, nothing is signed; no sources are given. The patternbooks are rarely referred to in the literature about icons, but they solve many problems about the consistency and integrity of Orthodox iconography. More information about patternbooks may be found in the "Introduction" to *The 'Painter's Manual' of Dionysius of Fourna,* translated by Paul Hetherington, printed and distributed by Oakwood Publications.

"Pecherska Lavra"—"The Monastery of the Caves" was founded by Saints Theodosius and Anthony in the eleventh century in Kiev, Ukraine. At that time the brotherhood dug out and lived in caves in the ground in a hill ove looking the Dnieper River. The monks were very famous for their sanctity, of whom 118 were canonized and many of the saints' relics are incorrupt.

Phelonion—The cloak worn like a poncho by priests and bishops.

Prologue, the printed—A large collection of lives of the saints, spiritual readings, sermons, points for meditation, etc. in the order of the days of the month that is prescribed by the *Typicon* to be read after the sixth ode during the canon at matins in two large volumes in the Church Slavonic language. It is not the same as *The Prologue from Ochrid* by Bishop Nicholas Velimirovic, a very valuable work which makes the essence of these massive tomes available in English.

Purple—Translates *"bagor"* which in the translator's opinion is more reddish like "maroon" than bluish like "violet."

Red—Translates *"krasen,"* generic "red." The word sometimes means "beautiful." Thus a robe can be understood as "reddish purple" or "beautiful purple."

Saccos—The bishops' vestment that resembles the deacons' sticharion or "dalmatic."

Scarlet—Translates *"kinovar"* and looks like cadmium red light.

Schema—The technical term in this book for specific monastic garments in addition to the tunic and cloak, that is, the cassock and mantle as depicted in icons. They are usually dark blue, gray or green and are sometimes specified to be depicted either only "on the shoulders," or on the shoulders and "on the head" like a cowl, in addition to the garment resembling a priest's stole down the front of the body. They are often embroidered with crosses, the lance and spear, and with some initial letters, e.g. IC XC NIKA. Very often they are trimmed with bright red piping. These garments are distinguished from the other "monastic robes" because a saint may not have received the "schema" during his or her earthly life.

Spiritual father—This expression was chosen to translate *"staretz,"* which literally means "elder," because in the text the word *"starets"* is often used together with the word "young." The ancient writers used this term for a "monk" (who may or may not be a saint) when he is depicted in an iconographic scene depicting the translation of relics of saints, for example.

Sticharion—The tunic as the under vestment worn by all clerical saints but is the major vestment of deacons. Deacon saints sometimes have another tunic under this vestment, and cloaks which appear as folds of material on top of their orarions on the left shoulder.

Synaxis—Translates *"sobor,"* the technical term for the liturgical commemoration honoring one or more of the persons included in a feast day or the holy angels. For example, the "Synaxis of the Mother of God" gives special honor to the Theotokos on the day after Christmas. The word literally means "assembly" or "meeting" and can also mean a synod of bishops or a cathedral church building.

Reddish brown—Translates *"dich"* and might correspond to burnt sienna.

Theologian—Unless specifically St. John the Theologian, this refers to St. Gregory the Theologian; see "Gregory."

Tunic—Translates *"ispod,"* a long garment that extends literally from the feet up to the throat and to the wrists. It may be any color. Depending on the category of saint it may be understood as a cassock, a sticharion, a long shirt, etc. Bishops' tunics very often have contrasting colored stripes running up from the bottom hem to the shoulder. It may also be a "middle garment" or translated as "short tunic". It is understood that saints wearing a breastplate wear a short tunic.

Typicon—The Orthodox liturgical book attributed to St. Sabbas the Sanctified which has directions for church services and the Orthodox life style, such as when to fast. It gives detailed instructions for monastic people and monasteries, but also the rules for lay people and parish churches or cathedrals. The *Typicon* has sections which might be called a perpetual almanac to determine the celebration of Pascha, detailed directions for the correct combination of services that fall on the same day, and the general calendar notations such as the number of hours in a day. The Mount Angel Abbey manuscript preserves the symbols distinguishing the rank in importance of feast days as they are found in the *Typicon*.

White—Translates *"belila."*

Year from creation—Until the time of Tsar Peter the Great Russian religious writers used the traditional number for their current year, that is, the number of years since God created the universe in 5508 B.C. The year of the Lord (A.D.) can be calculated by subtracting 5,508 from the year from creation, keeping in mind the Orthodox church year starts with September.

Yellow—is called "ocher", a dull earthy color, to avoid confusion with the bright color that comes to mind. When "yellow" is used in this text it means "bright yellow."

SYMBOLS AND ABBREVIATIONS

+   Read "died peacefully in" or "suffered martyrdom."

[ ]   Brackets enclose information inserted into *An Icon Painter's Notebook* text by the translator.

B.C.   Before Christ; all other dates are A.D., after Christ, the Christian era. "Year of creation" dates will have B.C.. or A.D. equivalents in brackets.

c.   Latin *circa*, read "about the year . . ."

MA   Followed by a number refers to the page number in the Mount Angel Abbey manuscript of a similar text.

NKJV   New King James Version of the Bible.

PG   The *Cursus Completus Patrologiae - Series Græca* of J. P. Migne, 1844 – 1866, Paris.

S.   Followed by a number refers to the page number opposite the illustrations in *An Iconographer's Patternbook: The Stroganov Tradition*, translated and edited by Fr. Christopher P. Kelley, by Oakwood Publications, 1992.

---

[1] Fedotov, George P. *The Russian Religious Mind: Kievan Christianity,* Harvard University Press, Cambridge, Massachusetts, 1947, page 203.

[2] See Sazonova, Yu. *Istoria russkoy literatury,* II, New York, Chekov Publishing House, 1955. (Compiled from Payne, Pierre Robert Stephen. *Ivan the Terrible,* Thomas Y. Crowell Co., New York, 1975.)

[3] Fedotov, George P. *The Russian Religious Mind, The Middle Ages, The Thirteenth to the Fifteenth Centuries,* Vol. II, Harvard University Press, Cambridge, Massachusetts, 1956, page 39.

Start of Golshakov Edition
Complete Text

FROM THE PUBLISHER, SERGE BOLSHAKOV

The taking of Russian iconography by His Majesty the Emperor under His Sovereign protection inspires a sincere feeling of gratitude toward His Imperial Majesty, who is concerned about everything precious in the legacy of sacred Russian antiquity and old-Russian art. We all hope to see a return of contemporary Russian iconography to the ancient, sanctified past along these traditional lines. It is for this reason that we dedicate this edition to His Majesty [Tsar Nicholas II of Russia] for the fatherly concern of His Imperial Majesty about the poor state of our iconography, which for us is a most memorable and important reason.

The purpose of our edition is to acquaint people with the patternbooks from our collection, not merely those who are interested in art, but first of all to satisfy the requests of our iconographers, who so often have turned to us for these indispensable iconographic patternbooks. The realization that the "Sophian," [1] "Summary" [2] and "Stroganov" [3] patternbooks are so very hard to buy made us even more aware of the need to republish them.

The figurative patternbook of our collection offers a new index of the "Stroganov," with some features distinguishing it from the previously published version plus an additional special section at the end with illustrations of murals. If anyone should compare one patternbook with the other, he will find that the content varies from those that are already published. The compiler of this our second patternbook without a doubt made use of the listings, such as the "Sophian" edition, especially the editor of the "Summary."

My most sincere and heartfelt appreciation is extended to A. I. Uspensky for aiding me in this edition, as well as to R. R. Shimanovsky (who prepared all of the drawings for printing except for the set of eight drawings revised by Diod. A. Shilov) and D. A. Shilov. [4]

Serge Bolshakov

Moscow, the year from Creation 7411 [1903] the 4th day of January.

NOTES

Tsar Nicholas was very interested in Russian history and culture, and he personally encouraged the renewed interest in old Russian style architecture, arts and crafts, all of which blossomed during his reign.

Подлинникъ

иконописный.

изданіе С. Т. Большакова,

подъ редакціей

А. И. Успенскаго.

МОСКВА.
1903 г.

ANTHOLOGY

ANTHOLOGY

Section 1

From a sermon for the Monday of the second week of the fast, page 250, a description of the divine Person, and of the perfect development of the physical body of our Lord, God and Savior Jesus Christ:

His height and other details of His appearance have been handed down by eyewitnesses from the beginning. The God-Man is three cubits tall, a little stooped, which reveals His humility, has clear eyes, a straight nose, a full head of light brown hair, but a black beard, and the fingers of His most pure hand are proportionately long, and there is a simplicity about Him resembling the woman who bore Him, and from whom He received physical life, and was made perfectly human.

From the same book, page 236, a description of the most pure Virgin Mary, the Mother of God:

She is of average height having the same poise as the One Whom she bore. A holy face, a little round, a bright forehead, a long straight nose, and a smooth complexion. The eyes are very clear, but black and well-colored pupils, like her eyebrows, a perfectly chaste mouth blushing with a reddish beauty, and the fingers of the God-bearing hands are slim, long, and tapering. Her gracious and radiant head is adorned with beautiful light brown hair.

NOTES

This anonymous passage is very similar to the text attributed to St. Germanus of Constantinople given in *The "Painter's Manual" of Dionysius of Fourna*, page 87, sections #523 and #524. It is also similar to the passages quoted by the fourteenth century writer Nicephorus Callistus in his *Hist. eccle. lib. II, cap. 23* from the work of the eighth century Monk Epiphanius.[5]

Section 2

From the book of the monastic St. Matthew of Jerusalem, volume 7, chapter 2, page 112, "Passions Excited by Paintings Kill the Soul:"

The one hundredth rule of the sixth council about painting explains that there is no place on the walls for paintings that excite the passions, or anything that impresses the sight with a sensuous feeling, or anything which should not be seen or heard at all, for that matter. The soul will believe what enters it. For this reason allow your eyes to see only the proper things that should be seen, as the Most Merciful One says, and one should take every means to protect one's heart [from evil].

NOTES

The Slavonic text appears to be a very close translation of the passage "Initial Letter Z[6]" chapter II, *Concerning Pictures* written by Hieromonk Mattheus Blasteres about the year 1335.[7]

Compare: "Let thine eyes behold the thing which is right," orders Wisdom, "and keep thine heart with all care." For the bodily senses easily bring their own impressions into the soul. Therefore we order that henceforth there shall in no way be made pictures, whether they are in paintings or in what way so ever, which attract the eye and corrupt the mind, and incite it to the enkindling of base passions. And if any one shall attempt to do this he is to be cut off. Ancient epitome of canon c. Pictures which induce impurity are not to be painted. Whoso shall transgress shall be cut off.[8]

Also: "Let thine eyes look aright, and keep thy heart with all diligence" (Prov. 4:25 and 23), wisdom bids us. For the sensations of the body can easily foist their influence upon the soul. We therefore command that henceforth in no way whatever shall any pictures be drawn, painted or otherwise wrought, whether in frames or otherwise hung up, that appeal to the eye fascinatingly, and corrupt the mind, and excite inflammatory urgings to the enjoyment of shameful pleasures. If anyone should attempt to do this, let him be excommunicated. (No interpretation of this is in the Greek edition.) Concord. Inasmuch as some men were wont to paint or draw on walls and boards lascivious pictures, such as women stark naked or bathing or being kissed by men, and other shameful scenes, which deceive the eyes of beholders and excite the mind and heart to carnal desires, therefore and on this account the present Canon commands that no such pictures shall by any means whatsoever be painted or drawn or sketched. If anyone should make such pictures, let him be excommunicated, since all the five senses of the body, and especially the first and royalest one, the eyesight, is easily lead to impress the pictures of those things which it sees into the soul. That is why Solomon recommends that our eyes look aright at things that are fine and good and beautiful, and that everyone of us keep his mind and heart away from the shameful objects of the senses.[9]

Section 3

From the book of Blessed Simeon, Archbishop of Thessalonica, "Against the Latins": Chapter 23—How one ought to paint according to the carefully preserved, honorable and customary tradition, which gives an explanation as follows:

Here [in the spiritual world represented in icons] all things are made new as it is said [in Scripture] and the holy icons [painted] outside of the [ancient] tradition after another [modern] style are such that instead of the original [simple] garments and hair they [i.e., artists] portray [contemporary, worldly] human hair styles and garments and beautify them [i.e., the icons], not after the example of the [traditional] original icons, but from [their own] imagination and without proper [spiritual] preparation, and they paint them more [complicated] and adorn them more [extravagantly] than the holy icons should be. In the year 7198 [1690].

NOTES
This excerpt is taken out of context and is part of a very long "Dialogue against Heresies" between the Archbishop and a Clergyman. Blessed Simeon actually lived in the fifteenth century, but an edition of his works was published in Moldavia in 1683.[10]

Section 4
From the book called *The Shield* by Joachim, Patriarch of Moscow. In his "Spiritual Testament" he writes as follows:

In the name of the Lord I proclaim that the icons of the God-Man Jesus, and the most pure Mother of God and of all the saints should be painted according to the ancient Greek tradition just as the ordinary icons we see are painted and the wonder-working icons which were painted by the ancients. And the standards are not to be taken from the example of the Latins and the Germans which are not similar to the originals [that is, Orthodox icons], but are new creations done according to their own passions. They do not paint taking the traditions of our Church into consideration and even where they find churches that are painted properly, they remove the good icons. Where we have the most pure Mother of God, and her betrothed husband the Righteous Joseph at the birth of the Lord Jesus Christ, they paint [foreign] heretics with uncovered head and curled hair, and a multitude of women with uncovered head and curled hair, and men according to their own foreign fashions. Such examples are never found in the Greek tradition, or in the ancient Russian tradition for that matter, and today they are not acceptable either, just as we believe that the most pure Mother of God remained a virgin even after the birth of Jesus. Such novelties [in iconography] are not acceptable in the Church, nor are they customary. It is not permitted to carve statues out of wood, such as can be physically embraced, because this has always been forbidden in the Eastern [Orthodox] Church.

NOTES
Joachim was Patriarch from 1674 until 1690 and tried to curb the westernization of Russia and the Orthodox Church during the reigns of Tsars Alexis and Peter the Great.

Section 5
From the writings of Theodosius of the Desert:
The divine service of iconographic representation has been received from the Holy Apostles, and for this reason it behooves both the priest and iconographer to live in chastity or in marriage according to the law. Just as the priest during the Liturgy by

[saying] the divinely-instituted words brings into being the Body [and Blood of Christ] which we receive in Holy Communion for the forgiveness of sin. Similarly the icon painter, instead of words, describes and depicts the body [of Christ or a saint] and brings to life [figuratively] that which we venerate for the sake of our great love for the [heavenly] Originals. But we do not serve [or worship them]. For it is a great crime [of idolatry] if someone should bow down and worship them. This is not acceptable as it says in the seventh rule. It is proper for the priest and the iconographer freely and not slavishly, always to research and trace [the icons] from the ancient patterns and finally to come with the icon to the patriarch, metropolitan, or bishop for approval. There the icon will be [certified] as a good representation, and the priest will testify for the iconographer's [Christian] life style, and he [the hierarch] will bless him to paint icons. This blessing will provide him with a position, and [the means] to live a virtuous life. He is not to paint "artistically" [that is, as opposed to "iconographically"], but to take someone who has not yet painted on as an apprentice, and to teach him his craft.

NOTES

The iconographer must be a worthy servant of the Church. This becomes even more obvious when one considers an icon painter shares something of the priesthood. Only after the priest fasts and says his rule of prayer at home does he go to stand at the altar to serve God by doing the Liturgy, making our Lord present in the Mysteries, so also the iconographer does his service of making our Lord and His saints visibly present in his studio only after his preparation at home by prayer and fasting, in a spirit of repentance, doing his work precisely and exactly without hurry. Just as the clergy and monastics order their lives according to the *Typicon,* so does the icon painter as well, and for this reason his patternbook has the same opening words in the month of September and many features of the *Typicon.*

Section 6

A short allegory patterned after the seven days of creation describing the human life span from birth to death in seven stages, in which a week represents seven years, and presents specific characteristics in the development both of men and women until their departure from human life. [That is,] from the birth of a person among men the number of seven weeks of years measures the perfection of the days of human life, during which a person completes his growth and development even until the completion of old age:

The first week, until a baby becomes seven years old: the child no longer remains innocent, the baby teeth fall out, little is understood, and all thoughts remain child-ish. The second week, when the person is fourteen years old, he or she discovers the burning lusts and passions of youth, and attains sexual maturity. The third week, that is, at twenty-one years of age, he passes from the understanding and growth of youth into that of manhood and begins to be wise. The fourth week, i.e., at twenty-eight, he becomes either a seeker of virtue, or a lover of money, greedy, arrogant, high-minded or full of deceit and violence. The fifth week, when a man is thirty-five, he is fully grown, and except for a few gray hairs, his growth is complete and he comes to the completion of wisdom. The sixth week, i.e., forty-two years, he is fully knowledgeable, introspective, powerful and rich. The seventh week, or at forty-nine years of age, he is a mature man, touched with gray hair, distant from all pettiness, and free from immorality, but begins to feel aches and pains and starts to decline physically. When a man begins his eighth week, or his fifty-second year, he enters into old age, the weakening of the body, the brittleness of his bones and then into the various stages of old age. During the ninth week or later, God willing, he will become neither senile nor have a feeling of wretchedness. Remembering all the "weeks" of his life, he considers his final dwelling place, but not does not leave the delusion and artificiality of this world of sorrows which until now he has loved with his whole heart. Indeed he has destroyed his soul by his wicked deeds. This world of delusion is revealed as meaningless, only understood as decrepitude and hardship, and he is overcome by assorted aches and pains, his teeth fall out, his eyesight weakens, he loses his hair, his entire organism changes, his blood does not flow, and he suffers the inevitable diseases, sicknesses, and sores of old age. These were all present in the body since youth and they increase steadily, just as the decrepitude, coughs, loss of strength, and the whole body weakening. His face becomes sad because of this and his struggles and hardships. Then he comes wretchedly to the end of his life, death. Alas, alas, O my soul! When we are separated from the body, and enter into the sleep of death, I do not know where I will go, or what I will be. I fear my deeds, for my deeds will judge me, and condemn me before God. Judge in righteousness and love the truth! The righteous will dwell in paradise, for "The Lord watches over the path of the righteous, but the path of the wicked will perish." For all eternity the condemned will be locked in hell and the shadow of death. Look, O man, what is your state? Be serious! What is a prince, or a leader, or a guide, or rich, or poor, or a man or a woman, not living in wisdom? Nothing but filth, worms, manure, chaff, dust and ashes! Only bare bones.

NOTES

This anonymous passage is typical of the popular pious literature found in the anthologies popular in seventeenth century Russia. There is no specific reference to iconography in this selection.

Section 7

From the sermon "On the Divinity and Humanity of Christ" by St. Cyril of Jerusalem, chapter 5, page 118, at the end:

The Persian Magi came to worship Christ at His birth. Abimalek presented gold as to a king. Hielisour presented frankincense as to God. Haeliab brought myrrh as to a dead man.

In another place he [St. Cyril of Jerusalem] writes about the birth of Christ:

The first [wise man], Melchior, was an old man. The second, Balthazar, did not have a large beard. The third, Caspar, was a young man without a beard.

Section 8

[On the icon of] the "Protection" [of the Mother of God] the Savior holds a scroll on which is written: "My ear is ready to hear your request, which anyone should ask in your name, My dear mother, who stands and prays for mercy for the human race." On the scroll of the Mother of God: "O Master of great mercy, O Lord, my Son and my God, bend Your ear and hear the prayer of Your mother who prays for the human race!"

Section 9

The following description of the divine-human nature and the perfect development of our Lord, God and Savior Jesus Christ was written by the monastic St. Maximus the Greek, a monk of the Holy Mountain [Athos], archimandrite of the Vatopedi Monastery:

He was a very handsome person. When He came of age, He was about six feet tall. He had a full head of brown hair, not very bushy, rather nicely kept. His eyebrows were not very dense. His eyes were bright and sparkling. Just like the description of His forefather David states, He was handsome with a well-shaped nose, a brown beard divided into two points at the end. He had long hair, which had never been cut nor had anyone ever touched His head except the hand of His mother during infancy. His shoulders were a little sloped, not very wide, but having simply a normal stature. His complexion was not very ruddy, with a round face like His mother's, and resembled her to some extent. He was characterized by wisdom, gentleness, without any anger, just like His mother was.

A description of the most pure Virgin Mary, the Mother of God by the same [monastic St. Maximus the Greek]:

She was of average height, had medium dark blonde hair, beautiful black eyes, black eyebrows, long fingers, a round face, long fingers on her hands, a straight nose, and the mouth of the Most Pure was chaste and rosy.

NOTES

This passage is a reworking of the ancient descriptions of our Lord and His most holy Mother and resembles the texts in Section 1 above. St. Maximus the Greek, born

Michael Trivolis in 1470 on the island of Corfu, was the most highly educated and most interesting personality of his time. In 1502 he entered the Dominican Monastery of San Marco in Florence, Italy where Savonarola was abbot. He returned to Orthodoxy, went to Mount Athos and was invited to Russia by Great Prince Vasily III in 1518. He was commissioned to correct the Church Slavonic service books. But because of intrigues and misdirected conservatism inflamed by his alleged heresies and for introducing errors, he spent many years in prison until his death in 1556. His writings were published in three volumes in Kazan, Russia between 1859 and 1862.

Section 10

January 18: [descriptions of] our fathers among the saints **Athanasius the Great** and **Cyril of Alexandria**, as recorded in the printed *Prologue*:

The appearance of St. Athanasius was humble, a little stooped with poor posture, short, but with a nice pleasant smile on his face, somewhat bald, sickly in bearing, not a long beard but broad, a full jaw, narrow lips, not very gray, but not very white either, but being somewhat brown.

St. Cyril had a slender physique, a soft face, scanty eyebrows but very rounded, wide forehead, flared nostrils, long fingers, thin lips, balding, a thick and long beard, somewhat brown, and simple.

January 30: The three hierarchs Saints **Basil the Great, Gregory the Theologian**, and **John Chrysostom**, as recorded in the printed *Prologue*:

St. Basil the Great had a tall frame, but very ascetic, a dark complexion, somewhat jaundiced, a hooked nose, bushy eyebrows, wide forehead, a narrow face and without anger, a dark visage and quiet demeanor, having a narrow beard, long and half gray.

St. Gregory the Theologian was physically short and had a pleasant appearance, a short nose, having straight eyebrows, gentle, and a slight build, not having a long beard, but parted simply, a little brown; balding, but with some white hair.

St. John Chrysostom was a very small person, but had a large head on wide shoulders. He was excessively thin, had flaring nostrils, his face was pale white, with deeply set eyes, but he was made impressive by the One Whom he served, and he had a happy disposition. To complete the picture he had a very high and wide forehead, marked by deep eyebrows, big ears, but a thin and shaggy beard touched with white, brown hair, and a strong jaw.

January 20: our monastic father **Euthymius the Great**, as recorded in the printed *Prologue*:

He has a pleasant appearance, a wizened figure, gray hair, and a beard down to his knees.

NOTES

The essence of these citations may be found in the Church Slavonic *Prologue* published in two large volumes by the Synodal Press in St. Petersburg, Russia, 1896.

Section 11

[September 13: an undated anonymous description of the icon] "The Founding of the Church of the Resurrection of Christ our God" [now called the "Holy Sepulcher" in Jerusalem]:

The church has five domes, or heads, and in the middle of the church stands the bishop St. James, the Brother of the Lord, who is blessing with both hands standing on the ambo, at his sides are two deacons with liturgical fans, around the church is a blue cloud with angels so that on the right side stand the ranks of bishop saints, martyrs, prophets, desert dwellers, nun saints, women martyrs, and all the saints, standing as if in a pile facing the cloud and the church, and looking towards the "Heavenly Jerusalem," which is located at the top in the right hand corner on cherubim, and in it is the Cross and the spear, sponge, nails. And under the Cross is an altar, and on the altar is the robe of the Savior, and angels with crowns in their hands which they are placing on the saints, who are in the church where St. James is. At the right side is King David in his place with a scroll, and to the left side is St. Gregory the Theologian, and under St. James is a great crowd of people of every description, old and with brown hair and young. Under them is a mountain and a sea, and on the sea islands, and on the islands churches, and the apostles are teaching all the nations and people, and in the sea one can see people all beaten flat, some are dismembered represented in this composition by just a head, or arms, feet, or breastplates. Under the sea is a mountain, where all the saints are, and in the midst of them are the ark of the covenant of the Lord, the altar, incense, and cherubim and seraphim, which are overshadowing the altar, and in the middle Solomon, and behind him the Israelites with loaves of bread and doves and lambs, which they are carrying to the Temple to be offered. Behind them are calves and a slaughtered ram which they are placing on the fire, and over them are children playing, wrestling, and sitting. At the right hand side under the Cross there are three small inset icons: first, the "Crucifixion of the Lord", second the "Laying in the Tomb", and third, the "Temptation and Expulsion of Adam from Paradise." On the left side the Archangel Michael is depicted opposite the "Heavenly Jerusalem" and the Cross, and under him is the "Resurrection of Christ", under this the "Coming of the Lord into the Midst of the Apostles", and under this a mountain and an abyss. In the abyss is a tomb to which three demons are chained.

Section 12

Descriptions of the prophets: 1 **Adam**, 2 **Enoch**, 3 **Noah**, 4 **Abraham**, 5 **Isaac**, 6 **Jacob**, 7 **Moses**, 8 **Aaron**, 9 **Joshua**, the son of Nun, 10 **Samuel**, 11 **Nathan**, 12 **David**, 13 **Josaphat**, 14 **Solomon**, 15 **Simeon**, 16 **Michaiah**, 17 **Elias**, 18 **Elisha**, 19 **Zachariah**, 20 **Isaiah**, 21 **Nahum**, 22 **Habakkuk**, 23 **Zephaniah**, 24 **Daniel**, 25 **Haggai**, 26 **Simeon**, 27 **John the Baptist**, 28 **Methusael**, 28 **Abimelech**, 30 **Zadok**, 31 **Balaam**, 32 **Lamech**, 33 **Zephaniah**, 34 **Jeremiah**, 35 **Azariah**, 36 **Josiah**, 37 **Obadiah**, 38 **Joel**, 39 **Gad**, 40 **Jonah**, plus the 73 [lesser apostles] who are found in Acts and so there are 113 figures in all.

Section 13

Patterns [for the depiction on a tier of an iconostasis] of the holy forefathers as they are described in writing:

To the right of the Lord Sabaoth is **Adam**, his cloak is green, his tunic is purple and on the scroll is written, "Adam the leader among the dead and for the living generation." Behind him is **Melchizedek**, who has gray hair, a shaggy beard like the Lord of Sabaoth, a crown on his head, a bishop's saccos, and Melchizedek holds a closed book. Behind him is **Abraham**, who has shaggy gray hair, a beard like St. John the Theologian, a green cloak, a purple tunic, and on the scroll is written, "Abraham ought to be praised." Behind him is **Isaac**, who is similar in everything to Abraham, but his cloak is green, his tunic is scarlet, and on the scroll is written, "He was led to be offered and was an image of the Crucified." Behind him is the righteous **Job**, who has gray hair, a beard like St. Nicholas, a cap on his head, his arms are raised in prayer, wearing a purple with white cloak, a blue tunic, a princes' fur coat and on his scroll is written, "Naked have I come from my mother's womb and naked will I return to the earth." Behind him is **Benjamin**, who is a young man resembling St. Gleb, and wears a scarlet princes' cloak, a purple tunic, and on the scroll is written, "Love the Lord, the God of Heaven, and keep His commandments!" Behind him is **Jared** with gray hair, a beard like St. John the Theologian, a white cloak, a blue tunic, and on the scroll is written, "You are righteous among the multitude of righteous." Behind him is **Methusalah**, who has balding gray hair, a gray beard like St. Basil the Great, a purple cloak, a blue tunic, and on the scroll is written, "[blank]" [or] he is writing on a scroll. Behind is him **Asher** who resembles St. Matthew the Evangelist, with an ocher cloak, a light gray tunic, and on the scroll is written "It is pleasing to God to hasten to lead from evil and defeat the enemy."

On the left side: the first mother **Eve**, has a scarlet cloak and a blue tunic. Behind her is **Jacob**, who has shaggy gray hair, a beard like St. Nicholas, an ocher cloak, a blue tunic, and on the scroll is written, "There will not lack a prince from among the Jews and an elder from his flesh, until the Lord comes". Behind him is **Lot**, an old man with a little gray hair, a big gray beard like St. Gregory of Nyssa, a green cloak, a purple tunic, and on the scroll is written, "The Lord led me out of Sodom and saved me." Behind him is **Seth**, who is an old man with gray hair and beard resembling St. Matthew the Evangelist, a green cloak, a purple tunic, and on his scroll is written, "Seth is the new seed of his parents to take the place of Abel." Behind him is **Noah**, an old man with balding gray hair, a beard like St. John the Theologian, a green cloak, a purple tunic, and he holds [a model of] the ark with both hands. Behind him is **Joseph**, the most handsome, who resembles St. Boris, with princes' robes with purple and royal purple, a blue tunic, and on the scroll is written, "He speaks of the promise of your glory." Behind him is **Abel**, who is a young man with a furry blue tunic reaching to the knees, bare foot and on the scroll is written, "The first among the dead, your lifeless blood cries out to the Lord." Behind him is **Shem**, an old man with gray hair like St. Matthew, a green cloak, a purple tunic, and on the scroll is written, "I covered the shame of my father with wisdom." Behind him is **Mahalalel**, an old man with gray hair like the forefather Jacob, apostles' garments, a crimson with white cloak, and on the scroll is written, "A word was offered, which commanded him before". Behind him is **Simeon**, on whose scroll is written, "Moderation in the body and understanding in the soul gives a man the promise from on high." Behind him is **Judah**, who has written on his scroll, "The Lord will dwell with mercy and be the salvation of Israel." Behind him is **Enoch** and on his scroll is written, "I hoped to call the Name of my Lord to me." Behind him is **Pharez** on whose scroll is written, "Gather wisdom in the fear of the Lord; if someone wishes to attain wisdom he will be on the throne together with kings." Behind him stands **Nephtali**, on his scroll is written, "Understand the wonderful works of the Lord, who created heaven and the earth and the sea and everything thing that is in them.

Section 14

Patterns for the holy prophets [on an iconostasis]:
Starting on the right side, the prophet King **David** has a beard like St. Nicholas, a royal crown on his head, royal robes, a blue cloak, a purple tunic, on the scroll is written, "Rise up O Lord in Your rest, You and the tabernacle of Your sanctuary!" Behind him is the prophet **Zachariah**, with a long beard, a cap on his head, a scarlet cloak, a blue tunic, and on the scroll is written, "Blessed is the God of Israel, for He has met and created the salvation of His people." Behind him is the prophet **Moses**, with balding brown hair, a beard like St. John Chrysostom, a crimson cloak, a blue tunic, and on the scroll is written: "I saw the burning bush that was not consumed" Behind him is the prophet **Isaiah**, an old man with gray hair resembling St. Andrew the Apostle, with a reddish brown cloak, a scarlet tunic and on the scroll is written, "Behold the Virgin has conceived in her womb and given birth to a son, and his name will be called Immanuel." Behind him is the prophet **Nahum**, an old man

with gray hair who resembles St. John the Theologian, with a crimson cloak, a blue tunic, and on the scroll is written "I saw you the true vineyard, from which has grown the vine of life which is Christ." Behind him is the prophet **Daniel**, who is a young man with curly hair resembling St. George. He has a hat on his head, a scarlet cloak, a blue tunic, and on the scroll is written, "I saw a great mountain from which came the rock which was hewn without being touched by human hands." Behind him is the prophet **Jonah**, an old man with balding gray hair, a beard like St. Nicholas, an ocher cloak, a blue tunic, and on the scroll is written, "I called out in my distress to the Lord my God." Behind him is the prophet **Jeremiah**, who resembles St. Andrew the Apostle, with an ocher cloak, a blue tunic, and on the scroll is written, "I have seen you, O Israel, the hand leading the holy child along the path of life." Behind him is **Zachariah** the Sickle-seer, a young man like St. Demetrius of Thessalonica, with a crimson cloak, a blue tunic, on the scroll is written, "Rejoice exceedingly, O daughters of Sion!" Behind him stands the prophet **Obadiah**, with curly gray hair and a beard like St. Menas the great martyr, a crimson cloak, a blue tunic, and on his scroll is written, "[blank]" [or] he is writing in a scroll. Behind him is the prophet Osee, and old man with gray hair, an ocher cloak, a blue tunic, and on the scroll is written, "When the sun comes to Siloam, and the oak tree is divided into twelve parts, there will be twelve springs of water flowing over the earth, the appearance of the Lord God, and for His sake the whole earth will be saved."

On the other side: the prophet King **Solomon**, who is a young man with curly hair, a royal crown on his head, in royal robes, a scarlet cloak, an ocher or green tunic, and on the scroll is written, "Wisdom has built herself a temple and strengthened it with seven pillars, and offered her sacrifices." Behind him is the prophet **Ezechiel**, an old man with gray hair, a beard like the Apostle Andrew, hair coming down over his shoulder, a crimson cloak, a blue tunic, and on the scroll is written, "I have seen you as a locked door, through which no one passes, except the one Lord God of Israel." Behind him is the prophet **Elias** with shaggy gray hair, a beard like St. John the Theologian, a purple cloak, an ocher tunic, and on the scroll is written, "I was very zealous for the Lord God Almighty." Behind him is the prophet **Aaron**, who has a long beard like Zachariah, a green cloak, a scarlet tunic, and on the scroll is written, "I have seen the staff of Jesse and the blossom from it, Christ." Behind him is the prophet **Zephaniah**, an old man with gray hair resembling St. John the Theologian, a crimson cloak, a blue tunic, and on the scroll is written, "I understood that He would be born from a virgin." Behind him is the prophet **Haggai**, an old man with gray hair like St. Elias flowing down over his shoulder, a reddish brown cloak, a crimson tunic, and on the scroll is written, "I understood the Lord would resurrect them." Behind him is the prophet **Michah** with a beard like Andrew the Apostle, hair flowing down over his shoulder, a reddish brown cloak, a blue tunic, and on the scroll is written, "And you, O Bethlehem, the land of Judah, are least among the rulers of the

Judah, but from you will come the leader." Behind him is the prophet **Malachias**, who has gray hair like St. Andrew the Apostle, a green cloak, a crimson tunic, and on his scroll is written, "Behold, I will send an angel before your face, who will prepare a path before you." Behind him is the prophet **Elisha**, who resembles Moses, with a crimson cloak, a blue tunic and on the scroll is written, "Elisha said, 'Whom do you seek? Go, follow him!'" Behind him is the prophet **Amos**, who is an old man with gray hair resembling St. John the Theologian, with a green cloak, a blue tunic, and writes in a scroll. Behind him is the prophet **Samuel**, who has gray hair like the prophet Zachariah, he is holding a ram's horn, his cloak is crimson, but on his shoulders it is ocher, the middle tunic is green, the tunic is reddish brown crimson. Behind him is the prophet **Joel**, who is an old man with gray hair like St. Elias, a big beard and much hair in one lock, a green cloak, a scarlet tunic, and there is an inscription on the scroll. Behind him is the prophet **Habakkuk**, celebrated on December 2, and on the scroll is the inscription, "God will come from the east, and the Holy One from the overshadowed mountain parts." [NKJV Hab. 3:3 "God came from Taman, the Holy One from Mount Paran."] Behind him the prophet Baruch, a small figure but not very small, and on the scroll is the inscription, "Behold God, and He will not allow another before Him."

Section 15

The names of the holy prophetesses are as follows:
1 **Sarah**, 2 **Rebecca**, 3 **Deborah**, 4 **Dinah**, 5 **Anna**, the mother of Samuel, 6 **Judith**, 7 **Miriam**, 8 **Elizabeth**, the mother of John the Forerunner, 9 **Anna**, the daughter of Phanuel, 10 **Mary**, the Theotokos, the mother of our Lord Jesus Christ.

Section 16

The life of Mary [the most holy Mother of God] was as follows:
Three years passed from her birth until her entrance into the Temple where she dwelt for eleven years being fed by an angel. Then she lived in the home of Joseph for twelve months where she accepted the Annunciation (celebrated on March 25) when she was fifteen years, two months old. She was forty-eight years old at the time of the Lord's Passion, and after His Ascension she lived in the home of St. John the Theologian for twenty-four years. In all she lived to be seventy-two years old when she fell asleep into eternal life. Amen.

She [Mary, the most holy Mother of God] was of average height, had brown hair, black eyelashes, long hands and fingers, a slightly round face, white and beautiful. She had her hair done simply, but beautifully. She was adorned more by good works than with a nice appearance. She was gentle, not vain, not putting on airs, or ornaments. She liked to wear dark red garments with bright trimming, but not from all different colors. This is witnessed by her head scarf which fell down over her shoulders and arms. She made vestments for the priests, a kind of cope called a phelonion, and she sang in the Temple to the Lord, and remained in prayer and fasting, and all night vigils, and hymns and in reading, and hand works in silence, with thanksgiving, so that for this reason she would be adorned with good works and in this way she was prepared to be a lady and a teacher for many of us. She is blessed by all the nations of the world being named the Mother of God, and the most pure and ever Virgin Mary.

Section 17

The Alphabet Book Sign 90: Concerning the Crucifixion of Christ:
Why do iconographers paint the left hand side of the footrest of the Savior pointing up, but the right side pointing down on icons of the Crucifixion of Christ on the Cross?

Commentary: When our Lord Jesus Christ was standing on the Cross He had His head bent down to the left so that He would attract all of the nations that would believe in Him and worship Him. And for the same reason the left foot rest is raised up, so that by believing in His Name their sins would be covered and that at His terrible second coming they would be lifted up in the air to meet Him. But the right side of the foot rest is pointing down so that those nations who do not believe in Him because of their ignorance would understand that they are condemned and will descend into hell.

NOTES

There were many "alphabet books" both as printed editions and in manuscript which were very popular and widely distributed in seventeenth century Russia. They doubled as reading primers and catechisms. From time to time one sees "three-barred" crosses that appear to be "reversed," that is, the bottom bar ascends from left to right. This is probably due to a misunderstanding of the passage just cited. The Slavonic text is misleading because it assumes the reader understands that "left" and "right" are actually from Christ the Savior's perspective and not the viewer's. Since a literal English translation would be misunderstood for the same reason, the words "left" and "right" have been reversed in this translation to avoid confusion.

Section 18

"The Praises to the Cross," these are the phrases that are arranged around the Cross: The King Commands. Christ Descends. He is lifted up to a verdant place. The thrice-sanctified Wood on which Christ was lifted up. The demonic powers flee the Cross, the Wood redeemed by the Blood flowing from God, a three-edged sword, the destruction of demons, the Cross is exalted, the demonic power is defeated by it, the debt to the debtor is small, peace conquers, this Wood terrifies the demons, the Cross is the beginning of Faith, found from God by the doe, the Tree of life and the salvation of the world, the Cross is exalted, the Christian family rejoices, the place of execution becomes a paradise, the Light of Christ illumines all, Lord's right arm is a mighty power.

[This is a series of acrostics, each of four words in the original Slavonic text starts with the same letter.]

А А А А	= "The Tree Presents the Ancient Heritage."
Б Б Б Б	= "by All the Faithful Restored to Paradise."
П П П П	= "He Grants the Worshipers Regeneration."
К К К К	= "the Cross is Might to Constantine in Faith."
С С С С	= "[Christ] Saves by a Word those who Glorify This."
Н Н Н Н	= "the Usurper in the Night of Ignorance in Need."
Ѡ Ѡ Ѡ Ѡ	= "the Finder Finds the Foundling, you are Found by the doe from God."
Д Д Д Д	= "the Good Wood Annoys the Devil."
В В В В	= "Great Rejoicing for those Believing in You."
Ц Ц Ц Ц	= "the Royal Bloom Blossoms in the Church."
Ѕ Ѕ Ѕ Ѕ	= "the Scourge of God whips the demons."
П П П П	= "I sing, I honor, I worship Fervently."
Х Х Х Х	= "Christ's Praise is the Chorus of Christians."
Ч Ч Ч Ч	= "The Honorable Honor is Honored by Humans."
О О О О	= "The Conqueror's Sword Protects the Grooms."

The image of the venerable and life-creating Cross of the Lord, on which He was crucified by the Jews, is equal to the height of heaven and the width of the earth, [symbolized by the] initials [each marked with a tilde as an abbreviation (or number) in Slavonic] Г Г Л С Ѣ С Н Б Н Д Н Б М В. [The words of the abbreviated text are not given.]

Christ rules as a king. Christ becomes a man. Christ defends us. Christ defeats the enemy. Christ conquers Allah. Christ reigns. Christ is glorified. Christ is exalted. Christ established Himself with us. And our Lord, being the God over all, controlling all, each as He pleased, and He created, and came down from heaven, and took flesh within the Virgin Mary, and was born from her, and freely came to the Passion, and was crucified on the Cross, and accepted burial, and resurrected on the third day, the great power of the mighty right arm of the Lord protects and keeps us. He is the one who suffered and tasted death for the sake of us sinners.

Rise up, O God! Judge the Earth! For You are the Crown Prince in all the nations. Arise, O Lord, my God! Let Your arm be raised! Do not forget Your poor people at the end!

Those who glorify the Word are saved by Him.

His Honorable Honor is honored by men honoring you [the Cross].

The Voice of God calls out, speaking to the generation.

Joyous is the Tree which presents the ancient heritage.

The Christ's praise is the chorus of Christians praising the Cross.

All the faithful are restored to paradise by the man on the path of salvation.

The good Wood annoys the devil.

The Cross is power, the might of Constantine in the Faith.

The unseen, unapproachable, unexplainable, indescribable Savior creates a
    net for Satan.

The royal blossom blooms in the Church, the foundling found by God.

I sing, I venerate, I worship Thy footstool, O Master Christ, our Savior.

O most glorious Tree, the Cross of the Lord, you might appear small, but
    the expanse of the Cross and the expanse of the heavens are equal.

My mind is awe-struck, and my thoughts are amazed, at the greatness of
    the Cross erected on the place of execution at the center of the whole earth.

I bow down to Your Cross, O Christ, and the spear and reed, because
    Your glory extends salvation to our hearts.

NOTES

All of these phrases and passages probably were taken from an "alphabet book" or
Orthodox church service composed to praise the Cross. It is possible that some
services and akathists used during the seventeenth century before Patriarch Nikon's
reform are no longer included in modern Slavonic church service books.

Section 19

An annotated description of St. Sophia or the Divine Wisdom in the Catholic and
Apostolic Church; and about virginity and chastity:

First it ought to be understood that virginity is a symbol of the divine nature.
Chastity and virginity are esteemed because our Lord was born of a chaste virgin
according to the flesh, a human being in form and similar [to all men], since to be
without flesh and a body is proper to God according to His divinity. By analogy a
human being is permitted to [become like a heavenly being] in our humanity by
unsullied chastity in our flesh. The highest endeavor is accomplished by virginity,
which is called the first rank in heaven, the place from which the fallen angels were
expelled, because each angel is higher than a mortal man. By analogy the state of
virginity is more honorable for a man than marrying which is demonstrated by the
[Lord's] divine example. It is better for us to live as Christians, and not to please ourselves, and to honor virginity more than the corruptible flesh from which one should

flee and where it is miraculous for a man to be without defilement. The bodily temple of Christ was formed without defilement from the most pure Virgin Mother of God in chastity, and after this she is still called a virgin, that is, a virginal soul. For this reason do not criticize the state of virginity, in which [the virtues of] virginity and chastity are attained, for virginal souls are beloved by Christ, because the Lord Himself taught us by saying, "Where ever I am, My servant will be also."

Saint Sophia, the Divine Wisdom, the Sophia of the Church of God is the most pure soul, the Mother of God. Commentary: The so-called "virginal soul," the inexplicable virginity in chastity, the truth of humble wisdom, it has over the head of Christ. Commentary: the Word is Wisdom, the only begotten Son, the Word of God, the descent of, the Lord is the expanse of heaven. Commentary: the Worship of heaven, He entered the pure Virgin, and took flesh from the Holy Spirit, because each of them loves virginity, they became similar to the Mother of God. Commentary: This woman gave birth to the Son, the Word of God, the Lord Jesus Christ, because loving virginity giving birth to active words, called the "not understandable teaching," because John the Baptist, who baptized the Lord, loved this. Commentary: And the order of virginity is demonstrated by life in God. Virginity has a fiery maiden's face. Commentary: Because divinity is a fire which burns up corrupting bodily passions, thus illuminating the pure soul. She has ribbons over her ears like angels have, because a chaste life is equal to that of the angels. The hair ribbons are the peace of the Holy Spirit, and on her head is a royal crown. Commentary: "Humble wisdom rules over the passions" is an explanation of the sash around her waist. Commentary: a most ancient image holds a scepter in her hand. Commentary: Royal status is symbolized by having fiery wings. Commentary: The highly intellectual prophesy quickly reveals the understanding of a bird that flies even higher when it sees a hunter, so also those who love virginity are never at rest from the nets from that hunter [of souls], the devil. She holds a written scroll in her left hand. Commentary: [A scroll] on which is written the unknown name, the preserving of mysteries, which is to know the so-called "traditional writings", because they are the unapproachable and unknowable—either by the angels or by mankind—divine mystery of virginity. The throne on which she is sitting is clothed with light. Commentary: The light reveals the peace and quietness of that future establishment and it has seven pillars. Commentary: The seven gifts of the Spirit, which are written in the prophesy by Isaiah, and she has her feet on a rock. Commentary: On this [rock] because [the Lord in Matthew 16:18] says, "I will establish My Church on the rock and even the gates of hell will not prevail against it," and again it says, "Faith in me is established on a rock, my mouth is bared against my enemies."

NOTES
Like the other passages in this and other anthologies we assume the editors in 1650

and 1903 included this excerpt for no other reason than to explain an icon and to edify the reader about the virtue of chastity. But the icon, in fact, introduces confusion into the Orthodox Christian understanding of the Person of our Lord Jesus Christ and how He should be depicted on icons. In short, something else, a "personification," has been given the place in an icon belonging to God, our Lord Jesus Christ. Tragically a "Sophian" heresy developed in Russia, which is a pantheistic teaching concerning a feminine aspect of the Trinity, which was condemned in 1935 by both the Russian Church Abroad and the Moscow Patriarchate, acting separately.[11] This section was retained since it is part of the Bolshakov *Iconographic Patternbook* and not to promote controversy or to endorse heresy.

Section 20

The Apostles are sitting [in the icon of] the "Descent of the Holy Spirit [for Pentecost]."

[Pictured] on the left side is the Apostle **Peter**, and behind and below him is St. **John**, a young man with a scarlet cloak and a blue tunic. Next to him is St. **Andrew**, an old man with a shaggy beard, gray hair past his ears, a green cloak and a blue tunic. Next to him is St. **Simon**, an old man with gray hair, resembling the prophet Moses in everything, with a reddish crimson cloak and a blue tunic. Next to him is St. **Bartholomew**, with brown hair coming down past his ears, a green cloak, and a blue tunic. Next to him is St. **Thomas** who is a young man with a scarlet cloak and a blue tunic. All the apostles have scrolls in their hands. Sts. John and Simon are looking backwards. Opposite him [St. Peter] sits the Apostle **Paul**, even if he were not there, they paint the "chosen vessel". Behind him is St. **Mark**, with a beard like St. Peter, slightly graying, a blue cloak, a reddish brown tunic, and he is looking backward. Behind him is St. **Matthew**, with gray hair, a shaggy beard, a green cloak, and a blue tunic. Behind him is St. **Luke**, with curly brown hair, a scarlet cloak, a blue tunic and he is looking backward. Behind him is St. **James**, with gray hair like Peter, a blue cloak, his cloak is blue, a greenish brown with white tunic. Behind him is St. **Philip**, who is a young man, with a crimson cloak and a blue tunic. They all have scrolls in their hands, and their other hands are in prayer and thanksgiving.

Concerning [the icon] of the "Descent of the Holy Spirit":

Why are all these details painted on the holy icons of "The Descent of the Holy Spirit" for the day of Pentecost? There is an old man sitting there in a dark place and his garment is red. He is wearing a royal crown on his head and is holding a strip of white cloth in his hands on which are twelve rolled up scrolls. Commentary: The man is called "The Universe", and he appears as an old man because he has been aged by Adam's fall into sin, and he is in the dark place which represents the whole world being in a state of unbelief, idolatry. His garment is red because it is stained by the

34

blood of all the sacrifices made to the idols, he has a royal crown on his head to symbolize that sin was ruling in the world until then, and he is holding a strip of white cloth in his hands on which are the twelve scrolls, which represent the twelve apostles, who each went to his specific country to teach the people to believe in Christ, and by their teaching they illuminated the whole world to the ends of the universe, and therefore the man has the name "Cosmos" which is Greek [for "universe"].

Section 21

The Evangelists [are depicted] on the royal doors [of the iconostasis]. St. **John** the Theologian is symbolized in the clouds by a lion and an ocher curtain. Opposite him is St. **Matthew** symbolized by an angel with a crimson cloak. Under St. John, St. **Luke** is symbolized by a lion in dark gray. St. **Mark**, who is symbolized by an eagle in dark gray, is opposite St. Luke, and they [that is, the animals] all have wings.

On the right side are St. **John** in a green cloak and a blue tunic, under St. John is St. **Luke** in an cloak of red brightened with blue lights, his tunic is blue and he has curly brown hair. On the other side are St. **Matthew**, who has gray hair, a shaggy beard, an ocher cloak, and under him is St. **Mark** with gray hair, a beard like St. Peter, his cloak is green, his tunic is reddish brown, and they are all sitting on golden thrones in palaces. The Apostle St. **John** the Theologian [has on his Gospel book], "In the beginning was the Word, and the Word was with God, and the Word was God. He was in the beginning with God. All things were made through Him, and without Him nothing was made that was made." [John 1:1-3 NKJV] St. **Matthew**, "The book of the genealogy of Jesus Christ, the Son of David, the Son of Abraham." [Matthew 1:1 NKJV] St. **Mark**, "The beginning of the gospel of Jesus Christ, the Son of God." [Mark 1:1 NKJV] St. **Luke**, "Inasmuch as many have taken in hand to set in order a narrative of those things." [Luke 1:1 NKJV]

On the pillars [or door posts of the royal doors are painted] the six deacons. On the right side are St. **Stephen**, under him is St. **Abib** with brown hair, under them is St. **Philip**, who is young. On the other side are the Archdeacon St. **Lawrence**, who is an old man with gray hair resembling St. Nicholas, under him is St. **Euplus** who resembles St. Nikita, and under them is the young man St. **Cyril**.

Section 22

How one ought to venerate the holy icons:
Since there are always people asking me about the origin of the veneration of icons, we answer them that in the beginning from time immemorial as the holy apostle and the chosen vessel St. Paul explains in his Epistle to the Hebrews as follows: That which were behind the veil, that is, in the Holy of Holies, above the ark are described the cherubim of glory, which were overshadowing the altar, and if the holy ark and

the altar appeared to be overshadowed by glory, it seems that this was for the glorification and worship of the God of heaven. The rest of this is explained when God appeared in the flesh, and the Lord Himself came to the Jews, and they asked Him, "Whose likeness is upon the coin?" And He answered them, "Caesar's," and then He said to them, "Render to Caesar the things that are Caesar's and render to God the things that are God's." And what belongs to Caesar but fear and taxes? And what is God's but honor and worship? And He did not say that they were not to make images, but rather they were to give similar things to the similar, and since they were merely symbols, they were not one and the same. For only two were pointed out for the sake of future generations, such as monarchs, etc. and the other for the sake of the sanctuary, such as where the cherubim of glory are found. For this reason neither do the apostles teach, nor do the evangelists proclaim [that images are forbidden], since it is not possible for any one who is born on earth not to be capable of being portrayed because it is proper to human nature and to the original essence of mankind to be portrayed. Here it is critical to understand correctly according to the evangelical saying that the Roman emperors were portrayed as statues, on the coinage and painted on panels and so likewise the rest of the kings and potentates and other famous men did not hesitate to have their likenesses portrayed, such as the testimony of "The Column of Heraclitus." How can anyone after the incarnation of the Lord Jesus Christ, our true God say that His most honorable and divine Body must not be portrayed and if His most honorable image, that is, of Christ the Savior, ought to be wiped out not be painted, then it is proper for Him to be without honor and to be discarded with the rest of the images, for it is said, for how can light be joined to darkness and Christ with Beliel? And it is the same with the images of His most pure Mother, the Theotokos, and of all of His saints, for the Lord Himself said, "where I am My servant will be also." Indeed, the following about the divine image in icons ought to be explained: God must always be worshipped because of His very nature, and not because of some traditional law, since from the beginning God created man according to His own image and likeness. What He means by His image and likeness can be explained by a simile, as when He says, "be merciful just as your heavenly Father is merciful," and again when St. Paul says, "be like me as I am like Christ." This is the image of the Holy Trinity the Source of Life: Father, Son, and Holy Spirit; Mind, Word, and Spirit. A man can not be a separated mind, word and spirit, whether a believer or non-believer. For this reason no man is worshipped, nor is the flesh worshipped in the image of God. If the flesh were to be worshipped, then the irrational nature of any living creature would be worshipped, for example, that of a horse or an ox, and for this reason we are making a distinction between what is higher and more worthy. Such is the divine likeness which we carry within ourselves, and we venerate it, that is, the mind, the word, and the spirit, which are the invisible image of the invisible God in our visible flesh which receives the glory and the honor and the veneration. Indeed when the Incarnation of the Word of God divinized human nature, according to the saying, "and the Word became flesh," and then by "the flesh" the visible God is described by the visible image which we venerate, and thus the veneration passes to the nature of the prototype. And if someone does not venerate the image of the God Who appeared in human flesh, he is not a believer because God the Word received flesh from the most pure and ever virgin Mary, and He was perfect God and perfect man.

Section 23

Chapter 43 from the "Council of the Hundred Chapters," the decree concerning painters and the venerable icons:

In accordance with the Tsar's recommendation, let the metropolitans, archbishops and bishops in the capital city of Moscow, and in all the cities, who are responsible for all of the different church offices among which are the painters of the holy icons, who are to be accounted the same as the other clerical ranks and are to be subject to the same church discipline, make sure that the painters preserve the features in their representations of our Lord, God and Savior Jesus Christ, and of the most pure Mother of God, and of the heavenly powers and of all the saints who were pleasing to God. Icon painters ought to be humble, gentle, reverent; not lazy, not frivolous, not quarrelsome, not envious; not drunkards, not thieves, not murderers; and more importantly they must preserve both their spiritual and physical chastity in every situation. If they are not able to do so until the end [of life], then they ought to marry according to the [clerical] rules[12] and live in the state of matrimony, and to visit their spiritual fathers frequently, and to confess [sacramentally] everything properly. They are to live according to their spiritual fathers' advise and teaching in fasting and in prayer and in self-control, with prudence, without any rancor or disorderliness, and with great diligence to paint the image of our Lord God and Savior Jesus Christ, the most pure Mother of God, the holy prophets and apostles, the hieromartyrs, the holy martyrs, the saintly nuns, the holy bishops, and the monastic saints, according to their image and likeness and substance. They are to view the icons of the ancient painters, and copy their icons from the best examples.

If some of the contemporary masters of icon painting will promise to live such a life, to keep all of the commandments, strive to do the work of God, and be gracious to the Tsar; and if the bishops will vouch for them, they are to be respected as more than laymen. These certified master painters will take on apprentices and will educate them in everything and will teach them in all reverence and chastity and introduce them to their spiritual fathers. The fathers will instruct them according to the tradition and regulations of the bishops, how one ought to live as a Christian, without any rancor or disorderliness, and thus let them be taught attentively by their masters, and if God has revealed that one of them is talented in this work, then let the master take him to the bishop. And the bishop having investigated everything thoroughly as to whether the apprentice is competent in his craft both in form and likeness, and the bishop has examined his life whether is being lead in chastity and in every virtue according to the rules [for clerics], without any disorderliness and immediately he will bless him and direct him, that he will live for the future in virtue and that he will do his sacred work with all sincerity and that apprentice will receive respect from him, as will also his teacher, as more than laymen. After all this the bishop instructs the master that he [the master] may not give preference to his own son, brother or any other relative. And if God has not given an individual the talent for teaching this work, or if he is not able to live according to the [clerical] rules, or if the master demonstrates his skill and otherwise is worthy in all respects, and presents [for inspection] the work of another apprentice not his own, and the bishop finds out, or discovers that the master is under a legal interdict, so that the other masters might be fearful, and not try to do the same, but the apprentice from that time forward will not be permitted to do iconography. And if an apprentice demonstrates a God-given talent for iconography, and learns to live according to the restrictions of the [clerical] rules, but the master begins to despise him because of jealousy, let the master not keep the respect he received. If the bishop finds out, he will place the master under a legal interdict, but the apprentice will receive greater respect.

If someone among these master iconographers hides his talent for teaching which God has given, and does not teach his apprentice properly, such a one will be condemned by God [like the lazy steward in the Gospel] to eternal punishment for concealing his talent. And if one of these same masters of iconography, or one of their apprentices, do not strive to live according to the prescriptions of the rules, but live in drunkenness, impurity, or any other kind of disorderliness, and this is discovered by the bishop, let them henceforth be dismissed from iconographic work, and never again let them be permitted to paint icons, but letting them fear the words spoken [in Scripture] that all those are cursed who do the work of God carelessly. And if someone at this time is not educated in iconography, but paints by his own will, or is self-taught, or does not paint like the accepted models, or produces work that is improper, or a scandal, or source of bewilderment to ordinary people, then let that one be commanded to be subject to a good master. And if God wills that he eventually learns how to paint according to the image and likeness, then let him paint, but if God did not give someone talent, then let him stop this work so that God's Name will not be blasphemed because of his painting. And if someone does not stop such [bad] painting, then let him experience the Tsar's wrath, and let him be condemned. And even if they begin to say, "We make our living at this and have to eat," do not accept their answers since they do not know what they are saying and they will not be excused from their sin. Not everybody can be an iconographer, and there are many other talents and skills given by God by which people can eat and make a living besides iconography, and by which God's image will not be insulted or reproached.

Therefore the archbishops and bishops are to test the master icon painters and personally inspect their icons in all of their cities and monasteries and villages within their jurisdictions, and to chose some of them within these bounds to be recognized masters so that their work can serve as a model for the rest of the iconographers so that there would not be any more bad work or disorderliness among them. And let the archbishops and bishops personally keep an eye on these painters, so that they would be most serious about their work and that of the other iconographers so that they would be respected more than lay people, so that even noblemen and commoners alike would respect these painters in every way, and then the people would have respect for their icons and then have respect for that which iconography represents. The bishops should be very concerned and diligent about this so that the more skilled artists and their apprentices would be painting from the ancient examples so that they would not be portraying the Divinity with creations of their own fantasies. This is because Christ our God was circumscribed in the flesh, but the divine nature was not, as Saint John of Damascus says, "Do not limit divinity, blind men do not lie since they are simple and do not see the visible, but I venerate and believe and glorify the flesh born from the holy virgin which is represented in the image." And who from among the skillful and creative master iconographers displays such a great talent which was given by God, but does not want to instruct and teach others in this work them, let him be condemned by Christ together with the one [lazy steward in the parable] who hid his talent into eternal punishment and for this reason let the iconographers teach their apprentices without any such wickedness so they will not be condemned to eternal punishment also.

NOTES

The "Council of the Hundred Chapters" during the reign of Tsar Ivan the IV (the "Terrible") in 1551 gave a lengthy answer in writing to many questions related to the internal and external discipline of the Church: Church courts, monasticism, liturgical practices, singing, icons, the sign of the cross, the correction of the books, the morals of the clergy, etc. The answers, published in a book of one hundred chapters, became the established Russian practice, the reform of which a century later in Patriarch Nikon's time resulted in the Old Believer movement.

Section 24

The *"Kormchaya Kniga"* chapter 124, An explanation of what iconographers ought to be by St. Isidore of Pelusium:
The iconographer must be chaste, live a spiritual life, be of good character, be marked

by humility and gentleness, and to do well in everything, but not foul-mouthed, nor blasphemous, nor an adulterer, nor a drunkard, nor a thief, nor be accustomed to any other kind of wickedness, because one must be godly to do God's work, since the Lord said to Moses in ancient times, that one must do the work of God joyfully, this joyous worker was the veil of the witness of the old testament, and today it is even more important in the age of grace to paint the image of our Lord God and Savior Jesus Christ, and the most pure Mother of God, and His saints who strove to receive the Holy Spirit. And if the iconographer were skilled in the correct ancient traditions and of the original masters godly wise men by whom from the beginning it was passed down according to the revelation of which here was a miracle or appearance, but of himself not one of the holy fathers add anything new, and if it were so important that they hesitated to change anything, but outside of the tradition of the holy fathers there is not acceptable tradition. And if someone wants very intensely to be skilled in the representation of the holy icons, but does not live a virtuous life, then such a one must not be permitted to paint icons. And again if some one lives a spiritual life but is not able to paint the icons beautifully, then he is not to be permitted to paint icons either, but rather he should make his living by some other trade.

NOTES

A book called the *"Kormchaya Kniga"* (Pilot Book) was published by Patriarch Nikon of Moscow in 1653 as the Russian Orthodox Church's first systematic corpus of canon law. This particular "Pilot Book" came from Serbia.[13] The distinguishing word in this citation is "systematic." As a title the words "pilot book" are very generic.

The *kormchiye knigi* (plural) include within themselves many bodies of church law, such as the regulations on marriage. The *kormchiye knigi* are made up of the countless manuscripts and many printed editions of collections of Orthodox canon law and commentaries that developed over the centuries that were translated into Slavonic in different countries at various times. The texts are a mixture of decrees of the Ecumenical Councils, Byzantine canons, opinions of the church fathers, combined with local bishops' decisions on various matters, with commentary. Patriarch Joseph of Moscow published an edition in 1650 and Patriarch Nikon published another edition in 1653. Modern editions are known variously; in English as "The Rudder," or "Pedalion," etc. Even though the rules about icons and iconographers collected together in this Section 25 are no longer included in our modern editions of canon law books, these rules are derived from Orthodox principles, and therefore are easy to remember and thus well known to iconographers in an oral tradition. The translator was convinced of general knowledge of the rules quoted here while speaking with iconographers who often said, "I'm sure there is a rule about" any topic that came up, even though they never saw the rules in print and could not name any sources. In fact, the translator himself read these rules for the first time while translating this book, and he does not know where else they are to be found, although he heard these and other rules quoted all of his life.

An Orthodox iconographer does not do any other painting except holy icons:
Iconographic representation is first of all a sacred task and if an artist is to be worthy of such holy work, then he ought not do any other sort of artistic painting except the holy icons. On no account should he do caricatures of people, or paint animals, snakes, reptiles, or any other kind of vermin, but only pleasant and edifying works which are like the traditional icons.

About icons that are placed over the gates, chapter 125:
It is not proper for Orthodox Christians to decorate the portals of their homes with animals, serpents, or pagan heroes. Instead Orthodox Christians are to place holy icons or the venerable Cross over the portals of their homes so that those who are entering or leaving the house may bow and venerate the Originals who are in heaven, a tradition which has been handed down by our fathers, and is the identifying mark of the Orthodox. The bishops, priests and spiritual leaders ought to supervise and teach all these things, as the Apostle says, submit yourselves to your leaders, consider the prohibition of following or subjugating yourselves to innovations, as the divine rule commands.

More about icon painters:
It is proper for iconographers who show themselves to be worthy of the sacred work of true representation, and of their position [as clergy], to be respected and to be assigned to the better seats and at dinners to be near the bishops and other notable people, like the rest of the servants of the church.

Chapter 126 (from the *Meditation,* St. Isidore to Eusebius, Bishop of Pelusium) Not to accept icons painted by unbelievers and not to sell the holy icons to unbelievers:
It is not proper for Orthodox Christians to accept an iconographic representation from unbelieving foreigners, Romans and Germans even if it happened somehow that it remained here in our faithful Greek or Russian territories from ancient times until now. But even then it will have been painted after the church schism; that is, the Greek from the Roman. And even if the iconographic representation is exactly according to the resemblance and skillful, do not venerate it, because it was painted by an unbeliever. Even if they do maintain the similarity [to Orthodox icons], their consciences are not inclined to chastity. About such things the holy Apostle Paul wrote in his Epistle to Titus as follows: "To the pure all things are pure, but to those who are defiled and unbelieving nothing is pure; and even their mind and conscience are defiled. They profess to know God, but in works they deny Him, being abominable, disobedient, and disqualified for every good work." [1: 15-16 NKJV] Do not paint icons for, and do not sell holy icons to unbelievers and foreigners, not to mention the despicable and pagan Armenians for silver or gold. This is a sin because it

does not honor but rather profanes the sacred, for it is written: "Do not give what is holy to the dogs." [Matthew 7:7 NKJV]

NOTES

This chapter is an anonymous "meditation" on a genuine text of the fifth century by St. Isidore of Pelusium to Bishop Eusebius which originally dealt with simony and false priests.[14] This section was retained to maintain the integrity of the Bolshakov *Iconographic Patternbook*. It is obviously a very harsh and negative elaboration on the principle that the Orthodox Church is the One, Holy, Catholic and Apostolic Church outside of which there is no Christianity; that is, saving grace. Closer study of the text reveals it is a very literal interpretation of Sacred Scripture and is actually addressed to those Orthodox who are ready to betray the Holy Church to her enemies.

Without knowing about this chapter, some iconographers instinctively refuse to sell their work to non-Orthodox people for the simple reason outsiders can not participate in the life of the Church, and can not be prayed for by name publicly during the preparation of the Gifts at the Divine Liturgy or during prayer services. This refusal is considered to be an act of charity because participation in Orthodox Mysteries by non-Orthodox (and careless Orthodox as well) will result in condemnation at the judgment. Naturally most Orthodox are discrete and try to present the teaching of the uniqueness of the Orthodox Church in a positive and attractive manner to non-Orthodox because they do not want to put stumbling blocks in the path of conversion. It is not for the Orthodox to accuse and condemn others, but rather by God's grace they desire to persuade others to repent and to become Orthodox freely and without threats. Some iconographers consider themselves preachers of the Gospel by their work. Called to be practicing missionaries, all Orthodox people must encourage everyone and anyone to become an Orthodox Christian, especially by good example and charity. Since there is no salvation outside the Church, sharing Orthodox books, icons, invitations to come to church, etc. with non-Orthodox are all necessary at times and must be done in a way that is appropriate, preserving the uniqueness of the Orthodox Church, and leading to the repentance of the heterodox. The grace that can and does flow through icons has led many non-Orthodox to become Orthodox in fact. Surely God will bless those who share their faith out of love for His Church and for the salvation of others.

The same principle is the reason why an iconography book should begin with the admonition to icon painters that first of all they must be pious Orthodox Christians. It is absolutely necessary for everyone to live the spiritual life of the Church in prayer and fasting together with participation in the Holy Mysteries to work out their salvation with fear and trembling. All the more the True Faith is assumed and is essential for iconographers. Those who are not Orthodox do not and can not participate in the Mysteries of the Church and therefore can not express the teaching of the Church truthfully since their words and actions do not express their minds and hearts. For this reason only Orthodox iconographers may provide icons for Orthodox churches and believers' homes.

Chapter 127, concerning on which objects it is proper to paint holy icons and on which not proper:
Represent and paint holy icons, which the God-bearing fathers decreed at the Seventh Council, on every kind of stone and wood, and on columns and on walls, and on the church vessels, which are of a solid substance or material, but do not paint icons on glass, and do not represent on it, because it is too fragile.

NOTES

This chapter forbids both the installation of stained glass windows which are supposed to be icons (not merely colored glass) and the religious folk art or craft of oil painting in reverse on glass more often found in Europe. These techniques are prohibited for the simple reason that liturgical things are supposed to be durable and not easily broken.

Do not offend the holy icons by a price in silver:
This ought to be known by a respectable painter or iconographer, if he is to live a life faithful to God, and if he is to be made worthy and resemble the ancient Godly-wise painters both in their painting and in their life style, then he should imitate the painters who did not offend the holy icons by an exchange of silver, but it will suffice to receive something for food and clothing and art supplies from the well to do.

NOTES

Except for those living in a perfect and ideal Orthodox Christian society or those who enjoy royal patronage, it is hard to imagine how the most pious and skillful iconographers, even those living in monasteries (which sell the icons in turn), can follow this chapter. In the sixteenth and seventeenth centuries there must have been many clever ways to get around this chapter which assumes the generosity and the universal obedience of all Christians to the next chapter.

Concerning the welfare of the painter:
Similarly it behooves every Orthodox Christian to make sure that those who in faith paint holy images in love, that this occupation will not result in the impoverishment of a respectable painter, but [every Orthodox Christian will provide] such that he will be comfortable and not in debt or lacking what is needed.

Section 25

The lettering on the Gospel book of the Savior:

Come, you blessed of My Father, inherit the kingdom prepared for you from the foundation of the world: "for I was hungry and you gave Me food: I was thirsty and you gave Me drink; I was a stranger and you took me in; I was naked and you clothed Me; I was sick and you visited Me: I was in prison and you came to Me." [Matthew 25:34–36 NKJV]

The lettering on the Gospel book painted on the icon of St. Nicholas the Miracle Worker (St. Luke, reading selection #24):

At that time, Jesus "stood on a level place with a crowd of His disciples and a great multitude of people from all Judea and Jerusalem, and from the seacoast of Tyre and Sidon, who came to hear Him and be healed of their diseases, as well as those who were tormented with unclean spirits. And they were healed." [Luke 6: 17-18 NKJV]

[About the lines and letters on the halo of the Savior:]

Around His divine head is a halo on which are painted nine lines marking an area in the form of a cross. This reminds us that He is like a king with His sacred nine choirs of angels arrayed before Him. It is in the form of a cross to remind us that the world has been saved by the Cross.

The three letters in the middle of these areas are written thus: Ѡ̈ [instead of Ѡ̆] For the Father, O for the Mind, and H for the Unapproachable Being. This is a witness to His divinity, to His humanity, and to His Saving Passion. Another witness to this is: Ѡ̈ - I came down from heaven, O - for those who did not know me, and H - was crucified on the cross."

NOTES

On old Russian icons one will often find the lettering on the Savior's halo as given here probably because of this passage in the patternbooks and not the more correct Greek "O Ω N" which is also common. The letters mean "The Being" or "I AM" in Greek and are the Septuagint translation of the most holy name of God in Hebrew "Yahweh." This section could not have been translated from Greek. The first ligature in Church Slavonic Ѡ̃ "OT" does mean "from," but the " O " is part of the ligature for the letter "u" in " оу́мъ " and the " H " is the first letter of the preposition " на " or "on" in Slavonic. These explanations are much more difficult to remember and to understand than to know that in Greek the letters mean "The Being" or "I AM."

DESCRIPTION OF ICONS IN THE ORDER OF THE CHURCH YEAR

THE ORDER OF CHURCH SINGING
AND CELEBRATIONS FOR THE ENTIRE YEAR

From the month of September to the month of August, in the order established by our God-bearing father Saint Sabbas at his holy monastery in Jerusalem.[15]

SEPTEMBER

"The month of September has 30 days."

1

The start of the **Indiction**;[16] that is, the New Year. The Indiction is painted as follows: the Savior is standing in the holy sanctuary. He is reading the book of Isaiah the Prophet, "The Spirit of the Lord God is upon Me, because the Lord has anointed Me to preach good tidings to the poor." [Isaiah 61:1] The Lord Sabaoth is above and the Holy Spirit is over the Savior, and around Him is a crowd of Jews of every description.

And the memory of our holy father **Simeon** Stylite [+ 459] *S. 2*, the archimandrite. He has gray hair and a beard like St. Nicholas the miracle worker, the monastic schema on his head and ringlets of hair around his forehead; he wears monastic robes, and is standing on a pillar, with one hand he is blessing and with the other he is holding a scroll with the inscription, "Bear trials and tribulations, brothers, and you will escape eternal torments." Over him is an inset icon of the Theotokos "Umilenia". And his mother Martha [+ 428] *S. 2*. St. **Martha** resembles St. Xenia; she has the schema on her head, her tunic is greenish brown, her mantle is purple, she has a rolled-up scroll in one hand and the other hand is raised in prayer.

And the holy martyr **Aeithalas** the deacon [+ 380]. St. Aeithalas resembles St. Cosmas.

And the holy deacon **Ammon** [+ beginning of the fourth century] has gray hair, a beard like St. Nicholas, and deacons' vestments.

And the memory of **Joshua** [+ c. 1425 B.C.], the son of Nun, is a young man with brown hair, a beard like St. Nikita. He wears a breastplate like St. Demetrius of Thessalonica. He has a helmet on his head, a cross in one hand and a spear in the other, and his cloak is scarlet.

46

And the Synaxis of the most holy Mother of God at Miasena; that is, the Theotokos of "**Ozurov**" [in 864]. There is a scarlet city to which a bishop who looks like St. Blaise is walking, and before him they are carrying the icon "Our Lady of Vladimir," the spiritual fathers and the people are carrying crosses. And at the bottom there is a lake and a mountain, and there is an army on a ship on the lake, and the icon of the Most Pure [Mother of God] is floating out of Lake Ozurov. And a bishop, who looks like St. Blaise, is bending down and taking it into his arms, and the people, spiritual fathers and people with brown hair and youths with crosses are coming out of the city to meet them.

And the holy martyrs **Callistus** and **Evodus** [+ beginning of fourth century] are young and resemble Sts. Demetrius and George, but are not armed, nor in armor, but are dressed like Sts. Florus and Laurus. Some others paint one as a old man with gray hair and the other as a young man with brown hair.

And the holy **forty virgin martyrs** [+ beginning of the fourth century], the ascetics, are painted like the other virgins or like St. Parasceva.

And the Great Prince **Theodore** Yaroslavich Vsevolodovich has brown hair and resembles St. Boris.

2

The holy martyr **Mamas** [+ 275] *S. 2* and his mother **Rufina.** St. Mamas is a young man like St. George, or St. Demetrius of Thessalonica; his cloak is scarlet and his tunic blue. St. Rufina looks like St. Anna.

And our father among the saints **John** the Faster [+ 595] *S. 2,* patriarch of Constantinople, has gray hair, a beard like St. Sergius of Radonezh, but others paint him with brown hair, and a beard like St. Basil of Caesarea, but shorter, a white cross patterned cloak, but others paint him in monastic robes.

And the 3,618 holy **martyrs** at Nicomedia [+ under Diocletian and Maximian] are standing as a group of men and women of every description.

3

The holy hieromartyr **Anthimus** [+ 320] *S. 4,* bishop of Nicomedia. St. Anthimus is an old man with gray hair, a beard like St. Blaise, parted at the end, and a cross patterned cloak.

Our holy father **Theoctist** [+ 467] *S. 4* has gray hair, a divided beard like St. Anthimus, or wide like St. Sergius of Radonezh and narrower at the end, his cassock is ocher with white.

And the holy and blessed **John** the "Hairy" of Rostov [+ 1580]. His garment is the same as St. Alexis the man of God, his beard is like St. Leontius of Rostov, long and curly, and very much hair.

And the holy virgin and great martyr **Basilissa** [+309] resembles St. Parasceva, simple hair, and there is a stone under her feet.

4

The holy hieromartyr **Babylas** [+251] *S. 4;* the bishop has gray hair, a beard like St. Blaise, and a green vestment.

And another holy hieromartyr **Babylas** [+ under Maximian] *S. 4* is an old man with gray hair like St. Gregory the Theologian, wearing a saccos, a purple cross patterned vestment, and three children with him are dressed in white loincloths (or rags) and are holding crosses.

And the holy prophet **Moses**, who saw God [+ 1531 B. C.]. The holy prophet the God-seer is middle aged, has balding brown hair, his cloak is reddish brown, his tunic is blue, in one hand he has a stone tablet, and in the other a scroll, "I prayed to the Lord God for a sinful people."

And the holy virgin martyr **Hermione** [+ c. 117], daughter of St. Philip the Apostle, wears simple hair and a single blue tunic.

And the holy martyrs, **Hermion** resembles St. Demetrius, and Eutych is like St. Menas.

And the holy martyrs **Mianus** and **Julian** [+ under Maximian Galerius].

5

The holy prophet **Zachariah** *S. 6,* the father of the Forerunner. Zachariah is an old man, he has long hair on his head and it is flowing down over his shoulders like Abraham, he has a long gray beard down to his waist, and at the end it is parted a little, long mustaches, on his head there is a little red hat with white folds around it. His cloak is scarlet, his short tunic is a mixture of green with white, and around this there is a gold band divided into twelve sections, his second tunic is blue, and his third tunic is bright crimson. In one hand there is a scroll on which is written, "Blessed is the God of Israel" and with his other hand he is pointing to the scroll.

And the holy Prince **Gleb** [+ 1015], who was murdered by his brother, is young with curly hair, and wears princes' robes.

And the holy martyr **Bebaia** [+ under Trajan] resembles St. Parasceva.

The holy martyr **Rhais** [or Raisa] looks the same.

And the holy martyr **Abdias** [+ between 408 and 420].

6

Commemoration of the miracle of **Michael** the Archangel at Colossae [fourth century] *S. 6,* which is Chonae. St. Michael is standing by a church and has his staff planted in a rock. The church is of white stone and has one dome, and there is a green mountain extending from the church and the second mountain is ocher. There are rivers that flow together from both mountains into that place [where the staff meets the rock], and there are nude people or people dressed only in loincloths floating in the rivers. There are still others with shovels, beams and crowbars, and the rivers are flowing into the rock with people, who are at the church doors, and other people are breaking up the mountain and swarming about. And our holy father Archippus, the sacristan. St. **Archippus**, [who is bowing down toward Archangel Michael in front of the church,] is an old man with balding gray hair, a beard like St. John the Theologian, and similar hair. He wears monastic robes.

And the holy martyr **Eudoxius** [+ 311] resembles St. Demetrius or St. Cosmas in appearance. He is dressed like a soldier, and in his hand he holds an open scroll which says, "O Lord my God, grant to all who call on Your Name, and also to myself, Your servant, forgiveness of sins."

And the holy hieromartyr **Cyril** of Gortyna [+ under Maximian] has a beard like St. John the Theologian, bishop's vestments, an omophorion and Gospel book, over him is a cloud, and on the cloud is the inscription "Go hither!"

Our holy father **David** [+ sixth century], who was previously a criminal, wears the schema, a beard like St. Blaise, and monastic robes.

And the holy apostle **Archippus** has balding gray hair, a long beard like St. Blaise, apostles' robes and an omophorion.

7

The holy martyr **Soson** [+ 304] *S. 8* is middle aged and has a beard like St. Cosmas. Others paint him with brown hair like St. Nikita, but according to the "Kievan printed pages" he is portrayed as a young man like St. Demetrius. His cloak is purple or scarlet, his tunic is blue, in his right hand he has a spear, and in the left a scroll on which is written, "O Lord Jesus Christ my God! Grant me Your gift to all of those who keep my memory, that they will be preserved from all adversity and granted forgiveness of sin, let [them fly up to heaven like] a bird."

And our father among the saints **John**, archbishop of Novgorod, miracle worker [+ 1186]. John has gray hair, a beard like St. Sergius of Radonezh, he has a white klobuk on his head, a monastic mantle, but it has white stripes around it in three places, his tunic is reddish brown, with one hand he is blessing and with the other he is holding a scroll.

And our father among the saints **Prochor**, archbishop of Radonezh, the new miracle worker has brown hair, a beard like the Theologian, and bishops' vestments with an omophorion.

8
"The day has 12 hours and the night has 12 hours."[17]
THE NATIVITY OF OUR MOST HOLY LADY, THE THEOTOKOS AND EVER VIRGIN MARY *S. 8.* St. Anna is laying on a bed, there are maidens standing holding gifts, and some others are carrying solar discs and candles, one girl is holding St. Anna under the shoulder. St. Joachim is looking out from a palace at the top, a midwife is bathing the Holy Theotokos in a basin up to her waist, another girl is pouring water into the basin from a vase. The outside of the palace is green, another palace is crimson, and near this palace Joachim and Anna are sitting on a throne and holding the most holy Theotokos and between the palaces there are stone columns and from these columns there are stretched red or green veils, around all this there is a fence colored white mixed with ocher.

And the remembrance of our holy father **Arsenius** [+ 1447], the abbot of the Konevits Monastery of Novgorod, miracle worker. He has gray hair, a blunt beard like St. Sergius, and he wears priests' vestments.

9
The holy and righteous ancestors of God **Joachim** and **Anna** *S. 10.* St. Joachim is middle aged and has a black beard turning to gray somewhat like St. Nicholas, his cloak is ocher or grayish blue, his tunic is scarlet or blue. St. Anna's cloak is scarlet, her tunic is green or blue. St. Anna is holding the most holy child [Theotokos] in her arms.

And the holy martyr **Severian** [+ 320] *S. 12* has brown hair like St. Cosmas, his cloak is blue, his tunic is scarlet lightened with white.

And our holy father **Joseph** of Polotsk [+ 1515] has gray hair but is not balding, he resembles St. Sergius, and has a beard like St. Sergius but somewhat smaller, broader and blunter. But in his "Life" it is written: "The saint was of average stature and had a handsome face, and he had a round beard, a little long and wavy, in youth it was brown, but in old age it became streaked with gray, he wears monks' robes, with the schema on his shoulders, and his cassock is ocher."

10

Martyrs **Menodora**, **Metrodora**, and **Nymphodora** [+ between 305 and 311] *S. 10.* On the first the cloak is purple or scarlet, the tunic is blue; on the middle one the cloak is grayish blue and the tunic is blue; and the third has a blue cloak and a scarlet tunic.

And St. **Pulcheria**, the empress [+ 453], is similar in everything to St. Helen, the empress.

And our holy father **Paul** the bishop [+ ninth century], his face, hair and beard resemble St. Gregory the Theologian, or St. Cornelius the Centurion in appearance and everything including robes.

On the same day the passing of our holy father prince **Joasaph**, the miracle worker of the Kamenny Monastery of Volotsk [+ 1453]. He is a young man wearing a black klobuk, with ringlets of hair around his face, his robes are monastic with the schema on his shoulders, and in his hand is a scroll, "Lord Jesus the King, look down from the heights of heaven."

11

Our holy mother **Theodora** of Alexandria [+ 490] *S. 12* has a cross in her hand, the schema on her head, her cloak is purple, the top is blue reddish-brown crimson, the tunic is light gray.

And the holy martyr **Ia** [+ c. 363] resembles St. Parasceva.

And the holy martyr **Euanthia** [+ first century] is the same.

And the holy martyr **Varisavus** [or Barisabos] has brown hair, a beard like St. Ephraim of Syria, and does not have the schema, but does wear a mantle and a cassock since he was the monk who carried the Blood of the Lord in a vessel among strangers and performed many miracles, and was killed for his conscience sake for saying the vessel contained great riches.

12

The holy hieromartyr **Autonomus** [+ 313] *S. 12* has a curly brown beard like St. Cosmas, his hair sticks out over his ears, a purple cloak highlighted with blue, his collar is ocher lightened with white, his shoulder piece and priest's stole are ocher, in his hands is a book, he is balding, he has a priest's vestment either with or without the omophorion.

The close[18] of the feast of the Nativity of the Theotokos.

And the holy hieromartyr **Cornutus**, bishop of Nicomedia [+ under Decius and Valerian] has gray hair and is old like St. Blaise.

And the holy martyr **Julian** of Galatia [+ under Diocletian] is a young man like St. Demetrius, in his hand is a scroll on which is written, "I thank You, O Lord, and grant everyone who receives my dust forgiveness of sin and freedom from suffering."

13

The holy hieromartyr **Cornelius** the Centurion [first century] *S. 12* is middle aged. He has brown hair like St. Florus, wears a priests' vestment which is blue highlighted with red and white, and has an ocher shoulder piece. His tunic is blue, his priests' stole can be seen; or a white tunic and bishops' vestments.

And the holy martyrs **Gordian** and **Macrobius** [+ under Licinius] are youths and soldiers like St. Demetrius.

And the holy martyr **Julian** the Presbyter [third century] is an old man with a priests' vestment like St. Cornelius with the omophorion.

[See section 15 of the Anthology in this volume for a description of an icon of the Dedication of the Church of the Resurrection in Jerusalem in 335.]

14

THE UNIVERSAL EXALTATION OF THE PRECIOUS AND LIFE-GIVING CROSS [in the years 326 and 628] *S. 14,* which was discovered by the Empress Helen. There is a church with one dome and eight bays, and in the middle of the church stands Bishop Sylvester, who looks like St. Blaise, holding the Cross over his head. There is a young deacon and a middle aged deacon who has a beard like St. Cosmas, who are assisting the bishop by holding him by his arms, and they are all standing on the ambo. On the right side behind the ambo on a platform are standing the Emperor Constantine and the Empress Helen, and on the other side are standing bishops, priests, and deacons, and below the ambo are princes and noblemen, and old, middle aged, and young men with brown hair wearing hats, and there is wide green palace, and a second palace colored crimson mixed with white, and a column, and on the column a man, who is holding a goblet in one hand and a saber in the other, all of which is painted scarlet.

And the holy women, the Princess **Juliana** and **Mary** the Prostitute, who resembles St. Anna or St. Elizabeth. St. Juliana resembles St. Olga.

And our holy father **Gregory** has gray hair, a thick forked beard, and wears monastic robes.

15

The holy great martyr **Nikita** [+ 372] *S. 14* has a beard and hair which flows down over his shoulders like the Savior, he is in a breastplate and armed, he has a scarlet cloak, a reddish brown or blue with light gray tunic, in his right hand he holds a lance and in the other a sword in its scabbard, but his sleeves and leggings are crimson with blue and white highlights, because he was burned to death for Christ's sake among the Goths by the King Athonarik during the reign of Constantine the Great and Licinius.

And the holy hieromartyr **Philotheus** the Presbyter [tenth century] is described in the "Kievan printed pages" as follows: Philotheus, archbishop and patriarch of Constantinople is on the 14th day of June.

On the same day as the discovery of the honorable relics of the holy first martyr and archdeacon **Stephen** [in 415]. There is a church in the middle of which is an open coffin, and St. Stephen is seen wearing a sticharion, and over him stands a bishop who is holding a book. He has gray hair and a beard like the Theologian, and on the other a deacon is incensing with a censer, and behind the bishop are priests and monks and lay people.

16

The holy great martyr **Euphemia** the All-praised [+ 304] *S. 16* wears a green cloak, her tunic is blue, in one hand she is holding the cross, and in the other a scroll on which is written, "Lord Jesus Christ, the True Light and the Joy of all, do not overlook those who call upon You in truth." Others write [the creed], "I believe in one God . . ."

And our father among the saints **Cyprian** of Moscow [+ 1406] wears a cap on his head, has gray hair and a long beard like St. Blaise which is parted, and he is wearing a saccos.

And the holy martyrs **Sebastiana** and **Meletina** [+ under Dometian] resemble St. Parasceva.

And the holy martyr princess **Ludmilla** [+ 927] resembles St. Helen or the princess, St. Olga.

17

The holy martyr **Sophia** and her three daughters **Faith** [or Vera], **Hope** [or Nadezhda], and **Charity** [or Love or Lyubov] [+ 137] *S. 16,* they are all wearing martyrs' robes; the first girl is wearing scarlet, the middle wears blue, the third green, and their hair is simple. Their mother St. Sophia is wearing a green cloak, a scarlet tunic, and on her head a shawl. St. Charity is holding a scroll which says, "O Lord Jesus Christ, I pray You, remember all the people who worship You and praise Your name forever and ever. Amen."

And the holy martyrs **Agathocleia** and **Theodota** [+ c. 230] resemble St. Parasceva.

On the same day the memory of the holy true believing princess Sophia, miracle worker of Suzhdal [+ 1542]. She is portrayed as a young woman in the schema and with monastic robes.

18

Our father among the saints **Eumenes** [+ seventh century] *S. 16,* bishop of Gortyna is an old man with gray hair, a beard like St. Blaise or like St. Gregory with curls at the end. He wears a cross patterned bishops' cloak, an ocher tunic with white, a stole and omophorion, and holds a book in his hands.

And the holy women martyrs **Sophia**, **Irene** and **Raida** [+ under the Emperor Hadrian] resemble St. Parasceva.

And the holy hieromartyr **Simeon** *S. 16* resembles St. Blaise in everything.

And St. Arcadius of **Novgorod** [+ 1168] has a beard like St. Gregory but his hair is not balding, a cloak like St. Blaise, bishops' vestments with the omophorion, and he is old and starting to gray.

19

The holy martyrs **Trophimus**, **Sabbatius**, and **Dorymedon** [+ 276] *S. 18.* St. Trophimus is an old man with gray hair, a beard shorter than St. Blaise, his cloak is green, his tunic is blue, and he wears a belt. According to the Kievan printed pages they are described as follows: "Trophimus is a young man like St. George, Sabbatius has a beard somewhat shorter than St. Blaise, and Dorymedon has hair and a beard like Sts. Cosmas and Damian." St. Sabbatius is a young man with hair like St. George, a green cloak, the short tunic is purple with scarlet, his tunic is scarlet. St. Dorymedon is also a young man like St. George, he has short hair coming down a little below his ears, his cloak is scarlet, his tunic is blue. They all have crosses in their hands.

And the holy true believing prince **Theodore** [+1291] of Smolensk and Yaroslavl and his children David [+ 1321] and Constantine *S. 16.* [Their relics were uncovered in 1463]. Theodore has a gray beard, long like St. Sergius but without waves, he wears the schema, his tunic is light gray, and he wears monastic robes. His sons are standing under his chest. They are wearing fur hats, brocaded red and blue cloaks; or they resemble Sts. Boris and Gleb.

And the holy martyrs **Agapia** and **Thecla** resemble St. Parasceva.

And the remembrance of the holy and blessed **Trophimus**, the fool for the sake of Christ, the miracle worker of Suzhdal. He has brown hair, a beard like St. Cosmas; he is nude except for a loincloth, his hands are in prayer, he has a full head of hair and it is bushy like St. John the Forerunner.

And the holy martyr **Zosimas** [+ under Diocletian] resembles St. Demetrius.

20

The holy great martyr **Eustathius** and those with him, his wife **Theopistes**, and their children **Agapius** and **Theopistus** [date unknown] *S. 20.* St. Eustathius is middle aged and has brown hair like St. George, a curly beard, and he is armed. His cloak is scarlet and is fastened over his left shoulder to under his right arm, he has green with light gray armor, which is decorated with a birds' feather pattern, his tunic is bluish, in his right hand he has a spear and a scroll on which is written, "O Lord God of powers, to everyone who keeps our memory grant a place in Your heavenly kingdom," and in the left hand a sword in its scabbard. His children are young and are standing in shirts. Their mother resembles St. Parasceva and wears a green cloak, a blue tunic, with one hand she is pointing to her family and the other hand holds a cross.

And the holy new martyrs and confessors the great prince **Michael** of Chernigov and his councilor **Theodore** [+ 1246] *S. 20.* St. Michael has brown hair, a curly beard, hair like St. John the Forerunner or like St. Blaise, which is shaggy and starting to gray. He is wearing a fur trimmed mantle with blue brocade and lined with scarlet mixed with white. His tunic is blue damask. His councilor St. Theodore has short gray hair going a little lower than his ears with a few stray hairs, a long beard like St. Blaise or St. Athanasius. He is wearing a fur coat with a blue lining with white ornaments, his tunic is scarlet damask. St. Michael is holding a cross in his right hand or in prayer and a sword in its scabbard in his left. St. Theodore is holding a [miniature] church in his hands in a gesture of prayer; but others portray a cross in one hand and a sword in its scabbard in the other.

21

The holy apostle **Quadratus** of Magnesia [+ under Hadrian] *S. 22* has balding brown hair, a curly brown beard or one like St. John Chrysostom; he is wearing apostles' robes, but on his shoulders is the omophorion, and in his hands the Gospel book, his cloak is reddish brown and his tunic is blue.

And the close of the feast of the Exaltation of the precious Cross.

And the holy martyr **Theodore** of Pamphilia in Pergium is similar in everything to St. George in a breastplate.

And the holy hieromartyrs **Hypatius** and **Andrew**, bishops [+ between 730 and 735], resemble Sts. Blaise and Tikhon.

22

The holy hieromartyr **Phocas** *S. 22*, bishop of Sinope [+ 171]. Phocas is an old man with gray hair like St. Blaise, a vestment without the omophorion; because some have said that he was only a priest, he is wearing a plain priests' vestment, his tunic is reddish brown, his vestment is light gray, over his tunic he is wearing the priests' stole, he is holding the book of the Gospels in one hand and in the other a scroll which says, "Lord Jesus Christ, preserve Your flock, and do not give to destruction those who have been covered by Your precious blood."

And the holy prophet **Jonah** [ninth century B. C.] *S. 22* has gray hair, a beard like St. Nicholas, his cloak is ocher lightened with white, his tunic is blue, and he holds a scroll in his hand.

And the holy presbyter **Jonah** [ninth century] *S. 22* is an old man with gray hair like St. John the Theologian, a purple cloak lightened with green and the shoulder piece is blue, his tunic is green lightened with white, he is wearing a priests' stole hanging down. The holy prophet Jonah is standing on the right side, John the Presbyter in the middle, and Phocas on the left.

And our holy monastic father **John** Eukhatsky is an old man and has a beard like St. Gregory the Theologian.

23

The conception of the holy glorious prophet and forerunner of the Lord, **John** the Baptist *S. 24*. There is a church and in the church his father the prophet Zachariah has incense and is at the altar performing the holy service, and standing opposite him is the archangel Gabriel humbly, and in his hand he is holding a staff, and Zachariah is praying toward the altar with his arms raised, and over them are scarlet cherubim, and behind Zachariah are standing old men near him, and one of them has a beard like St. Blaise, and another like St. Nicholas, and they have garments and head coverings of green and scarlet, and behind them is standing a leader who resembles St. Nicholas and he has a white klobuk on his head, a scarlet cloak, and near him stands another who resembles St. Blaise and has a blue klobuk, and there are other men with brown hair and youths and women with babies, and on one side there is a purple palace and on the other side is a green palace. The altar is covered with a scarlet cloth adorned with white pearls, and on the altar are a book and a chalice which are blue. Over the altar there is a canopy like a tent which is scarlet highlighted with blue and white outside and blue inside.

On the same day the falling asleep of the great prince **Alexander** Yaroslavich of Vladimir.

And the holy virgin martyrs **Irais** [or Rhais] is a young girl of ten years and Euphrosyne resembles St. Eudokia.

And the holy monastic women and virgins sisters **Xanthippa, Polyxenia**, and **Rebecca** resemble St. Parasceva.

On the same day the passing of the holy and blessed prince **Demetrius** of Galich and Moscow, who is a young man with a mustache, wears princes' robes and has his arms lifted in prayer.

24

The first woman martyr and equal to the apostles **Thecla** [first century] *S. 24* the all-praised. St. Thecla is a maiden with a blue headband, but has straight hair which comes down over both shoulders. She wears a cloak of greenish brown lightened with reddish brown, and in her hands she has the book of Epistles or the Gospels, she has bare feet and her garment has wide sleeves.

And our holy father **Coprius** [+ c. 530], who was brought up in monasticism by a goat, is an old man of 90 years, gray hair, a longer beard than St. Blaise, and monastic robes.

On the same day the passing of our holy father **Galacteon**, miracle worker of Vologda [+ 1612], who has gray hair a forked beard like St. Sergius, he has the schema, and monastic robes.

25

"The day has 11 hours and the night 13 hours."

Our holy mother **Euphrosyne** of Alexandria [+ middle of fifth century] *S. 26* wears a klobuk around her head, she is wearing an upper monastic cloak of greenish brown with reddish brown, her tunic is blue with reddish brown and her cassock is light gray, and in her hands she holds a rolled up scroll.

And a second **Euphrosyne** of Suzhdal [+ 1250], who resembles the first saint, everything as a monastic saint.

And the passing of our holy father, the abbot **Sergius** of Radonezh the miracle worker [+ 1392]. There is a white church, which has a palace on one side and a wall on the other, and there is a coffin, and the miracle worker Sergius is laying in the coffin, and he is wearing monastic robes, and on his head is a green schema, his tunic is reddish brown and at his head there is standing a bishop who has balding gray hair and resembles St. Athanasius, and his vestment is patterned with crosses, and behind him are priests and deacons; young and old and some with brown hair, and in the middle of them behind the coffin stands an abbot who resembles St. Sergius in his garments and wears a klobuk, and a deacon and behind him a priest and in the middle a spiritual father resembles St. Blaise who is bending down and placing the lid which covers the coffin, and other spiritual fathers are crying, and they have their hands covered, and others are bowing toward the coffin.

And the holy monastic martyr **Paphnutius** of Egypt and the 547 martyrs with him [under Diocletian]. They are all standing in a group, old, middle aged, and young all dressed in monastic robes. St. Paphnutius is in their midst with a beard like St. Blaise and wearing only a cassock.

And our holy fathers **Abraham** and **Coprius** the founders of the monastery on the Pechene, the miracle workers of Vologda on the Pomyeli River. St. Abraham has gray hair, a beard like St. Cyril of the White Lake, and St. Coprius is like St. Alexander Nevsky, [19] with brown hair and the schema, and monastic robes.

58

26

The passing of the holy, glorious and all praised apostle and evangelist **John** the Theologian [+ beginning of second century] *S. 28*. There is an ocher mountain, St. John is lying down, covered with soil and only his head can be seen with a halo, and bowing down over him are his disciples, two old men who resemble St. Nicholas, three middle aged men with curly beards, and one of them has a beard like St. Basil of Caesarea, two young men, and they are all wearing apostles' robes, and one of them, the disciple Plato is covering the head of the Theologian, and the others are crying, behind the mountain one can see the city of Ephesus, and in it are palaces and a church. [On a portrait icon] the head of the Theologian is balding, he has a long nose, arched eyebrows, a thick gray beard spreading out with little curls, a dense mustache, he holds the open Gospel book in his hands on which is written, "In the beginning was the Word."

27

The holy martyr **Callistratus** [+ 304] *S. 28* and his 49 companions. Some portray him like St. Florus, and others give him gray hair like St. Blaise, his cloak is scarlet, his tunic is blue, and in his left hand he holds a scroll and in the right a cross. And his 154 [20] companions are arranged about him and are of every description.

And the passing of our monastic father **Sabbatius** [+ 1435] *S. 28,* miracle worker of Solovki, is an old man with gray hair, and a beard down to his fingers that is wider than that of St. Basil. There is a church and a palace, and on the other side there is a green mountain, and the brothers are crying. There are two old men and one young man, a monastic priest in robes is wearing a klobuk, he has a censer in his hand, and in the other a book, but there is no deacon, and a spiritual father in the center is covering the coffin with a lid.

And the holy martyr **Epicharis** [under Diocletian] *S. 28* resembles St. Parasceva, and there is a stone under her feet, and water is flowing from it.

And our father the monastic St. **Herodion** the Desert Dweller, who lived at the Ilo Lake, the miracle worker of Vologda [+ 1541].

28

Our holy father **Chariton** [+ 350] *S. 30* the confessor is an old man with gray hair, a beard a little longer than St. Basil, his upper cloak is purple lightened with green and reddish brown, an ocher tunic lightened with scarlet and gray, in one hand he holds a scroll and he is blessing with the other.

And the holy martyrs; **Alexander** looks like St. George, **Zosimas** and **Mark** resemble St. Cosmas, **Nikon** is like St. Damian; **Neon** and **Diodorus** [under Diocletian].

And the holy Prince **Byacheslav** [or Wenceslaus] of the Czechs, who was killed by his brother Boleslav [in 935], is an old man with hair starting to gray that comes down past his ears, a beard like St. Basil but curly, and princes' robes.

29

Our holy father **Cyriacus** the Hermit [+ 556] *S. 30* has a beard like the Theologian but divided at the end, a light gray tunic, one arm is covered to the fingers, but he is holding a scroll of the law with the mantle.

The holy martyrs **Dadas** and **Gabdelas** the crown prince, and the sister of Gabdelas, Casdoe the princess [+ in the middle of the fourth century in Persia]. St. Dadas resembles the prince St. Boris, St. Gabdelas looks like the Crown Prince Demetrius of Russia, and St. Casdoe like St. Catherine.

And the holy prophet **Baruch** has a gray beard and a scroll in his hand on which is written, "Behold, He is our God and none can be compared to Him."

30

The holy hieromartyr **Gregory** of Great Armenia [+ 335] *S. 30* has brown hair like St. Basil of Caesarea, but his beard is lighter than Basil's beard with some graying, he is wearing the omophorion, he has purple with reddish brown bishops' vestments, his tunic is green with light gray, and his stole is ocher.

And our holy father **Gregory** [+ 1451] *S. 30,* who lived on the Pelshma River, the miracle worker of Vologda, is an old man with a beard a little narrower than St. Sergius, his hair is thick and gray and goes down below his ears, he has the schema on his shoulders, with one hand he is blessing and holds a scroll in the other.

And the holy women martyrs **Ripsima** and **Gaiana** [+ fourth century] resemble St. Parasceva.

OCTOBER

"The month of October has 31 days."

1

Today [we celebrate the feast of] the **Protection** [or Veil] of the most holy Mother of God [tenth century] *S. 32.* The "Protection" of our Lady, the most holy Mother of God and ever virgin Mary is depicted as follows: there is a church with five domes, and there are some palaces by it. In the church on the icon the most holy Mother of God is praying to her Son and God, above her the Savior is on a cloud, in her left hand is a scroll on which is written: "O Heavenly King, my Son and my God, accept everyone who calls upon Your Name and mine in every place and glorify them" and the other hand is blessing. There are two red cherubim, over the Mother of God is an omophorion, also called the "protection," which is scarlet adorned with gold and it is held at the ends by two angels. Under the feet of the holy Mother of God are the royal doors of a church opposite the ambo and on the ambo stands **Roman** the sweet singer [+ end of fifth century] who is a young man and has a scarlet vestment with a blue tunic and in his hand is a scroll on which is written, "Today the Virgin stands in the Church" and to the right side of the Virgin is the choir of prophets led by St. John the Forerunner, and on the other side is the choir of apostles lead by St. John the Theologian, and behind the choir of apostles are the ranks of martyrs, monastic fathers and all of the saints around the ambo. On the left side of the ambo stands the fool for Christ **Andrew** [+ 956], his hair is like [the holy forefather] Abraham, he is gesturing with his right hand and is pointing out the Mother of God to Epiphanius. St. **Epiphanius** is a young man like St. George and has a scarlet cloak and a blue tunic.

And the holy apostle **Ananias** [first century] *S. 32* has gray hair, a smaller beard than St. Athanasius, he is wearing the omophorion, he has a bright purple cloak, a blue tunic and has a book in his hand.

And our holy father **Sabbas** Stylite [+ 1460], the miracle worker of Vishersk. St. Sabbas resembles St. Demetrius of Priluki in his hair and beard and has similar monastic robes; but some paint him as a column dweller on a pillar.

And our father among the saints **Theodosius**, archbishop of Astrachan, the new miracle worker. Theodosius wears a bishop's cap, not very much gray hair, a beard larger than St. Sergius, he wears a crimson and gold bishops' vestment patterned with many crosses, with the omophorion and the Gospel book and a blue tunic.

2

The holy hieromartyr **Cyprian** [+ 268] *S. 34,* has a longer beard than St. Cosmas, brown hair with curly ends, bishops' vestments with omophorion and the Gospel book in his hand.

And the holy martyr **Justina** [+ 268] *S. 34,* her head covering comes down over her right shoulder, her cloak is green, her tunic is blue, her hair is pushed back behind her ears, one hand is raised in prayer and the other holds a cross.

And the holy blessed **Andrew**, the fool for Christ [see October 1]. His face resembles St. Andrew Stratelates, in his hand is a scroll which says, "I prayed for those in poverty, difficulties, servitude, and for peace for all."

And the holy hieromartyr **Dometian** of Persia, has a beard like St. Florus, and priests' vestments.

3

The holy hieromartyr **Dionysius** the Areopagite [+ 96] *S. 34,* has curly gray hair like St. Clement, wears bishops' vestments, greenish brown with white, the tunic is lightened ocher.

On the same day our holy father **Dionysius** of Novgorod the miracle worker, has a beard like St. Basil of Caesarea and monastic robes.

4

The holy hieromartyr **Hierotheu**s [first century] *S. 34,* bishop of Athens, resembles St. Blaise, his beard is curly at the end, his vestment is patterned with many crosses, and his tunic is reddish brown.

And the holy hieromartyr **Dometian** of Persia wears priests' vestments.

And the holy martyrs **Domnina, Berenice, Callisthenia** and **Prosdoce** [+ fourth century] resemble St. Parasceva.

And our father among the saints **Gurias** [+ Dec. 4, 1563; uncovering of relics 1595], archbishop and miracle worker of Kazan, has gray hair, a beard like St. Basil of Caesarea, he wears a cap [decorated] with cherubim, an omophorion, he holds the Gospel in his hands, and wears bishops' vestments.

And our father among the saints **Barsonophiu**s [+ Apr. 11, 1575; uncovering of relics 1595], bishop of Tver, is an old man starting to gray with a beard like St. Gurias divided at the ends, a similar cap and bishops' vestments.

5

The holy martyr **Charitina** [+ 304] *S. 36* has a green cloak and a scarlet tunic.

And the holy martyr **Mameltha** [+ 344] is similar [to St. Charitina].

On the same day we celebrate the **three hierarchs** [Sts. Peter, Alexis, and Jonah] of Moscow. [This feast was established in 1596; a fourth hierarch, St. Philip of Moscow, who died in 1569, was added in 1875.]

And the holy monastic fathers of the Pecherska Lavra in Kiev **Dominian, Hermes,** and **Matthew** [eleventh century].

6

The holy apostle **Thomas** [first century] *S. 36* has a young face like St. Demetrius of Thessalonica, a scarlet apostles' cloak, a blue tunic and in his hand the Epistle book.

7

The holy martyrs **Sergius** and **Bacchus** [+ between 290 and 303] *S. 36.* St. Sergius has brown hair, a longer beard than St. Cosmas, a blue cloak, and a blue tunic with white. St. Bacchus is a young man like St. Demetrius of Thessalonica, with a blue cloak, a green short tunic and a scarlet tunic. They have crosses in their hands.

And the holy martyr **Maximus** is young and in armor like St. George.

And our monastic father **Sergius** [+ 1412] who lived on the Obnora River, the miracle worker of Vologda, has gray hair and a beard like St. Alexander of Svir.

And the holy virgin martyrs **Pelagia** and **Taisia.**

8

Our monastic mother **Pelagia** [+ 457] *S. 38* resembles St. Eudokia, has a blue klobuk on her head and a lightened greenish brown tunic.

And a second St. **Pelagia** [+ 303], a virgin from Antioch, has a single garment with a belt.

On the same day the passing of our monastic father **Tryphon** [+ 1612], the archimandrite of the Dormition Monastery, which is on the Vyatke, the new miracle worker.

9

The holy apostle **James** Alphaeus [first century] *S. 38,* has a beard smaller than St. Basil of Caesarea, a whitened ocher cloak, and a blue tunic.

And our holy father **Andronicus** [+ beginning of fifth century] *S. 38* has gray hair like St. Sergius, monastic robes, the mantle is tied up, the tunic is whitened ocher.

And our holy father **James** of Kostrom, which is on the Yellow River, wears the schema, and a beard like St. Euthymius of Suzhdal.

And our monastic mother **Athanasia** resembles St. Eudokia.

And the two holy servant girls **Pamplia** [and Pamplia] who resemble Sts. Elizabeth and Anna.

And our holy father Nicander, the miracle worker of Pskov, is an old man with gray hair, wears the schema, has a beard like St. Basil which is curly at the end, and monastic robes.

10

The holy martyrs **Eulampius** *S. 38* an**d Eulampia** *S. 40* [+ 303]. St. Eulampius resembles St. George; his cloak is green, his short tunic is blue with a scarlet [long tunic]. St. Eulampia, his sister, resembles the martyr St. Barbara, her cloak is blue, her tunic is scarlet. They have crosses in their hands.

And our holy father **Basil** in appearance and beard resembles St. John the Theologian, but with monastic robes.

And the holy martyr **Theopentus** the soldier [+ under Maximian], resembles St. Demetrius.

And the holy bishop **Martin** the Merciful of Constantinople, has a brown beard similar to St. John Chrysostom, and bishops' vestments.

11

"The day has 10 hours and the night 14."

The holy martyr **Philip** the Deacon [first century] *S. 40* is a young man and wears deacons' vestments.

And our holy father **Theophanes** the confessor of Nicea [+ 847] *S. 40* has gray hair, a beard shorter than the Theologian and it is curly at the end.

On the same day [we keep] the memory of the holy fathers of the **Seventh Ecumenical Council** [787, also kept on July 16] *S. 42.*

And our monastic father **Amphilochius** the abbot of Glushetsk and Vologda [fifteenth century] *S. 40* is similar to St. Dionysius of Glushetsk.

And the holy virgin martyrs, the sisters **Zinoida** and **Philonuida** [disciples of St. Paul]. St. Zinoida holds a scroll on which is written "O Lord God of our fathers, I thank You that You have always heard me, and healed the suffering and those possessed by evil spirits."

On the same day [we keep] the memory of the holy patriarchs of Constantinople **Nectarius** [381 - 397], **Sisinius** [426 - 427], **Arsacius** [404 - 405], **Atticus**, and **Acacius** who has brown hair like St. Tikhon; St. Atticus resembles St. Basil.

12

The holy martyrs **Probus** *S. 42,* **Tarachus** *S. 44,* and **Andronicus** [+ 304] *S. 44.* St. Probus resembles St. Cosmas, his cloak is green, his tunic is scarlet. St. Tarachus is old and has gray hair, a beard like the Theologian but narrower, a soldier with honor, a purple cloak, a green tunic and stands in the middle. St. Andronicus has brown hair, a beard longer than St. Florus, a scarlet cloak, a blue tunic. They hold crosses in their hands.

And the holy monastic martyr **Anastasia** wears a garment without tailoring and no schema.

And the holy martyr **Dominica** [+ 286] resembles St. Parasceva.

And our monastic father **Cosmas** of the Holy City, the bishop of Maiuma and the composer of canons [i.e., church hymns, + after 776] is represented as an old man with gray hair, a wide beard down to his knees and wide, at the end it is forked and narrow, he wears an ocher cassock and he holds a scroll in his hand.

13

The holy martyrs **Carpus** and **Papylus** [+ 251] S. 44. This hieromartyr Carpus was a priest, an old man with gray hair, a beard like St. Blaise and it is forked at the end, his vestment is purple patterned with many crosses. St. Papylus the deacon has gray hair and resembles the martyr St. Menas. He wears a deacon's sticharion, his cloak is purple reddish brown high lighted with blue. In one hand he holds incense and in the other a censer. And St. **Agathonica**, the sister of St. Papylus, resembles St. Parasceva.

And our holy mother **Parasceva** of Rzhevsk *S. 46* wears monastic robes, has a blue klobuk with crosses on her head, her tunic is greenish brown with scarlet, in one hand is a scroll and with the other she is holding to her chest. She was a hegumena [abbess].

14

The holy martyrs **Nazarius, Gervase, Protase** *S. 46,* and **Celsius** *S. 48* [their relics were uncovered in 387 and are now in Milan]. St. Nazarius is an old man with gray hair coming down past his ears, a rounded beard like St. Nicholas, a green cloak, his armor is decorated with a birds' feather pattern, the towel which reaches from over the left shoulder to down under the right arm is scarlet with white, his sleeves are blue and his tunic are blue, his knees are bare, his leggings are reddish brown, he has a sword in its scabbard in his left hand, and in his right a lance with a banner. St. Gervase resembles St. George in a breastplate, his cloak is reddish brown high lighted with blue, his armor and quiver are decorated with gold, and he himself is young and resembles St. George, his right sleeve is scarlet and in his hand a lance and in the other a shield, his tunic is scarlet, his leggings are purple with green and blue, a sword in a scabbard can be seen in the tunic by the shield. St. Protase resembles St. Demetrius of Thessalonica, he has a green cloak, a blue short tunic and a scarlet tunic. In the "Kievan printed pages" they are described similarly. St. Celsius has a beard like St. Cosmas and his hair flows down past his ears, a scarlet cloak, a blue tunic, he holds a cross in his right hand and his left hand is empty. The printed *Prologue* and the *Monthly Reader* say he was a child.

And our holy father **Nonus,** bishop of Cypress, has brown hair like St. Tikhon the miracle worker [June 16].

And the holy bishop **Nirsus** is an old man with gray hair, a beard like St. Gregory the Theologian, bishops' vestments, and he lived to be eighty years old.

On the same day [we celebrate] the monastic saint and prince **Nicholas** Svyatosh of Kiev [+ 1143]. He has the schema, wears monastic robes, on the schema is the cross, and he has a beard like St. Theodore of Yaroslavl.

15

Our holy father **Euthymius** the New [+ 889] *S. 48,* is an old man with gray hair, a beard longer than St. John the Merciful, monastic robes, the tunic is lightened ocher.

And the holy hieromartyr **Lucian** the presbyter [+ under Maximian] S. 48, resembles St. John Chrysostom but with redder hair, he wears a cross patterned vestment, a blue tunic brightened with light gray, the omophorion and holds the Gospel.

And the holy virgin martyr **Bibea** [beginning of the second century].

And our father among the saints **John,** bishop of Suzhdal, the miracle worker, has gray hair, a beard like St. Sergius, he wears a cap, bishops' vestments, the omophorion and the Gospel book like St. Leontius of Rostov.

16

The holy martyr **Longinus** the Centurion [first century] *S. 50* resembles St. Cosmas, has brown hair, is armed, has a scarlet cloak, checked armor, the sleeves are blue, his leggings at the knees are reddish brown, in his left hand is a sword in a scabbard, he has a white head covering, in his right hand he holds a lance and a scroll on which is written, "Truly this was the Son of God. You are the One who suffered Your great passion for the sins of the whole world."

And the holy righteous **Longinus** the new miracle worker of Yarensk, has brown hair, a beard like St. Cosmas, a green garment like St. Alexis the Man of God.

17

The holy prophet **Hosea** [or Osee + 820 B.C.] *S. 50* has gray hair, a beard similar to the prophet Elias, a whitened ocher cloak, a blue tunic and in the left hand a scroll.

And the holy monastic martyr **Andrew** of Crete [+ 767] *S. 50* has gray hair, a beard longer than St. Blaise and forked at the end, bishops' vestments, the Gospel book in one hand, and he is blessing with the other.

And the holy monastic martyr **Abdius** has gray hair, a beard longer than St. Sergius, monastic robes, the tunic is green with greenish brown.

And the translation of the venerable relics of the friend of the Lord **Lazarus** [first century]. He resembles St. John Chrysostom somewhat in appearance, but his garments are like the Apostle Paul.

And the holy miracle workers **Cosmas** and **Damian** [+ end of the third century], who were from Aravit, resemble Sts. Florus and Laurus and have similar garments to the latter.

And the holy martyr **Leontius** has a [black] beard like the [holy fore-] father

Joachim, a red cloak with greenish brown, the tunic is light gray, in the right hand is a cross and in the left a sword in its scabbard

The holy martyrs **Anthymus** and **Patrick**. St. Patrick is a young man like St. George, while St. Anthymus resembles St. Florus, his cloak is scarlet, his tunic is green, he has a cross in his right hand and a piece of cloth in the left.

18

The holy, glorious, and all-praised apostle **Luke** [first century] *S. 50* has curly hair, he is middle aged, has a beard like St. Cosmas, apostles' robes, the cloak is green with scarlet, the tunic is blue, in his hands is a Gospel book on which is written, "Inasmuch as many have begun to order a narrative of those things believed." [Luke 1:1]

19

The holy prophet **Joel** [800 B.C.] *S. 52* resembles the prophet Elias in beard and hair, has a reddish brown cloak, the tunic is scarlet.

And the holy martyr **Varus** [+ 307] *S. 52* resembles St. George, has a blue cloak, a scarlet tunic, and with him are seven other martyrs: two are old, three are middle aged, and two are young. And the blessed **Cleopatra** [+ 327] resembles St. Parasceva and her son **John** resembles St. Varus.

And our holy father **Marinus** the Elder has brown hair like St. Cosmas, a black klobuk without the schema, and monastic robes.

And the holy hieromartyr **Sadoc** [or Sadoth + 344] *S. 52* and those with him. St. Sadoth is a priest, has a beard longer than St. John Chrysostom, priests' vestments, holds the Gospel book with both hands, a blue tunic with reddish brown, but also in his hand is a scroll on which is written, "I believe in my God, that if a Christian who protects and conceals my relics and calls on the name of God for my sake, he will attain salvation."

And our holy father **John** Rilsky [+ 946] *S. 54* has gray hair, a longer beard than St. Hilarion, monastic robes, the tunic is lightened ocher and his hands are held in prayer.

And the holy righteous **Lot** [c. 2100 B.C.], has gray hair, is balding, has a beard like St. Blaise, and apostles' robes.

20

The holy great martyr **Artemius** [+ 363] *S. 52* has a lot of gray hair past his ears, a shorter beard than the Theologian but straight at the ends, he is armed, his cloak is scarlet and wraps around from over his right shoulder down to under his left arm, he has purple leggings, on his left arm he has a shield and behind the shield one can see a sword in its scabbard, in his right hand he has an unrolled scroll on which is written, "O God from God, One from One, crowned King by the King, Who for your sake in piety has suffered."

And the holy martyr **Cleopatra** *S. 54* resembles St. Parasceva, in front of her is a child wearing a white shirt, in her hand is a cross, bare knees, and red or blue shoes.

And the memory of Saint **Cornelius** the Centurion, who is mentioned in the Acts of the Holy Apostles, has gray hair like the martyr St. Menas, is armed, his breastplate is decorated with a birds' feather pattern, he holds a shield in his hand, his cloak is scarlet and his tunic is blue.

21

Our holy father **Hilarion** the Great [+ 372] *S. 54* is an old man with gray hair, a longer beard than the Theologian, and narrower at the end, monastic robes, the tunic is ocher mixed with white. And again St. Hilarion the Great has a scroll in his hands on which is written, "Be diligent about your souls, I beseech you brothers and sisters, during the present age so that you will enjoy eternal life."

And the holy father **Hilarion** [+ 1164], bishop of Meglin, has a beard like St. Athanasius, gray hair, a blue cross patterned vestment and light gray, in the middle dark gray, white and blue, a bishops' omophorion, and the Gospel book in his hands.

And the holy martyr **Licirion** has brown hair like St. Florus and wears a single garment.

22

Our father among the saints and equal to the apostles **Abercius** [or Averky + 167] *S. 54*, bishop of Hieropolis and miracle worker, is an old man with gray hair, a beard shorter but wider than the Theologian, he has a bishops' cap on his head, a reddish purple cross patterned vestment, a blue tunic, the omophorion and Gospel book.

And the **seven holy youths** at Ephesus who slept for 372 years, all are young *S. 56*. They are standing slightly bowed in a cave facing Emperor Theodosius [408 - 450], and the emperor is bowing to them on his knees and is looking at them, the emperor has gray hair, a beard the same size as St. Nicholas and does not hang down straight. According to the "Kievan printed pages" the emperor is young, his cloak is blue, his tunic is scarlet, and has a cap and curly hair. Behind the emperor stands a bishop with gray hair and a beard like St. Sergius, on his head is a black klobuk, his tunic is light gray, and he is also looking at the youths, in his hand he holds the Gospel book, the other hand is in prayer. Behind the bishop are three men, one has gray hair and a long beard like St. James the brother of the Lord, and on him is a blue brocade coat, his tunic is embroidered scarlet, a green hat, and the other two men who are seen behind the bishop resemble Sts. Boris and Gleb, the third is young like St. George and has a scarlet hat adorned with white, a green cloak, the mountain is ocher with whitened wild color [in Slavonic *"dika"*]. The first youth from the Emperor resembles St. Demetrius of Thessalonica, his cloak is scarlet, around his waist is a sash hanging down, his tunic is blue, one sees only the left hand of the one with the sash. The youth behind him resembles St. George, with a green cloak, a scarlet tunic, since this one also has a sash, his garment appears to be divided. The third youth resembles St. Demetrius of Thessalonica and has a similar sash, his cloak is purple with lightened reddish brown, his tunic is blue. The fourth youth is similar to the first youth and all seven of them are young, and their knees are bare, and in the cave they are carrying vessels, the seven of them, and they all wear caps, and their names are as follows: **Maximilian, Jamblicius, Martinian, Dionysius, John, Constantine,** and **Anthony.**

On this day we celebrate the miraculous icon of the most Holy Mother of God of **Kazan** [specifically the miraculous intercession by the Mother of God for the city of Moscow in 1612].

And the 40 holy martyred women, **Anna, Elizabeth, Theodotia, Glykeria** and the others [+ second or third century]; all resemble St. Parasceva.

23

The holy apostle **James** [first century] *S. 56,* the brother of the Lord according to the flesh, who was the first bishop of Jerusalem, the first hierarch who was appointed by the Lord Himself to the episcopacy, has a long beard like St. Basil, but curly at the ends, he has a white bishops' cloak high lighted with blue, a reddish brown tunic, the omophorion and Gospel book, with one hand he is blessing and with the other he is holding the Gospel.

And the holy blessed **James** [+ 1540], who was a fool for Christ's sake and miracle worker of Borovichi. James is young and naked except for a cloth around his waist.

And our holy father **James,** the abbot of the Iron School and miracle worker of Kostrom, has gray hair, a beard like St. Blaise, has the schema, curls of hair around his head, and monastic robes.

24

The holy martyr **Arethas** [+ 523] *S. 58* and those with him. St. Arethas has gray hair like St. Andrew the Apostle, a beard longer than St. Nicholas, a breastplate with a birds' feather pattern, the sleeves of his [short] tunic are scarlet, his leggings are black, on his left shoulder he has a purple cloak lightened with blue, in his left hand he has a sword in its scabbard, but in the right hand together with the cross he is holding a scroll against his heart on which is written, "O Lord, Jesus Christ, have mercy on those who remember our martyrdom and grant them forgiveness of sins."

And the holy martyr **Syncletia** [+ 523] (and her two daughters) is similar to St. Parasceva; she has a chalice with her blood in her right hand and a scroll in the other on which is written, "I will praise You, O Lord my God, for You have made me worthy to taste the honorable sacrifice." Her daughters resemble Sts. Faith and Charity [see September 17].

Patriarch **Proclus** has a beard like St. Nicholas, gray hair the omophorion and gospel, and on his head is the schema.

And our father among the saints **Athanasius** [+ 1311], patriarch of Constantinople *S. 58,* has a beard not much longer than St. Sergius, gray hair, in a blue saccos, his tunic is reddish brown.

And the holy righteous **Elesbaan** [+ c. 555], king of Ethiopia, has gray hair, a beard like St. Nicholas, and his virgin daughter **Mary,** they have monastic robes, but St. Elesbaan wears a royal crown.

And the holy martyr **Ralius,** brown hair and garments like the martyr St. Nikita.

The holy martyr **Roman** is an old man with a long graying beard, and martyrs' robes.

The monastic martyr father **Razas** is a young man.

25

The holy martyrs **Marcian** and **Martyrius** the notaries [+ 355] *S. 58.* St. Marcian resembles St. Florus with brown hair, a scarlet cloak, a purple with white short tunic, and a blue tunic. St. Martyrius is a young man like St. Demetrius of Thessalonica, has a blue cloak, a green short tunic and a lightened scarlet tunic. They hold crosses in their right hands and their left are raised in prayer.

And the memory of St. **Proclas** [first century], the consort of Pontius Pilate. She resembles St. Helen and wears a crown.

The monastic saint **Abraham** *S. 60* has gray hair, a long beard like St. Athanasius, but thinner, in one hand is a scroll and with the other he is blessing, his tunic is reddish brown and ocher with white.

And our father among the saints the metropolitan **John** wears a white klobuk, a saccos, a beard like St. Blaise but not forked.

26

The holy glorious great martyr **Demetrius** of Thessalonica [+ 306] *S. 60,* who was stabbed in the ribs with a spear. He is a young man wearing a greenish brown with white breastplate with a feather pattern, his cloak is green, he is girded with a towel, in his right hand he has a lance as well as a scroll on which is written, "O Lord, do not destroy the city and people; if You save the city, I will be saved with them, and if they are lost, I will be lost with them." In his left hand is a sword in its scabbard and his knees are bare.

And the passing of our father among the saints **Jonah** the bishop and miracle worker of Perm. He has curly gray hair, a beard like St. Demetrius Priluki, he wears a bishops' cap and vestments.

27
"The day has 9 hours and the night 15."
The holy martyr **Nestor** [+ 306] *S. 60* is young like St. George, his hair is disheveled, he is in armor, the breastplate is lightened ocher with a feather design, he has a broad sash from over the right shoulder to under the right arm, his cloak is purple with white, his tunic is scarlet, in his right hand is a lance passing from the left shoulder by the right side, but in the left hand is a shield, and his leggings are black.

And the holy martyr **Mark** [time and place unknown] has brown hair like the martyr St. Nikita, and is dressed in armor.

And the holy martyrs **Capitolina** and **Eroteis** [+ 304], her maid servant. St. Capitolina is like St. Parasceva, and her servant St. Eroteis is like St. Juliana.

And the passing of the holy true believing Prince **Andrew** [+ c. 1390] of Smolensk and Pereyaslavl, the miracle worker, resembles the martyr St. Nikita in his beard, and hair down over his shoulders, he has princes' robes, in one hand the cross and in the left a sword.

28

The holy martyrs **Terence** S. 60 and **Neonilla** S. 62 [time and place unknown]. St. Terence has brown hair, a beard like the Apostle Paul, a green cloak, a purple tunic with lightened reddish brown, his right hand is in prayer, and he is pointing up with the fingers of his left hand. St. Neonilla has a green cloak, and a scarlet tunic with white.

And the holy martyr **Maximus** [+ under Decius] is an old man who is beginning to gray.

And the holy great martyr **Parasceva** [+ under Diocletian] S. 62 called "Friday," has a scarlet cloak, a blue tunic, a white shawl on her head, a scroll in her hand on which is written, "O Lord Jesus Christ my God, let every one who calls on You by means of me Your servant, save him from every need and forgive him his sins," and in the left hand a cross.

And our father **Arsenius** [+ 1266] S. 62, archbishop of Serbia, has a beard and hair like the Apostle Andrew, bishops' vestments with omophorion and Gospel book, a cap on his head and a light gray tunic.

And the holy martyr and bishop **Cyriacus** of Jerusalem [+ under Julian the Apostate], resembles the Apostle Matthew, bishops' vestments, a cross in the right hand, and the Gospel in the left.

And our holy father **Stephen** [eighth century] of St. Sabbas' Monastery and writer of canons, has gray hair like St. Nicholas and monastic robes.

And Saint **Gregory,** bishop of Crete, has gray hair, a beard like St. Sergius, and bishops' vestments.

29

The holy monastic martyr **Anastasia** the Roman [+ under Valerian] S. 62, wears a blue cloak, a scarlet tunic with white, and has a cross in her hands.

And our holy father **Abraham** the Recluse and his daughter **Mary** [+ 360]. St. Abraham has gray hair, his beard is curly like the Theologian, his tunic is reddish brown, and both wear monastic robes.

And our holy father **Abraham** [eleventh century] S. 64, archimandrite of Rostov, the miracle worker, has thick yellowish hair, a beard like St. Sergius, monastic robes, and his tunic is reddish brown.

And the holy martyrs **Claudius, Asterius, Neon** and the virgin **Neonilla** [+ 285], all are young.

Saint **Stephen,** King of Serbia [1275 - 1320], resembles King David [the prophet] in everything.

And the monastic saint **Anna** [+ 826], also named "Euphemiana," resembles St. Eudokia.

30

The holy martyr **Zenobius** and his sister **Zenobia** [+ 285] *S. 64.* The hieromartyr Zenobius is an old man with gray hair, a beard shorter than St. Athanasius, a purple cross patterned bishops' cloak, and St. Zenobia is a young woman resembling St. Barbara, in her hand is a scroll on which is written, "O Master Lord God, protect Your city, which You have redeemed by shedding Your Blood," a green cloak, a purple tunic with white, and a cross in her hand.

And our holy father **Gregory** of Lopotov, has gray hair, a beard like St. John the Theologian, and monastic robes.

And the holy martyrs Eutropius [+ 250], and Anastasia of Thessalonica; St. Eutropius struggled for three years as a monk and the virgin Anastasia twelve years as a nun.

31

The holy apostles **Stachys, Amplias**, and others [first century] *S. 64.* The holy martyr **Epimachus.** St. Stachys has brown hair, a beard like St. Florus, his cloak is purple, a blue tunic, like St. Luke the Evangelist, there is a scroll in his hand. St. Amplias is young like St. Demetrius of Thessalonica, his cloak is lightened scarlet, his tunic is blue, his hands are held in prayer. St. Epimachus has brown hair like St. Cosmas, a scarlet cloak, a blue tunic, his hands are held in prayer. But in the printed *Prologue* he is described as being very young and having a very handsome face.

And the holy fathers **Spyridon** and **Nicodemus** of the Pecherska Lavra [twelfth century]. They have sandals on their feet, the monastic saint Spyridon has a gray beard longer than St. Sergius and forked at the end, St. Nicodemus has a beard like St. Sergius but it is narrower, gray hair, monastic robes, black klobuks, and the schema.

And the monastic saint mother **Maura** [fifth century] resembles St. Eudokia.

And our holy father **Marous,** the miracle worker, has brown hair, a curly beard like St. Paul the Apostle, the schema on his head, monastic robes. He performed miracles by his prayers [saving people] from plagues, fires, earthquakes, exorcising demons, and healing all sicknesses.

NOVEMBER

"The month of November has 30 days"

1

The holy miracle workers and unmercenaries **Cosmas** and **Damian** [from Asia, no date] *S. 66*. St. Cosmas has a scarlet cloak, a greenish brown short tunic, and a blue long tunic. St. Damian has a blue cloak, a lightened ocher short tunic, and a scarlet long tunic. Both have medium beards, both hold spoons in their right hands, open containers in their left hands and they have ocher sandals on their feet. And their mother, the monastic St. Theodota, resembles St. Eudokia.

And the holy women and martyrs **Cyrenia** and **Juliana** [+ under Maximian] resemble St. Elizabeth.

And the holy martyr **Hermeningild** [+ 586] is a young man like St. Demetrius and wears a royal crown and purple robes.

2

The holy martyrs **Akindynus, Pegasius** *S. 66,* **Aphthonius,** and **Elpidephorus** the counselor, and **Anempodistus** [+ c. 345 in Persia] *S. 68*. St. Akindynus is an old man with gray hair like St. John the Theologian; he has a short beard, a purple cloak mixed with white, a blue tunic, and a wide sash down from the left shoulder to under the right arm. St. Pegasius resembles Moses the God-seer; he is a man with brown hair, a dark greenish brown cloak with white, a blue tunic, and the 7,028 martyrs with them. They are a group of old and middle-aged men, but St. Elpidephorus the counselor resembles St. Theodore of Chernigov and wears similar robes.

3

The holy martyrs **Akepsimas** the bishop *S. 68,* **Joseph** the presbyter, and **Aeithalas** the deacon [+ fourth century in Persia] *S. 70*. St. Akepsimas is an old man with a shorter beard than St. Andrew, but with gray hair similar to St. Andrew, a greenish brown cloak with white, a scarlet tunic with white, a Gospel book in his hands, bishops' vestments with the omophorion. St. Joseph is seventy years old, resembles St. Blaise, and wears priests' vestments. St. Aeithalas is sixty years old but has brown hair and wears deacons' vestments.

And the monastic saint mother **Snadulia** [+ c. 350 or 380] resembles St. Anna.

And the holy martyr **Porphyrius** has brown hair like St. Cosmas.

And our holy father **Joannicius,** the desert dweller of the Vologda district, the new miracle worker, wears monastic robes.

4

Our holy father **Joannicius** the Great [+ 86] *S. 70* is an old man with gray hair and a long and broad gray beard which is parted at the end, a purple mantle lightened with greenish brown and reddish brown, and he holds a scroll in both hands.

And our holy mother **Sophia,** princess of Suzhdal and miracle worker, resembles St. Eudokia in everything and wears monastic robes.

5

The holy martyrs **Galacteon** and **Epistemis** [+ under Decius] *S. 72.* St. Galacteon is young, wears monastic robes, an ocher tunic with white, there is a scroll in his right hand, his schema is embroidered all around, his left hand is raised in prayer. St. Epistemis wears the schema on her head, monastic robes, her mantle is a lighter color than Galacteon's cloak, the tunic is ocher with whitened reddish brown, in her right hand is a cross, and the fingers of the left hand are raised up in prayer.

And our father among the saints Archbishop **Jonah** [+ 1470] *S. 72* wears a white klobuk, he has a longer beard than St. Sergius, he is an old man with gray hair and bishops' vestments.

And the memory of our holy father **Galacteon,** abbot of Vologda, miracle worker, is an old man with gray hair, has a narrower beard than St. Sergius; he wears the schema and monastic robes.

6

Our father among the saints **Paul** the Confessor [+ 350] *S. 72,* patriarch of Constantinople, is an old man with gray hair, has a narrower beard than the Theologian; he wears a bishops' vestment with a cross pattern, his tunic is green with white, with an omophorion and holds a Gospel book.

And our holy father **Luke** [+ 820] is a young man and wears monastic robes.

And the passing of our holy father **Barlaam** of Khutin of Novgorod [+ 1192] *S. 74,* miracle worker. St. Barlaam is a young man with black hair, a beard down to his chest, trimmed. There is a church with one dome, green lightened with white. Barlaam wears the schema, his tunic is greenish brown with white. At the head of the Saint there is a bishop with a book, who resembles St. John Chrysostom, and is balding but has some curls of hair coming down on his shoulders, he wears a white cross patterned cloak, the shoulder piece is gold, so that the collar may be decorated, and a Gospel book is in his hands; there is a young deacon next to him. And at the Saint's feet is an abbot in a klobuk, who is an old man with gray hair, a beard like the Theologian, an ocher tunic; behind him there is a young spiritual father with a black mantle, an ocher tunic with white, and one can see a few more of them behind the abbot, from the side of the young spiritual father they are all similar, they have a greenish brown tunics with white, and in the midst of them in the center there is one with brown hair, not a long beard, and by the abbot one sees the head of a young man; all are wearing klobuks, there are two palaces, one on each side.

And the holy martyr **Victor** has brown hair like St. Nikita, in his hands is a scroll on which is written, "I do not desire temporal things, but I long for heavenly delights."

And the holy seven virgin martyrs **Tecussa, Alexandra, Polactia,** and **Claudia, Euphrosyne, Athanasia, Matrona**; they are all similar young maidens.

And the passing of our father among the saints **Herman,** archbishop of Kazan, miracle worker [+ 1568], who has brown hair, a beard like St. Nikita the martyr, wears a bishops' cap and vestments.

7

The holy martyr **Hieron** [+ under Diocletian] *S. 76* and the **33 martyrs** with him. St. Hieron [or Neron] is a young man who resembles St. Demetrius, his upper cloak is blue, his tunic is greenish brown with white, there is a cross in his hand, his left arm is raised, the fingers are in prayer. And the holy 33 Martyrs who suffered in Melitene and the three children with them. There stands a column of old men with gray hair, young men with brown hair and children; all wear martyrs' robes, and in front the three children wear [long Russian] shirts.

And our holy father **Lazarus** the Faster [+ middle of eleventh century] *S. 76* is an old man with gray hair, a longer beard than the Theologian, his tunic is ocher with white. According to the "Kievan printed pages" he has monastic robes, a blue [blank space], and is young like St. Demetrius.

And the holy martyrs **Absinyania** and **Thessalonica** resemble St. Parasceva.

8

The Synaxis of St. **Michael** the Archangel *S 78*, the leader of the heavenly armies. His cloak is scarlet and his tunic is blue. And the other bodiless powers. The archangels have curly hair and curls go down over their ears, scarlet cloaks, blue short tunics, and scarlet long tunics with white. They are holding the Savior Immanuel in a cloud, beneath the Savior is a scarlet cherub, with seraphim on either side; all of the angels have wings and staffs. If you want to paint the great synaxis of angels; that is, illustrate the nine choirs of angels, then 1 cherubim, 2 seraphim, 3 thrones, 4 dominions, 5 many-eyed [powers], 6 authorities, 7 principalities, 8 archangels, and 9 angels. A design of how to paint this [great synaxis of angels is not found] in this pattern book.

9

The holy martyrs **Onesiphorus** S. 78 and **Porphyrius** S. 80 [+ under Diocletian]. St. Onesiphorus is a young man like St. Demetrius and has a blue cloak and a scarlet tunic. St. Porphyrius has brown hair like St. Florus, a short beard, a green cloak, and a blue tunic with white. Our holy monastic mother **Matrona** S. 80 stands between them, and wears a purple cloak, the schema on her head; they hold crosses in their hands and their arms are raised in prayer.

And our holy mother **Theoktista** [+ ninth century] wears the schema like St. Eudokia and holds a scroll on which is written, "Now dismiss Your servant according to Your word in peace."

And our holy monastic father **John** Kolovos is a young man like St. Galacteon; but others paint him like St. Basil of Caesarea, i.e., an old man with gray hair, wearing the mantle and a cassock to the knees.

And the holy monastics **Eustolia** and Sosipatra were of imperial rank, but fully professed nuns.

And the holy martyr **Alexander** of Thessalonica resembles St. Demetrius, but unarmed.

10

The holy apostles **Erastus, Olympas, Herodion, Quartus** and others [first century] S. 80. St. Erastus resembles St. John Chrysostom, he has a greenish brown cloak with white, the omophorion and a book in his hands, as do all the others; St. Olympas is young like St. Demetrius of Thessalonica; St. Herodion resembles St. Luke the Evangelist, with a greenish brown cloak, a blue tunic, the omophorion and Gospel book. In the "Kievan printed pages" they are described as follows: Erastus has a wide beard like St. Blaise; Olympas and Herodion have beards like Sts. Cosmas and Damian; and Quartus has a beard like St. John the Merciful.

And the holy blessed **Maximus** [+ 1433] *S. 84,* the fool for Christ's sake, the miracle worker of Moscow, has a beard and hair like St. Peter the Apostle, balding, he is nude except for a wide sash and his hands are held in prayer. His burial is described as follows: a bishop who is an old man with gray hair and a beard like St. Cyril of the White Lake is burying him, and with him are priests and deacons and a crowd of all kinds of people.

11

The holy martyrs **Menas** [+ 304], **Victor** [+ under Emperor Antoninus], and **Vincent** [+ under Diocletian] *S. 82.* St. Menas is an old man with curly gray hair, a beard like St. Nicholas, there are little wisps of hair coming out from behind his ears, his cloak is greenish brown with white, his tunic is scarlet, in one hand is a lance, in the left hand is a sword in its scabbard, his leggings are purple. St. Victor resembles St. Cosmas, has a scarlet cloak, a short ocher tunic with white, in one hand the cross, the left is in prayer, the fingers are raised, the tunic is blue. St. Vincent is a young man like St. Demetrius, has a scarlet cloak with white, a blue tunic, a cross in the right hand, and a sword in its scabbard in his left hand.

And the holy martyr **Stephanida** [suffered with the St. Victor just mentioned] resembles St. Parasceva.

And our holy father **Theodore** [+ 826] *S. 82,* abbot of the Studion, is an old man with graying hair, a simple short beard like St. Nicholas, monastic robes, a greenish brown tunic with white, with one hand he is blessing, and in the other a scroll is curling down. But according to the printed *Prologue* he was emaciated, had a white face, parted hair, balding, and a scroll on which is written, "I promise you, that if you want to be courageous in the day of the Lord, you must pray for it unceasingly."

And our holy monastic father **John** the candle bearer of Solovki, miracle worker, is of short stature with brown beard turning gray, and is emaciated.

12
"The day has 8 hours and the night 16."

Our father among the saints **John** the Merciful [+ 620] *S. 84,* archbishop of Alexandria, is an old man with gray hair like St. Blaise, the beard is a little long, his cloak is blue with white, an ocher tunic, in his hands is the Gospel, and on his shoulders the omophorion.

And our holy monastic father **Nilus** [+ c. 450] *S. 84* is an old man with gray hair, a large beard like St. Joannicius the Great, narrower and denser with curls at the end, his tunic is greenish brown with white, he has a scroll in his hand on which is written, "Be alert, brothers, and do not sin!"

On the same day the holy blessed **John,** the fool for Christ's sake, miracle worker of Ustyuzh, is a young man, short shaggy hair, in a [long white Russian] shirt, but his right shoulder is bare as well as his knees.

13

Our father among the saints **John** Chrysostom [+ 407] *S. 84,* patriarch of Constantinople, has a beard like St. Cosmas, the hair of his head is curly, he wears a saccos which is patterned with many gold crosses in circles, he is blessing with one hand and he holds the Gospel book with the other.

And the holy martyr **Antoninus** is an old man; the martyr **Nicephorus** is a young man; the martyr **Germanus** [or Herman] has a stunted body; and **Manena** was a maiden [+ 308].

14

The holy glorious apostle **Philip** [first century] *S. 86* is a young man like St. Demetrius of Thessalonica, his robes resemble St. Thomas the Apostle, his cloak is scarlet with white, his tunic is blue, and he has a scroll in his left hand.

And the holy hieromartyr **Hypatius** of Gangria, is an old man with gray hair like St. Blaise, the end of his beard is frizzled, his vestment has many crosses, in his left hand is the Gospel, the right is in prayer, and his tunic is ocher.

And our father among the saints **Gregory** Palamas [+ 1360] *S. 86,* archbishop of Thessalonica, is an old man, he has curly gray hair like St. Clement, a beard like St. John the Theologian, a vestment with a cross pattern, a white tunic with a little scarlet, he holds the Gospel book in both hands, and he wears the omophorion.

And the holy true believing Emperor **Justinian** [+ 565] and the Empress **Theodora** [+ 548]; the emperor has a forked, curly, brown turning to gray beard down to his waist like the Emperor St. Constantine. St. Theodora resembles St. Helen the Empress.

15

The holy martyrs **Gurias, Samonas** *S. 86* [+ 306], and **Abibus** the deacon [+ 306] *S. 88.* St. Gurias has a beard like St. John the Theologian but a little longer. He is not balding, his hair comes down over his ears, he has a greenish brown cloak with white, the short tunic is scarlet lightened with white, but his tunic is green, in his hand a cross, the right hand is in prayer, the fingers are pointing up. St. Samonas has brown hair like St. Cosmas, a scarlet cloak lightened with blue and white highlights, like the apostles he is wrapped about with this cloak, his tunic is purple lightened with white and scarlet, in his right hand is a cross, but the left hand is stretched across his bosom. St. Abibus [or Habib] resembles St. George the martyr in his features, but he is dressed like St. Stephen the protomartyr, his right hand is stretched out to the side and he is holding incense away from himself in it, and the left hand holds a censer.

And holy father **Eupater** [or Hypatius] *S. 88* is an old man with gray hair like St. Blaise, but his beard is forked at the end, his vestment has many crosses, his tunic is ocher, in the right hand is the Gospel book and the left hand is held in prayer.

16

The holy apostle and evangelist **Matthew** [first century] *S. 88* is an old man with gray hair, has a beard like the Theologian, a greenish brown cloak with white, on the thigh it is ocher with white, a blue tunic, the Gospel is in his hands, bare feet; or in his hand is a scroll on which is written, "Blessed are those who honor my memory, for they will be glorified for ever and ever."

And our holy monastic father **Nikon** of Radonezh [+1428], the disciple of St. Sergius, is an old man with gray hair, a longer beard than St. Nicholas, but shorter than St. Sergius.

And the holy apostle **James** [first century], the brother of St. John the Theologian, his hair and beard are like St. Cosmas, his upper cloak is green, his tunic is blue and there is a scroll in his hand.

17

Our father among the saints **Gregory** the Miracle Worker [+ 270] *S. 88*, bishop of Neo-Caesarea, is an old man with balding gray hair, a simple beard longer than St. Nicholas, a purple cross patterned cloak, an ocher tunic, omophorion and Gospel book.

And the holy father **Gregory** of Neo-Caesarea, is an old man with gray hair, a beard like St. Blaise, there are two curls at the end, black [perhaps cross patterned] vestments, omophorion and Gospel, a reddish brown tunic, ocher priests' stole, his hands are in prayer.

Sts. **Eucharistus** and his wife **Mary,** who resembles St. Anna.

18

The holy martyrs **Plato** and **Romanus** [+ 306] *S. 90.* St. Plato has brown hair, a beard longer than St. Cosmas, a scarlet cloak with white, and with white highlights, a light blue tunic, in one hand a cross, the left hand in prayer, the fingers are raised. St. Romanus has brown hair, a beard longer and wider than St. Cosmas, a greenish brown cloak with white, a scarlet tunic, the hands are like St. Plato, and there is a young child with them.

On the same day the passing of our holy mother **Helen,** the abbess of the Diyevochi Monastery in Moscow, who resembles St. Eudokia.

19

The holy prophet **Obadiah** [or Abdias + 716 B.C.] *S. 90* resembles the martyr St. Menas, has a reddish brown cloak lightened with ocher, and a blue tunic. The prophet Obadiah is holding a scroll on which is written, "The day of the Lord is approaching for all the nations which He has created: behold this will be the kingdom of the Lord."

And the holy martyr **Varlaam** [or Barlaam + 304] *S. 90* is an old man with gray hair, a beard like St. Blaise, a scarlet cloak with white and a blue tunic.

And our holy monastic fathers **Barlaam** the desert dweller, and **Joasaph** the crown prince of Great India. St. Barlaam of India is an old man with gray hair, a beard like St. John Damascene, on his head is the schema with crosses, a purple cloak, a reddish brown tunic, with one hand he is blessing and in the other is a scroll on which is written, "I have shown you the precious pearl which is Christ, the most precious Gem which illuminates the entire creation." Opposite him stands the crown prince Joasaph, who is a young man resembling St. Demetrius of Thessalonica. St. Joasaph is looking toward St. Barlaam, he has a magnificent royal crown on his head, admonitions, in his right hand he is holding a cross which he is showing to Barlaam, and in the left a scroll on which is written, "I have abandoned all the beautiful things of my kingdom, and have purchased this priceless gem which is Christ, and have followed the narrow path." He is wearing monastic robes and the schema on his head.

20

Our holy father **Gregory** Decapolites [+ 820] *S. 92* is an old man with gray hair, balding, on his shoulders small wisps of hair, his beard is like St. Nicholas or St. Blaise, but longer, an ocher cloak with white.

And our father among the saints **Proclus** [+ 447] *S. 92,* patriarch of

Constantinople, is an old man with gray hair, a beard like St. John the Merciful, he wears a purple saccos with blue circles with gold in which are crosses, he is holding the Gospel with both hands.

And the holy martyrs **Eustace** the deacon, **Thespesius** and **Anatolius,** laymen [+ 312]. They are young men like Sts. George and Demetrius, they are brothers according to the flesh, St. Eustace has a scroll on which is written, "O most gracious Lord, grant mercy and healing to the sick, comfort to the suffering." St. Thespesius has a scroll which says, "O most gracious Lord, grant mercy to all who call upon You!" St. Anatolius' scroll has "We beseech You, O Christ, grant a blessing to those who keep our memory, grant them the heavenly reward."

And the holy martyr **Azades** the eunuch [+ 343] is a young man with a beard like St. Cosmas. Sts. **Thecla** and **Anna** resemble Sts. Anna and Elizabeth, and there are three maidens.

21

THE ENTRY INTO THE TEMPLE OF OUR LADY THE MOST HOLY MOTHER OF GOD AND EVER VIRGIN MARY *S. 94.* The entrance, the Theotokos, Joachim as usual, Anna behind him, a little bowed down and with both her hands stretched out towards the Theotokos, the Most Pure [Mother of God] is a three year old child, and behind her are seven maidens with candles, which they are carrying triumphantly, and there are other maidens behind Joachim and Anna. The prophet Zachariah has his left hand stretched out to the Most Pure, and with the right he is blessing the Most Pure, and Zachariah is wearing three robes, green, reddish brown and a scarlet tunic. The temple has three domes and five columns, but itself is ocher with white, and at the top the Most Pure is sitting on the steps, an angel is giving her something to eat, above the Most Pure is a canopy on four columns, and on this a cross, the top of the canopy is ocher with white, and under the Most Pure are seven steps, but Zachariah is standing at the temple gates.

And the holy martyr Empress **Augusta** resembles St. Catherine, on her head is a royal crown and under the crown a scarf, her hands are in prayer.

22

The holy apostle **Philemon** [first century] *S. 94* and those with him. St. Philemon is an old man with balding gray hair, a beard like St. John the Theologian, he wears the omophorion, a greenish brown cloak with white, a blue tunic, and the Gospel in his hands.

And St. **Michael** the Soldier [+ 866] resembles St. George.

And the murder of the holy true believing Great Prince **Michael** of Tver [+ 1318], who is a little gray, a beard like St. Michael of Chernigov, a cap on his head, in his right hand the cross, and a sword in its scabbard in his left.

And the holy martyrs **Pilicia** and **Olympia** resemble Sts. Elizabeth and Anna.

23

Our father among the saints **Amphilochius** [+ 394] *S. 96,* bishop of Iconium, is an old man with gray hair like St. Blaise, his beard is forked at the end, he wears a purple cloak lightened with scarlet and with white, his tunic is very lightened ocher, he has small curls on his head, the omophorion and Gospel.

And our father among the saints **Gregory** [+ end of sixth century] *S. 96,* bishop of Agrigentum, his hair goes down a little below his ears, his beard is longer than the Theologian, he wears a blue cross pattern cloak, his tunic is lightened ocher, he is holding the Gospel with both hands, and the omophorion.

And the holy true believing Great Prince **Alexander** Nevsky [+ 1263] *S. 98,* resembles St. Cosmas, he is in the schema, he wears monastic robes, curls can be seen a little, he has a schema with the tunic, the schema itself is on the shoulders of the body, he has a purple cloak, a light gray tunic, and is grasping a scroll in his hand. [Note: This description is not in the usual format. St. Alexander Nevsky was portrayed as a monk until the Holy Ruling Synod of Russia resolved in June of 1724 that in painting icons of Alexander Nevsky no one on any account is to portray this saint as a monk, but rather in the robes of a Great Prince.]

And the holy martyr **Procopius** is either a middle-aged or young man, he wears martyrs' robes, he is a soldier and resembles St. Michael the Merciful, under his feet is a serpent with three heads. His body is located in the city of Ternova.

And the passing of our father **Amphilochius,** the abbot of Glushetsk, miracle worker. He is an old man with gray hair, a beard like St. Basil of Caesarea, he is a little stooped, he wears a purple cloak, an ocher tunic, and holds a scroll in his hand.

24

The holy great-martyr **Catherine** *S. 96* has a royal crown on her head, simple hair like a maiden, a blue cloak, a scarlet tunic, and has the royal bands down to her ankles, also on her shoulders and on her sleeves. The sleeves are wide, in her right hand is the cross, and in the left is a scroll on which is written, "O Lord God, hear me, grant him who remembers the name of Catherine forgiveness of sins and in the hour of his death lead him forth with peace and grant him a place of rest."

And the holy great-martyr **Mercurius** [+ under Decius and Diocletian] *S. 96* resembles St. George in armor, his cloak is purple with white, a blue tunic, the breastplate has a feather pattern, ocher with white, in his right hand a sword, and in the left the scabbard, his leggings are purple.

And a second martyr St. **Mercurius,** the miracle worker of Smolensk [+ 1238], resembles St. Demetrius of Thessalonica, large in stature, but not a large beard, divided a little, a cap on his head with black herringbone pattern, a purple brocade fur trimmed coat, white lapels, in the right hand is a large bare saber, but he is leaning against it like a staff, and in the other hand the scabbard.

And the holy martyr Empress **Augusta** resembles St. Catherine, on her head is a crown, under the crown a shawl, like the empress St. Helen.

And the holy virgin **Mastridia, Porphyrius** the commander with two hundred soldiers. There is a column of old, middle aged, and young men, all are in armor, St. Porphyrius is old and has a beard like St. Blaise.

25

Our father among the saints hieromartyr **Clement** [+ 101] *S. 98,* pope of Rome, and Peter of Alexandria [+ 311] *S. 98.* St. Clement has curly gray hair that goes down below his ears like St. George, a beard like St. Blaise, but simple, a purplish cross patterned cloak, an ocher tunic with white. St. Peter has a head of curly gray hair, he has a white cap on his head, a beard like St. Nicholas, a greenish brown cross pattern cloak with white, and he holds the Gospel with both hands.

26

Our father St. **Alypius** the Stylite [+ seventh century] *S. 98* is an old man with gray hair like St. John the Theologian, monastic robes, the mantle is greenish brown with white, some paint him on a column.

And the consecration of the church of the holy great-martyr **George** which is in Kiev at the Golden Gate [in 1037]. St. George *S. 100* is in armor, with a scarlet cloak, a breastplate with a feather pattern colored ocher with white, a blue tunic, purple leggings, and sitting on a horse. The horse is white, the lance is poking the dragon, and behind him is a mountain, and before him is a city, before which a maiden is leading the dragon into the city, another maiden is opening the gates, on a tower is a middle aged king, and the queen, and the people behind him with lances and axes, the name of the city is *"Rakhlyey."*

27

The holy great-martyr **James** the Persian [+ 421] *S. 100* has brown hair like St. Boris the Prince, his cloak is dark gray brocade, a blue tunic, in his right hand is a cross and a scroll which says, "Holy, holy, holy are You, O God Almighty, grant peace to those people who suffer for Your Name" and in his left hand a sword in its scabbard.

And our holy father **Paladius** the Monk [+ end of sixth century] *S. 100* is an old man with gray hair like St. Sergius, his beard has little curls, his tunic is ocher.

On the same day [we celebrate a miracle in 1170 of the icon of the] **Sign** of the most holy Mother of God.

And our holy father **Acacius** of Sinai is a young man like St. Galacteon or St. John the Basket maker [see January 15], and wears monastic robes.

And our holy father **Damian** the desert dweller [also known as Diodorus of George Hill + 1633] has brown hair and a medium beard.

And our holy father **Irinarch,** the recluse of Sts. Boris and Gleb Monastery, miracle worker of Rostov, has gray hair, a beard like St. Paphnutius Borovsky, in the schema and monastic robes.

28
"The day has 7 hours and the night 17."
The holy martyr **Stephen** the New Confessor [+ 767] *S. 102* is an old man with gray hair, a beard longer than the Theologian, is holding with both hands (some say only in the left hand) a scroll on which is written, "O Lady, accept the prayer of your servants," with his mantle he holds the "Vladimir" Icon of the most holy Theotokos with the Pre-eternal Child Jesus Christ, he has monastic robes and the schema.

And the holy martyr **Hirenarchus** [+ under Diocletian] S. 102 resembles the young man St. Demetrius, he has a scarlet cloak, a blue tunic, in his hand is a scroll on which is written, "The God of powers will hear His servant and grant him the petitions of his heart," and with him are seven women and two children.

And [the finding of the relics in 1193] of the holy true believing Prince **Vsevolod** of Pskov [named Gabriel in baptism], the miracle worker, has brown hair that goes down below his ears, a beard like St. Basil of Caesarea, but wider, he wears a brocaded fur coat and a blue tunic, a cap on his head, in his left hand is a [miniature] church which is green with white and has only one dome, [dedicated to] the Holy Trinity.

And the holy father **James** or [Jacob + 1392] *S. 100,* bishop of Rostov, wears a cap, a beard like the Theologian and gray hair, bishops' vestments with the omophorion and Gospel book.

29

The holy martyr **Paramon** [+ 250] *S. 102* has brown hair, a beard like St. Cosmas, a scarlet cloak, a short tunic of greenish brown and purple with white, and a blue tunic.

Our holy father **Acacius** [who is mentioned in *The Ladder of Divine Ascent* of St. John Climacus] *S. 104* has a graying beard like St. Barlaam of Khutin, a green tunic with reddish brown and white.

And the memory of the holy mother **Parasceva** of Rzhevsk.

And the holy father **Ananius** the presbyter who baptized St. **Hirenarchus** and the two children, and together with them died by martyrdom for Christ. St. Ananius has brown hair, a beard like St. Cosmas, priests' vestments, and standing before him are two children standing in [long white Russian] shirts.

And the holy father **Bessarion** is a young man like St. Galacteon with monastic robes.

30

The holy glorious and all praised Apostle **Andrew** [first century] *S. 104* "the first called," has dense hair like St. Florus, a longer beard than the Theologian, gray hair divided a little in two, a greenish brown cloak with white, from the waist ocher with white, he is holding a scroll with both hands, his cloak is billowing out on the left hand side, and he has bare feet.

And our father among the saints **Theodore,** archbishop of Rostov, miracle worker, has gray hair, a shorter beard than St. Blaise, wears a white klobuk, bishops' vestments, with the omophorion and Gospel book; but some paint him with brown hair.

DECEMBER

"The month of December has 31 days."

1

The holy prophet **Nahum** [c. 700 B.C.] *S. 106* is similar to St. John the Theologian, his cloak is purple with reddish brown, his tunic is blue, and in his left hand is a scroll. Nahum has a scroll on which is written, "The mountains quake before the Lord, the hills melt, and the earth shrinks from His presence."

The holy martyr **Ananias** resembles St. George and wears martyrs' robes.

And St. **Philaret** the Merciful [eighth century] is an old man with a gray beard and hair like St. Demetrius, but a little longer and wider, and wears monastic robes, although some paint him as a prince.

2

The holy prophet **Habakkuk** [or Abbacum c. 700 B.C.] *S. 106* is a young man like St. George, his head is bowed toward the prophet Nahum, his cloak is scarlet, his tunic is blue and in his left hand is a scroll on which is written, "Your obedient servant Habakkuk listened, O Christ." The prophet Habakkuk's scroll might have another text which says, "God will come from the south, from the holy overshadowed mountain, heaven will conceal His glory, and His praise will fill the earth."

And the holy martyr **Myrope** [or Marobia + 251] is similar to St. Anna.

And our holy father **Athanasius** [+ 1176], the recluse of the Kiev Caves, is an old man with gray hair, a beard like St. Sergius, and monastic robes.

3

The holy prophet **Zephaniah** [or Sophonias c. 600 B.C.] *S. 106* is an old man with gray hair; he resembles St. John the Theologian, having a small beard, a round face, his cloak is purple lightened with red, the thigh of which is blue; he is blessing with one hand, and with the other he is holding a scroll on which is written, "Rejoice greatly, O daughter of Sion, speak out, O daughter of Jerusalem, rejoice and adorn yourself!"

And our holy father **Sabbas** [+ 1407, canonized 1549], abbot of Zvenigorod (Storozhev), is an old man with gray hair, a beard like St. Macarius of Yellow Lake, the miracle worker, balding, and wears monastic robes.

And the holy hieromartyr **Theodore** [+ between 606 and 609], bishop of Alexandria, is similar to St. Blaise.

And our holy father **John** the Silent, who lived in the Lavra of St. Sabbas, who previously was a bishop, is an exceedingly old man with white hair, having a round beard, monastic robes or he may wear bishop's vestments since he left the episcopate voluntarily.

4

The holy martyr **Barbara** [+ 306] *S. 106* wears a royal crown on her head, a green cloak, a scarlet tunic, and in her hand is a scroll on which is written, "Almighty Lord Jesus Christ, make every Christian, who honors the day of my martyrdom, worthy that no plague or any other evil will enter his house."

And our holy father **John** of Damascus [+ 777] *S. 106* is an old man with gray hair, a beard like St. Euthymius, monastic robes, the tunic of which is greenish brown, he is blessing with one hand, and in the left he holds a scroll on which is written, "The whole creation rejoices in you, O all blessed!" Other icons have "If the One born from her is truly God, then she is in truth the Mother of God" written on the scroll.

And the holy martyr **Ananias** is like St. George with martyrs' robes.

And the holy martyr **Juliana** [the companion of St. Barbara] is similar to St. Parasceva.

5

Our holy and God-bearing father **Sabbas** the Sanctified [+ 532] *S. 108,* is an old man with gray hair, a beard smaller than St. Blaise, but sticking out from both cheeks, monastic robes, his tunic is ocher with whitened reddish brown.

And our holy father **Karion** [or Cyrion or Larion] the monk [fourth century], is an old man with a beard like St. Nicholas, and his son St. **Zachariah** is a young man; they are wearing monastic robes.

On the same day our holy father **Spyridon,** abbot of Vologda, miracle worker, is an old man with gray hair, a beard like St. Blaise, but divided at the end, wears the schema and monastic robes.

6

Our father among the saints **Nicholas** [+ 342] *S. 108* of Myra in Lycia, miracle worker, gray hair, not a large beard, a curl of hair coming from his balding head, small curls of hair on his temples, a purple cloak lightened with blue, a blue tunic, in his one hand is the Gospel, and with his other hand he is blessing.

On the same day the memory of the holy blessed **Nicholas,** who was a fool for Christ's sake in Pskov, the miracle worker in the time of Tsar Ivan Vasilievich [the Terrible], his features, i.e., his beard and balding head resemble the Apostle Paul, he has graying hair and is completely nude.

7

Our father among the saints **Ambrose** [+ 397] *S. 108,* bishop of Milan, has brown hair, a beard like St. Basil of Caesarea but divided, a blue cloak with many crosses, a scarlet tunic with white, the omophorion and Gospel.

And our holy father **Anthony** of Siya [+ 1556] is an old man with balding gray hair, a scanty, straggling beard, five curls like St. Anthony of the Pecherska Lavra, but longer, and monastic robes.

And the holy monastic martyr **Athenodorus** the monk [+304] resembles St. Cosmas, he has monastic robes without the schema, at his feet lies the hand of Eparchus with a sword.

And our holy father **Nilus** of Stolbensk Lake [+1554], miracle worker of Novgorod, resembles St. Macarius of Yellow Lake, he has gray hair, a long beard, and monastic robes.

8

Our holy father **Patapius** [seventh century] *S. 110* is an old man with gray hair, a beard like St. Blaise, with both hands he is holding a scroll, he has monastic robes, and his tunic is reddish brown with blue.

9

The Conception by St. **Anna** *S. 110,* when she conceived the holy Mother of God, according to the announcement of the angel. St. Joachim is praying in the desert in front of a mountain, he has a graying beard like St. Cosmas, a purple cloak lightened with blue, and a blue tunic; the angel of the Lord is flying to him. And in a second area St. Anna is praying to the Lord in the garden, the angel of the Lord is flying to her, she has a scarlet cloak and a blue tunic. In the middle of both areas Joachim is kissing Anna, on the scroll near Joachim and Anna is written, "O Seer of the hearts of all, O Creator of everything visible and invisible, hear us, O merciful One, and grant us the grace of childbearing, so that the one who will be born from us may be brought to You as a gift, as a donation in chastity."

And the holy prophetess **Anna** [+ 1100 B.C.], the mother of the prophet Samuel, resembles the St. Anna with St. Joachim.

And our holy father **Cyril,** his features, beard, etc. resemble St. Cyril of White Lake.

10
The holy martyrs **Menas, Eugraphus,** and **Hermogenes** [+ 313] *S. 112.* St. Menas is an old man with gray hair, a beard like St. Nicholas, curly hair, like St. George in a breastplate, a purple cloak, a green tunic, in his hand a cross, and in the other a sword in its scabbard, his leggings are yellow, his shoes are ocher. St. Eugraphus is a young man like St. George.

11
Our holy father **Daniel** the Stylite [+ 480] *S. 112,* has gray hair, a beard broader than St. Blaise, wears the schema, monastic robes; he stands bare-headed on a column, there is one door.

And our holy father **Luke** the Stylite [+ between 970 and 980], of Constantinople, has a beard like St. John the Theologian, but he is sitting on a column like St. Daniel.

The **Sunday of the Holy Forefathers**. [See December 16.]

12
Our father among the saints **Spyridon** the miracle worker [+ 348] *S. 114,* bishop of Tremithon, is an old man with gray hair, a beard wider than St. Blaise, on his head is a white hat, his cloak has many crosses, his tunic is scarlet with white.

And the holy martyr **Razumnik** or [in Latin] Synesius [+ under Emperor Aurelian], the reader of the holy [Roman] church, looks like St. Demetrius.

And the passing of our holy father **Therapont** of Monza, which is on the Kostrom River, the new miracle worker, is an old man with gray hair, a beard like St. Basil of Caesarea, but a little longer and wider, on his shoulders is the schema, purple monastic robes, and his tunic is dark green.

"On this day the sun waxes until summer:
the days grow longer and the nights get shorter."

13
The holy martyrs **Eustratius, Auxentius, Eugene, Mardarius,** and **Orestes**

[+ under Diocletian] *S. 114.* St. Eustratius resembles St. Florus in a breastplate, a purple cloak with white, a scarlet tunic, his leggings are purplish, in one hand is a cross, in the left is a shield. St. Auxentius is a young man like St. Demetrius, his upper cloak is scarlet with white, his tunic is blue. St. Eugene has brown hair like St. Cosmas, his upper cloak is purple with white and crimson, his tunic is ocher with white. St. Mardarius resembles the holy martyr Nikita, his cloak is purple, his tunic is crimson. St. Orestes resembles St. George, his cloak is greenish brown with white, light gray, his tunic is green.

And our holy father **Arsenius** [eighth or ninth century] *S. 116,* who was in Latros, his beard, etc. are similar to St. Sergius, his cloak and tunic are light gray.

And the holy virgin martyr **Lucy** [+ 304].

And the memory of our holy father **Arcadius,** the new miracle worker of Novotorzhesk, is a young man like St. Galacteon; he wears the schema and monastic robes.

14

The holy martyrs **Thrysus** and **Leucius** *S. 116,* and **Philemon** and **Apollonius** *S. 118* and **Arianus** and **Callinicus** [+ between 249 and 251]. St. Thrysus has a beard wider than St. Nikita, but a little longer at the end, his cloak is reddish brown, with white, his tunic is green, his left hand is held in prayer. St. Leucius is a young man like St. Demetrius, his cloak is reddish brown with white, his tunic is green, and his left hand is in prayer.

And the holy martyr **Theodora** the Empress *S. 116,* resembles St. Helen in everything.

15

The holy hieromartyr **Eleutherius** [+ under Hadrian] *S. 118* is an old man with gray hair like St. Blaise, he wears a bishops' vestment with many crosses, a blue tunic, and his mother St. Anthia resembles St. Anna.

And the holy hieromartyr **Stephen** [+ middle of eighth century] *S. 118,* archbishop of Surozh, is an old man with gray hair, a wide beard like St. Blaise, a purple cloak with white, his tunic is ocher with white, in his hand is a Gospel book, and he is blessing with his right hand.

16

The holy prophet **Haggai** [or Aggaeus + 500 B.C.] *S. 118,* is a man with gray hair like the prophet Elias; he is old, balding, having a rounded beard, a greenish brown cloak, a blue tunic; there is a scroll in his hand which says, "Thus says the Lord God Almighty, 'Place your heart on your path, construct a temple for Me, and I will consent to live in it, and I will be glorified.'"

And the holy martyr **Marinus** [+ 283] is a young man like St. Demetrius; he was a government councilman.

The Sunday of the **Holy Forefathers** *S. 122*. Next to Daniel [see December 17] stands the first forefather, his features, hair and everything resemble the Prophet Elias, his upper cloak is purple, his tunic is blue, in his left hand is a scroll. And the forefather next to him resembles St. Andrew the First-called, his upper cloak is darkened scarlet, his tunic is ocher with white. The third forefather has brown hair, a simpler beard than St. Blaise, his upper cloak is green, his tunic is purple with white. Behind them are many other holy forefathers, but one can see only their heads and they have apostles' robes.

17

The holy prophet **Daniel** [c. 500 B.C.] *S. 122* and the three holy youths **Ananias, Azarias,** and **Misael** *S. 120*. All three are young men; they are standing in the furnace, among them is the Angel of the Lord, from the right hand side the youth has a green cloak, a blue tunic, and the youth on the left hand of the angel has a blue upper cloak, a crimson tunic, the youth in the middle of them has a scarlet cloak, a green tunic, they have wide sashes, on their heads are hats, the bottom parts of the hats are white. And the angel is standing behind them but the youths are standing only as high as the angel's chest, and above them one sees the angel with his arms over them. The Chaldeans are overcome by the heat, one has a crimson cloak, the second a blue cloak and the third an ocher one with white. from the bosom the sleeves are purple; they are covering their faces, but looking toward the angel. On the left side of the furnace a king is sitting on a high throne, beneath his feet there is a stairway with four steps; he has brown hair, a longer beard than St. Constantine, a purple cloak, a blue tunic, he holds his arms up in prayer toward the angel. Between the furnace and the king are standing four executioners, they have helmets on their heads, they are wearing breastplates. The first has an upper cloak of plain scarlet, his leggings are blue, the second after him has a green cloak, and the others all look alike. Next to the furnace there is a golden body on a tall column resembling a mannequin, in his hand is a lance, and in the left is a shield. And there is fire burning the executioners, which is touching their bodies, and over the king's throne there is a scarlet canopy.

The prophet **Daniel** *S. 122* resembles the martyr St. George, on his head is a scarlet hat with a white turban, a scarlet cloak, a green tunic, his left hand can be empty, or it can hold a scroll, "Blessed is the Lord God of Israel," the right hand is in prayer, the fingers are pointed up, he has a wide girdle.

Sunday of the **Holy Forefather**s *S. 122.* There stand Adam, Seth, Abel, David, Solomon, and behind them a multitude of kings and prophets with varying appearances.

Sunday of the **Holy Forefathers** *S. 124.* The first bishop standing is an old man with balding gray hair, in his features, etc. he is similar to St. Blaise, he has a scarlet bishops' vestment with many crosses, a light gray tunic; the one next to him has brown hair, a shorter beard than St. Basil of Caesarea, a hat on his head, a vestment with many crosses, a blue tunic; the third one has brown hair, in appearance and hair like St. Florus, he has a blue cloak with many crosses, a purple tunic with white, the fourth looks like St. Basil of Caesarea, he has a purplish cloak with many crosses, a blue tunic; the fifth resembles St. Athanasius, he wears a black vestment with many crosses, a green tunic, all have crosses in their hands, and there is a multitude of other bishops but one can see only their heads.

18

The holy martyr **Sebastian** [+ 287] *S. 124,* has brown hair like St. Cosmas, a scarlet cloak, a blue tunic, in his right hand is a cross and in his left is a fold of his cloak.

And St. **Gregory,** bishop of Suzhdal, has gray hair, a beard wider and longer than St. Blaise, and bishops' robes; Bishop Capiton of Korsun, has gray hair, a beard like St. Blaise, and bishop's robes.

And our holy father **Michael** the Councilman, is similar in everything to St. Sabbas the Sanctified, but his beard is shorter.

And the holy martyr Martin is a young man like St. Demetrius of Thessalonica.

19

The holy martyrs **Boniface** [third century] *S. 126* and **Aglae.** St. Boniface resembles St. Cosmas, balding, but others depict him like the holy martyr George, with a scarlet cloak, a blue tunic. St. Boniface has a scroll in his hand on which is written, "Almighty Lord Master, save Your people from the wrath of idolatry, and from all suffering and sorrow." St. Aglae is like St. Parasceva.

And the holy martyr **Timothy** [fourth century] is a young man like St. George and in his hand is a cross; the "Kievan printed pages" have the same.

And our father among the saints **Gregory** [+552], archbishop of Omerits, is an old man with gray hair, a beard wider and longer than St. Blaise, and bishops' robes with the omophorion.

And a second holy martyr **Timothy** *S. 126,* has brown hair like St. Cosmas, etc. He is dressed like St. Stephen the protomartyr, and holds a censer in his right hand.

20

The holy hieromartyr **Ignatius** the God-bearer [+ 107] S. 126, archbishop of Antioch, is an old man with gray hair, a beard like St. Blaise, a scarlet cloak with many crosses, a blue tunic with white, he holds an icon of the Savior in his left hand and he is blessing with his right.

And our holy monastic father **Philogonius** [+ 324] is similar to St. Michael the Councilman [December 18].

And the memory of our holy father **Ignatius,** miracle worker on the Loma of Vologda, is an old man with gray hair, a beard like St. Cyril of White Lake, he wears a klobuk and monastic robes.

21

The holy martyr **Juliana** [+ 304] *S. 126* has purple cloak, a green tunic, and in her hand is a cross, but some portray her being tormented by a demon like the martyr Nikita.

And the passing of our father among the saints **Peter** [+ 1326] *S. 128,* metropolitan of Moscow, miracle worker. The Saint is lying in a coffin, and there are two [figures] holding the lid. St. Peter has gray hair, a beard like St. Sergius, a blue saccos with many crosses, the omophorion and Gospel book, on his head is a white klobuk. A group of young men is carrying the coffin; some are like St. George, two in the middle resemble St. Cosmas, one is old, and balding, his beard is smaller than St. Blaise. There is a white church with one peak at very top, but the coffin is green and reddish brown. At the head of the coffin a bishop is standing, and he is reading a scroll, he has gray hair like St. Blaise; on his right hand is a young deacon and on the other hand a priest with balding gray hair, a beard like St. Athanasius, a purple vestment with highlights, an ocher tunic, next to the bishop is a deacon with balding gray hair, and one head can be seen, and between the bishop and the priest there is a young man like St. George, and another four heads can be seen. At the feet of the Miracle worker stand princes resembling Sts. Boris and Gleb, with white hats, their hands held in prayer, next to them a prince resembling St. Vladimir, with gray hair, a green brocade cloak, a scarlet tunic, and behind him a man with balding brown hair resembling St. Paul, wearing an ocher cloak with white, and of the others one sees only their heads. There is a palace with three peaks, before it is a wall, and behind the wall a bell tower, the top of which is scarlet, the side is bluish, and the other top is blue.

22

The holy great-martyr **Anastasia** [+ 304] *S. 128*, the deliverer from bonds [There is no description in Bolshakov's text. "The holy great martyr Anastasia has a scarlet cloak, a light blue tunic, and a scarf on her head. She has a palm branch in her hand." *MA 153*.]

And the holy martyr **Theodota** [+ 304], similar to the above, green cloak, crimson tunic with white, and a cross in her hand.

And the holy monastic martyr **Chrysosgonus** [+ 304], similar to St. Michael the Councilman [December 18], and a cross in his right hand.

23

The holy **ten martyrs** of Crete [+ 262] *S. 130*. The first martyr has brown hair, a beard shorter than St. Athanasius, a blue cloak, a crimson tunic, blue leggings; the martyr next to him is like St. George, a green cloak, a scarlet tunic, purple leggings; and between them are others with beards like St. Blaise, ocher cloaks, and the rest can not be seen entirely, but they all have crosses in their hands, and only the heads can be seen of some of them, some have gray hair and three have brown hair.

And our father among the saints **Niphon** [+ fourth century], patriarch of Constantinople, his face, head and beard resemble St. Paul the Apostle, except for his robes and he is not balding; some portray him as a monk, in his hand is a scroll, "Lord, God of powers, grant forgiveness of sins to every soul which calls on my name." Sometimes St. Niphon has another scroll on which is written, "He is cursed who leaves God's Church, he will be pursued by demons."

And our father among the saints **Philip,** metropolitan of Moscow and all Russia, miracle worker, has a white klobuk or a cap on his head, a short rounded beard, black but graying, in the saccos, omophorion and Gospel.

24

The holy nun-martyr **Eugenia** [+ 262] *S. 130* and her children John and Arcadius. St. Eugenia has a blue schema, a greenish brown tunic with white, her hands are in prayer but according to the "[Kievan] printed pages" she is holding a cross.

And our holy father **Nicholas** the Monk [+ ninth century] is an old man like St. Sergius, he is wearing the schema on his head, and monastic robes.

25

THE BIRTH IN THE FLESH OF OUR LORD, GOD AND SAVIOR JESUS CHRIST *S. 132.* The Nativity of Christ is painted as follows: three angels are looking at the star, the foremost angel has a blue cloak but the two other angels have crimson, the angel is announcing to the shepherds, one has a crimson cloak and a blue tunic, the other two shepherds have crimson cloaks, the Most Pure [Mother of God] is lying in a cave, she has a purple cloak, the Christ Child is lying in a manger, the manger is ocher, the cave is black, and in it can be seen half of a horse [that is, an ass] and on the other side can be seen half of a cow [that is, an ox], three angels are over the cave, there is an ocher mountain with white, on the right side the Magi are bowing down, there are three of them, one is old, has a beard like St. Blaise, wears a hat, a green cloak, a scarlet tunic, the second one in the middle has a short rounded beard, wears a hat, a scarlet cloak a light gray tunic, the third is young like St. George, wears a hat, a purple cloak, a blue tunic, and all three are carrying containers in their hands colored dark ocher. Under them is a mountain, and in the mountain is a cave, St. Joseph the Betrothed is sitting on a stone, he has a beard like the Apostle Peter, a green cloak, a crimson tunic, with one hand he is closing his cloak, and with the other he is gesturing down. And before him is standing a shepherd with gray hair, a beard like St. John the Theologian, balding, wearing a furry garment with many curls, blue with black, in his hand are three crutches, but he is extending one to Joseph, behind him is a young shepherd wearing a scarlet cloak, and he is grazing goats, and the goats are black and white and striped. And in a field of the mountain the midwife Solomia is sitting, her cloak is open to the waist, the tunic is white, her arms are bare, and she is holding Christ in one arm. The other midwife has one hand in a basin of water, she wears a scarlet cloak and a blue tunic.

26

The **Synaxis of the most holy Mother of God** *S. 134* and St. **Joseph** the Betrothed is pictured as follows: "What will we offer You, O Christ, [who for our sake appeared on earth as a man? Every creature You made offers You thanks: the angels offer You a hymn; the heavens - a star; the Magi - gifts; the shepherds - their wonder; the earth - its cave; the wilderness - the manger; and we offer You a Virgin Mother. O pre-eternal God, have mercy upon us!"] etc., as is customary. And the Most Pure [Mother of God] is sitting on a scarlet carpet and around it is a circle of blue, and the Christ Child is on her arms, He is blessing with both hands in both directions, above Him is a heaven with stars and angels, an ocher mountain, the shepherds are looking on, there is a green mountain, the Magi with gifts are facing the

98

Most Pure. [Below the] cave which holds a manger, there is an empty space with a maiden, and on the other side another empty space with a maiden entwined with grass and flowers. St. John of Damascus is standing somewhat below [and between them], he is blessing with on hand, and in the other there is a scroll, and on the scroll is written, "All creation rejoices in you, O full of grace." And St. Euthymius the Great is standing on the other side, he is blessing with one hand, in the other is a scroll on which is written, "Today the Virgin gives birth to the Transcendent One." And there is a crowd of many people standing between them, princes and nobleman, bishops and monks, and women with children, and soldiers, old men with gray, some with brown hair, and middle aged, and children, and the multitude of them have their hands held in prayer, and there is an inscription which says, "We magnify the Virgin Mother as Theotokos."

And the memory of the righteous **Joseph** the Betrothed, **David** the King, and **James** the brother of the Lord according to the flesh. David has a scroll in his hands on which is written, "You and the ark of Your holiness, and Your priests will be clothed in righteousness."

And the holy hieromartyr **Euthymius** [+ 840], bishop of Sardis, has gray hair, a beard like St. Athanasius, bishops' robes, an omophorion and Gospel.

27

The holy protomartyr and archdeacon and first server **Stephen** S. 134 is a young man in deacon's robes with a censer and a bald spot on the top of his head, but according to the "[Kievan] printed pages" he has a cross in his hand. St. Stephen has a scroll, "O Lord, do not hold them responsible for this sin, for they do not know what they are doing or [whom] they are killing."

And our holy monastic father **Theodore** the Branded [+ 840] S. 136 resembles St. Sergius of Radonezh.

28

The holy **twenty thousand martyrs** S. 136 who were burned in the church in Nicomedia [+ 302]. There is a church and a palace as is customary, Bishop **Anthimus** is standing in the center of the church, he has a beard like St. Blaise, a balding head, a vestment with many crosses, and before him are old people and some with brown hair, some middle aged and some young, and he is giving them Holy Communion, and behind him is a middle aged deacon with a short rounded beard, and behind the deacon is a multitude of people, and down below the church there is a multitude of people lying down, and one can see fire burning under them, and the executioners all around are throwing wood under them, [this happened] in the reign of Diocletian and Maximian the infamous.

And the holy martyr **Domna** resembles St. Parasceva, and the holy martyr Stephanida resembles her as well.

29

The **fourteen thousand holy martyrs** *S. 138* who were killed for Christ's sake by Herod in Jerusalem. King Herod is sitting on a throne and before him executioners are killing children and they are cutting them with swords, and they are impaling them on lances before the king. And one sees women crying behind the mountain, they have uncovered hair, and behind the king is the holy city with towers, and by the soldiers there are many slaughtered children under their feet, the dead are in the blood.

Our holy monastic father **Marcellus** [+ 486] *S. 138,* abbot of the monastery of the "Unsleeping Ones," resembles St. Sergius of Radonezh in his beard, hair and robes.

30

The holy martyr **Anysia** [+ end of third century] *S. 140* resembles St. Parasceva in everything.

And our holy father **Zoticus** [+ middle of fourth century] *S. 140,* nurse of lepers, does not have a very big curly beard similar to St. Theodore the Stratelates, and monastic robes.

And our holy monastic mother **Theodora** of Caesarea [+ not later than 755] is similar to St. Eudokia.

And our holy mother, another St. **Theodora** the Greek [+ 940], is similar to the first.

31

Our holy mother **Melania** [+ 439] *S. 140* of Rome has the green schema on her head, monastic robes, a light gray tunic, her hands are held in prayer.

The holy apostle **Timotheus** has a beard like St. Cosmas, a purple cloak with white, a blue tunic, the omophorion on his shoulders, with one hand he is blessing, in the other a book, and his feet are bare, or else he has black sandals.

But according to the "Kievan printed pages" there are **crosses** in the hands of all the monastic women and martyrs.

On the same day the holy and righteous **Joseph,** the betrothed of the holy Mother of God, and **James** the brother of the Lord, and the Prophet **David,** and others who are described elsewhere.

JANUARY

"The month of January has 31 days."

1

THE CIRCUMCISION IN THE FLESH OF OUR LORD, GOD AND SAVIOR JESUS CHRIST *S. 142.* In the temple there is a priest who resembles St. Blaise, he has robes like St. Zachariah and is facing the Most Pure [Mother of God], and the Most Pure is holding the Infant whose legs are bare, and the priest is holding a knife in one hand, and a platter in the other, and St. Joseph is standing behind the Mother of God, and other women can be seen.

And our father among the saints **Basil** the Great, archbishop of Caesarea in Cappadocia [+ 379] *S. 142,* has black hair, a hooked-nose, gnarled features, rounded eye brows, a long and thin beard sparse at the end, he is middle-aged, but graying a little, the beard extends to his fingers, his cloak is white with purple crosses, a green tunic, he is blessing with one hand, and is holding the Gospel with the other, he has the omophorion on his shoulders.

And the holy martyr **Basil** [+ 362], who is from Ankyra in Galatia, has brown hair; he resembles St. Cosmas, and wears martyr's robes.

"The day has 8 hours and the night 16."
2

Our father among the saints **Sylvester** [+ 335] *S. 144,* the pope of Rome, who baptized the Emperor St. Constantine, wears a purple saccos, has a plain beard like St. Nicholas, the hair on his head is very curly and unruly, and comes down over his ears.

And the holy and righteous **Juliana** of Murom [+ 1604] resembles St. Elizabeth.

3

The holy prophet **Malachias** [400 B.C.] *S. 144,* is an old man with gray hair, a beard like St. John the Theologian, a blue cloak, a scarlet tunic with white, in his left hand is a scroll on which is written, "Behold, I send my angel before your face, who will prepare your way before you." ...Thus was his development in his youth, having a handsome face, but not very tall, but a little bent in stature, with curly hair flowing down, and a high forehead [from the printed *Prologue*].

The holy martyr **Gordius** [+ fourth century] *S. 144* has a short beard, apparently since he was not fully mature, he is very young like blessed John the fool for Christ, his hair is curling out from his ears a little, he has a scarlet cloak, a green tunic, in one hand a cross, and in the other a scroll. In the *Prologue* it is written of him, "He was an officer in the army over a hundred soldiers in armor."

4

The **Synaxis** of the Seventy Apostles *S. 144 to S. 173a*. The first apostle is an old man with gray hair who resembles the prophet Elias, he wears a purple cloak with white and a blue tunic; next to him is an apostle who resembles the Apostle Paul, with a bright crimson cloak, a blue tunic; and the third apostle has brown hair, resembles the Apostle Mark, with a blue cloak, a scarlet tunic with white. The fourth apostle resembles St. John Chrysostom, graying a little bit, a purple cloak with white, a blue tunic; the fifth apostle is a young man resembling an archangel, his cloak is a reddish purple with white, a blue tunic. And behind them stand old men and young men all wearing an omophorion.

And our holy monastic mother **Apollinaria** [+ 470] resembles St. Eudokia.

And our holy father **Theoctist** *S. 173a* is an old man with gray hair, a beard a little longer than St. Anthymus, it is narrow at the end, he wears an ocher cassock with white and monastic robes.

5

The holy martyrs **Theopemptus** and **Theonas** [+ 303] *S. 174*. St. Theopemptus has brown hair and resembles St. John Chrysostom, the hair from his left ear flows down over his shoulder, he wears a bishops' vestment with many crosses, an omophorion and holds the Gospel. The martyr Theonas resembles St. George, he has a scarlet cloak, a green tunic, and a cross in his hand.

Our holy mother **Syncletica** [+ 350] wears a klobuk on her head, monastic robes, her tunic is greenish brown with white.

The holy prophet **Micheas** [ninth century B.C.] is an old man with gray hair, a beard like the Theologian, a dark green cloak and a blue tunic.

6

THE HOLY THEOPHANY OF OUR LORD, GOD AND SAVIOR JESUS CHRIST *S. 176*. Christ is standing naked without a loincloth in the Jordan, He is bowing His head to the Forerunner, there is a green mountain, the Forerunner is bowing from his right to Christ, he is baptizing Him with his right hand, and the left hand is lifted in prayer, the fingers are extended to heaven, and he is looking to heaven,

102

the mountains on the other side are ocher with white, angels are standing before them, one angel is holding a white cloak, he is wearing a purple cloak and a blue tunic; the second angel is holding a purple cloak, and he is wearing a scarlet cloak and a green tunic; the third angel can be seen only a little; and all are bowing toward Christ. The Holy Spirit from the cloud is approaching John's right hand, and Christ Himself is blessing the Jordan with His hand, and the other hand is covering His body a little, the Forerunner is wearing a greenish brown cloak, the tunic is shaggy goat hair, purple with black. There are two fish in the Jordan; one is going up, and the other is going down, from the Lord of Sabbaoth there is a scroll, "This is My beloved Son in Whom I am well pleased."

7

The **Synaxis** of the holy, glorious, prophet, and forerunner John the Baptist *S. 178.* There is a crowd of people being baptized in the River Jordan, men with brown hair and young boys are sitting there, one of them, a youth dressed in a loincloth is jumping head first into the river, and all similarly are dressed in loincloths, and some of the youths are taking their clothes off by the side of the river, and the Forerunner is baptizing them with his hand bowing down, and Jews are standing behind the Forerunner, in front of them is a gray haired man with a beard like St. Sergius, a scarlet cloak and a blue tunic, there is a cloth on his head, and among them an old man with a smaller beard than his with a lightened purple clock and a scarlet tunic with white, and others have brown hair like St. Longinus the Centurion, and all are in white head scarves, and others are seen without clothes, the mountains are greenish brown with white.

8

Our holy father **George** the Chozebite [+ seventh century] S. 180 is an old man with gray hair, a beard like the Theologian, and monastic robes.

And our holy mother **Domnica** [+ 474] *S. 178* wears monastic robes, a blue klobuk, and a greenish brown tunic with white.

And the holy nun-martyr **Basilissa** [+ 313] is similar to St. Domnica.

And our holy father **Gregory** of Crete [+ 820] is an old man with gray hair like St. Sergius and monastic robes.

And on the same day the passing of the holy hieromartyr **Isidore** the Presbyter and the 72 with him, suffering in Yuriev in Lithuania by the godless Germans in the year 6980 [1472]. St. Isidore has gray hair, a beard like St. Blaise curling at the end, a crimson priests' vestment, with an ocher shoulder piece, a blue tunic, and the others are standing as a crowd of old people, middle aged and youths.

9

The holy martyr **Polyeuctus** [+ 259] *S. 180* resembles St. Florus, wears a scarlet cloak, a blue tunic, and holds a cross in one hand raising it on high.

And the holy prophet **Zacchaeus** [should be Shemaiah at the time of King Solomon] is an old man with gray hair, a beard like the Theologian, a green cloak, a reddish brown tunic and in his hands a scroll on which is written, "Thus says the Lord, 'I will lead evil Rehoboam and I will consume Rehoboam and his generations.'"

10

Our father among the saints **Gregory** [+ 394] *S. 180,* bishop of Nyssa, is an old man with gray hair, a beard a little longer than St. Blaise, bishop's vestments, on his shoulders the omophorion, and he had a physical resemblance to his brother St. Basil of Caesarea, both were starting to gray.

And our holy father **Dometian** [+ 601] *S. 182,* bishop of Melitene, is an old man with a gray beard, a beard a little shorter but wider than St. Blaise, and bishops' vestments.

And our holy father **Paul** Komelsky [+ 1429] *S. 182,* who was the miracle worker on the Obnora River of Vologda, is an old man with gray hair, a beard like St. Sergius but shorter, monastic robes, his tunic is ocher with white, and in both hands he holds a scroll on which is written, "Do not sorrow, brothers, if someone suffers in this place, for I will trust that the mercy of God will not leave him, and it will not abandon him even if he sins."

And our holy father **Marcian** the Presbyter [+ after 471] *S. 180* is an old man with gray hair, a shorter beard than St. Athanasius, priests' vestments but without the omophorion.

11

Our holy and God-bearing father **Theodosius** [+ 529] *S. 182,* the originator of the common life, is an old man with gray hair, a longer beard than St. Blaise, but a little wavy, he is blessing with his right hand, but in the left he is holding a scroll on which is written, "Pay attention to yourself and your flock," and his tunic is ocher.

And our holy father **Michael** of Klops [+ 1456] *S. 182,* miracle worker of

Novgorod, has a beard like St. Varlaam, he is starting to gray, in the schema and monastic robes.

And our holy father **Martyrian** [+ 1483], abbot of White Lake, miracle worker, has a beard like St. Blaise, gray hair, monastic robes, but some paint him in priests' vestments but without the omophorion.

12

The holy martyr **Tatiana** [+ c. 225] *S. 184* resembles St. Parasceva; she has a scarlet cloak and a blue tunic.

And the holy martyr **Peter** [+ 310] resembles St. Florus, and according to the printed Prologue, "he is young like St. Demetrius the soldier."

And the holy martyr **Taisia,** is a maiden, who was an adulteress, who made herself a commoner, but is wearing a royal crown.

13

The holy martyrs **Hermylus** and **Stratonicus** [+ 315] *S. 184*. St. Hermylus resembles St. George, has deacons' vestments, in his right hand he has incense and in the left a censer. St. Stratonicus has brown hair like St. Cosmas, a blue cloak and a purple tunic.

And the holy martyr **Peter** [the same person as on January 12] is a young man like St. Demetrius.

And our holy father **Stephen** [eighth century], who lived near the Jordan, is an old man with gray hair, a beard like St. Sergius, in his hands is a scroll on which is written, "Brothers, do not forget God! You know that this world will pass away."

14

The holy **Fathers** *S. 186* killed [between the years 300 and 311] at Sinai and Raithu by the Glazates. There is a church with three peaks, the very top is ocher, it is decorated with gold, there is a white church behind the mountain, the holy fathers are lying down in a little hill, the first is an old man with gray hair and a beard like St. John the Theologian, a tunic and cloak ocher with white, next to him there is a similar one, with gray hair, the third one is also gray, and has a plain long beard, his name is Adam and has a halo, the fourth is a young man whose name is George, and has a halo also, and others are lying with them, but one can see only their heads, and all are in the schema, the mountain is ocher with white.

The holy **Fathers** *S. 188* killed [during the fifth century] at Sinai and Raithu by the Saracens. The Holy Monastics are standing, the middle one is an old man with gray hair, balding, a beard longer than St. Blaise, a purple mantle, a greenish brown with white tunic; next to him is an old man with gray hair like St. Sergius, an ocher tunic, his hands are held in blessing; the third is an old man with gray hair, a beard like St. Athanasius, but wide at the end with two curls; next to him one with curly hair, a beard like St. Nicholas, and of the rest one can see only some heads, old men and youths, middle aged and some with brown hair.

And our father among the saints **Sabbas** [+ 1236] *S. 186,* archbishop of the Serbs, is an old man with gray hair, balding, a beard like St. Blaise, a cross pattern vestment, his tunic is ocher with white, the omophorion and Gospel.

And the holy martyr **Agnes** resembles St. Parasceva.

And the closing of the feast of the Holy Theophany.

15

Our holy fathers **Paul** of Thebes [+ 341] *S. 188* and John the "Hut-dweller" [+ middle of fifth century] *S. 190*. St. Paul is an old man with gray hair, balding, has a longer beard than St. Blaise, his hands are held in prayer to his heart, the fingers are pointing up, his cloak is ocher and striped, like pine bark, but the coat under it is purple, and countering the stripes there is white, and they reappear back and forth like palm tree bark is woven, his forearms and knees are bare. St. John the hut-dweller is a young man, he wears monastic robes, in his hands is a gold Gospel book, and his tunic is reddish brown with ocher.

16

The veneration of the precious **chains** of the holy and all-glorious apostle Peter *S. 190*. St. Michael the Archangel is girded up, he has a purple reddish brown cloak, where it comes down over his shoulder it is purple with white, with his right hand he is taking Peter's left hand and leading him out of the prison, and Michael's left hand is raised as in prayer. Peter has a greenish brown cloak with whitened reddish brown, his tunic is blue, the prison is ocher, and from the middle the ocher is whitened, there are two soldiers standing in the door, both are young with breastplates, they are looking at each other, one has a greenish brown with white cloak, a feather [patterned breastplate], a blue tunic, purple leggings, there is a lance in his hand; the other has ocher armor decorated with gold, a scarlet tunic, purple leggings, there is a greenish brown mountain lightened with reddish brown.

And the holy monastic true believing crown prince **Peter** of Rostov; his features are similar to St. Peter of Murom, he wears the schema, he has a round beard like the holy ancestor of God Joachim, and is very old and gray.

And the holy martyr **Neonilla** resembles St. Elizabeth.

And the holy martyrs the three youths, the triplets **Speusippus, Eleusippus,** and **Meleusippus** [+ under Marcus Aurelius], are young men like Sts. George, Demetrius and Varus; the first has a purple cloak, a crimson tunic, and a blue hat on his head; the third one is looking at them, he has a crimson cloak with white, an ocher tunic and a white hat on his head.

17

Our holy father **Anthony** the Great [+ 356] *S. 192,* is an old man with gray hair, in the schema, a beard like the Theologian, the right hand is held in prayer, the fingers are pointed up, and in the left is a scroll on which is written, "Behold, I have fled afar off and I have dwelt in the desert," and his tunic is ocher with white.

And our holy father **Martyrius** the "Black Robed" and God-bearer is a young man wearing monastic robes.

And our holy father **Anthony** the Roman [1067 - 1147], miracle worker of Novgorod, is an old man with gray hair, a long beard wavy with curls, like St. John the Theologian, with the hair is a schema, he is standing on a stone in shoes, and monastic robes.

"The day has 9 hours and the night 15."

18

Our fathers among the saints **Cyril** [+ 444, also on June 9] and **Athanasius** Great [+ 373, also on May 2] *S. 192,* the archbishops of Alexandria. St. Athanasius has gray hair like St. Peter the Metropolitan [of Moscow], a reddish brown cross pattern saccos, the omophorion and Gospel. St. Cyril resembles St. Basil of Caesarea; he has a cap on his head, his beard is divided at the end, the omophorion, the Gospel, and his tunic is green.

And the three holy youths **Pesiotus, Palesitus,** and **Elasinus;** they are all young men like the three youths in the fiery furnace [see December 17], with curly hair, all three are wearing robes by which they are distinguished to graze herds of animals, and their grandmother St. Neonilla is similar to St. Parasceva.

And the holy martyr **Theodula** resembles St. Parasceva.

And the memory of our father among the saints **Acacius,** bishop of Tver, the new miracle worker, is an old man with gray hair, a beard like the Theologian, and bishops' vestments with the omophorion.

19

Our holy monastic father **Macarius** [+ 391] *S. 194,* the presbyter of Alexandria, is covered with hair and entirely nude; his beard goes down to his knees, and from his knees two strands reach the ground, he is holding his hands to his heart, the hair on his head goes down over his shoulders.

And there was a second **Macarius** [+ 395] *S. 194,* the presbyter of Alexandria: an old man with gray hair in a klobuk, a longer beard then the Theologian, monastic robes, with a reddish brown greenish brown tunic, in his left hand is a scroll and the right is empty; but in the printed *Prologue* is written, "The Saint had the appearance of being only twisting sparse curls of hair and his moustache reached the end of his beard."

And our holy father **Mark** of Athens, who fasted on the mountain *"Phryachyesti,"* is an old man with gray hair like the prophet Elias, a gray beard down to the ground, a little wavy but straight, but he himself is all curly hair and nude, he has the right hand to his heart, and with his left hand he is covering his privates.

And St. **Euphrosyne** [+ 303] resembles St. Parasceva.

And the holy blessed **Theodore** [+ 1392], the fool for Christ's sake, the new miracle worker, is a very old and gray man with a beard like St. Nicholas and wears princes' robes.

20

Our holy father **Euthymius** the Great [+ 473] *S. 194* is an old man with gray hair, a beard longer than St. Blaise, straight, it is parted at the end, monastic robes, an ocher tunic with white, he is blessing with one hand, and in the other is a scroll on which is written, "Brothers, endure terrible troubles," but in the printed *Prologue* it written of him, "He had a very white complexion, gray hair, a beard down to his knees."

And our holy father **Euthymius,** the new miracle worker, who lived in the city of Archangel, was a old man with gray hair, a beard a longer than St. Sergius, in a black klobuk, with his right hand he is blessing, and he is clutching a scroll in the left.

21

Our holy father **Maximus** the Confessor [+ 622] *S. 194* is an old man with gray hair, a beard like St. Blaise divided at the end, a greenish brown cloak, a light gray tunic, he has a cross in his right hand and in the left a scroll on which is written, "And so I will hymn and worship the Father and the Son and the Holy Spirit."

And the holy martyr **Neophytus** [+ 303] *S. 196* is a young man like St. Demetrius and has ordinary robes.

And the holy martyr **Agnes** [+ 304] resembles St. Parasceva.

And the memory of our holy father **Maximus** the Greek [+ 1556], the miracle worker of Radonezh, is an old man with gray hair; he has a wide beard that covers his shoulders and chest, he wears a kamilavka, monastic robes, and has a book in his hands.

22

The holy apostle **Timothy** [first century] *S. 196,* has a beard like St. Sylvester; but others describe him as follows: he is a young man like St. Demetrius of Thessalonica, with brown hair like St. John Chrysostom, a purple cloak lightened with red and on the thigh lightened with reddish brown, a blue tunic, the Gospel and omophorion.

And the holy hieromartyr **Athanasius** the Persian [+ 628] *S. 196,* is an old man, he has a beard like St. Blaise, priests' vestments, and a scroll in his hand.

And the memory of our holy father **Gennadius** [+ 1565], the miracle worker of Kostrom, is a very old man with gray hair, in the schema, a shorter beard like St. Basil of Caesarea, and monastic robes.

23

The holy hieromartyr **Clement** [+ 312] *S. 196,* the bishop of Ancyra, is an old man with gray hair, a beard longer than the Theologian, a cross pattern vestment, a scarlet tunic with white, he has a cap, omophorion, and Gospel, in his hand is a scroll on which is written, "Lord, Jesus Christ, grant all who honor my memory the richness of Your generosity forgiving them their sins."

And the holy martyr **Agathangelus** *S. 198* is an old man with gray hair, a smaller beard than St. Blaise, a scarlet cloak and a blue tunic.

And our holy monastic father **Salamanes** the Silent [+ c. 400] is an old man like St.

Sergius, in his hand is a scroll on which is written, "Lord, Jesus Christ, have mercy on all those who serve Your name and worship You as our true God."

24

Our holy mother **Xenia** of Rome [fifth century] *S. 198* and her two servants. She resembles St. Euphemia, has a bluish klobuk, monastic robes, a greenish brown tunic with whitened ocher, in her hand is a cross and in the other a scroll.

And the holy monk martyr **Paul** of Galaidos resembles St. Theodosius.

And the holy martyr **John** of Kazan [+ 1529] is a young man with a scarlet cloak, a blue tunic, a cross in one hand and a scroll in the other.

And the holy martyrs **Peter** and **Stephen** of Kazan; both are old men.

On the same day the passing of our father among the saints **Gerasimus,** bishop of Perm, miracle worker, who was smothered by his household staff, his holy body is lying with the adornments of working many miracles for those who come in faith. He is an old man with gray hair, a beard somewhat larger than St. Nicholas, he has the schema on his shoulders, a purple mantle with the fountains. Others paint him in bishops' vestments, a cap, a green tunic, and a scroll in his left hand.

25

Our father among the saints **Gregory** [+ 389] *S. 198,* archbishop of Constantinople, the Theologian, has a humble face, a little bit pale, a high forehead, his mustache and beard are not long but very dense and wide, the edges reach his shoulders, gray hair, bishops' vestments, a green cross pattern saccos, omophorion and Gospel, an ocher tunic.

And his holy sister **Gorgonia** resembles St. Euphemia.

And the holy martyr **Felicitas** [+ 164] resembles St. Parasceva, and her seven sons.

And our holy father **Moses**, archbishop of Novgorod [+ 1396], miracle worker, has brown hair, a beard like the Theologian, and bishops' vestments. Some paint him with as an old man with gray hair, in a white klobuk, with the omophorion and Gospel.

26

Our holy father **Xenophon** [fifth century] *S. 198* and those with him. He is an old man with curly gray hair, a longer beard than the Theologian, monastic robes, the tunic is ocher with white, in his hands is a rolled up scroll; his wife **St. Mary** *S. 200* resembles St. Xenia with a greenish brown tunic with scarlet; their children stand up to their waists, both are very young in black klobuks, monastic robes, greenish brown tunics with white, their names are **Arcadius** and **John,** their hands are stretched out to their father and mother, who are looking at them.

On the same day [we remember the transfer in 845 of the relics of] our holy father **Theodore** of the Studion.

And our holy father **Joseph** of Thessalonica [+ 830].

27

The translation [in the year 438] of the precious relics of our father among the saints **John** Chrysostom, patriarch of Constantinople, *S. 200.* Three deacons are carrying the coffin of the Saint, at the head is a young man like St. Stephen, the second has brown hair, a beard a little smaller than St. Paul the Apostle, a green sticharion, the other deacon has a beard like St. Nicholas, but not balding, behind the coffin a very old and gray deacon is walking, balding with a beard like the Theologian, and he is carrying a big cross. At the head of the Saint there is a bishop standing who has brown hair in a cap, a beard like St. Cyril of Alexandria, and behind him are four priests, two are old and gray like St. Blaise, and two are middle aged like St. Cosmas, the bishop has a cap on his head, and in his right hand incense, and in the left a book, and they are carrying the coffin to a city. A king is greeting it who is similar to St. Constantine the Emperor, both in robes and beard, and before him a bishop is standing who has gray hair like St. Blaise, in a saccos, the priests and the deacons have brown hair and are young men, and behind the king are princes resembling Sts. Vladimir, Boris and Gleb, and another like St. Mercurius, they are carrying crosses and icons of the Savior "Not Made By Human Hands" and before the king "Our Lady of the Sign." The mountain is ocher with white and behind the mountain there is a green widow's garden and greenery and every kind of flower can be seen, and behind the garden there is a green city, very white and in the city there is a white church with one peak.

28

Our holy father **Ephraim** the Syrian [+ 373] *S. 202* has brown hair with a little gray, the beard is smaller than St. John Chrysostom, in the schema, and monastic robes.

And our holy father **Paladius** [fourth century].

And our holy father another **Ephraim** of Novotorzh [+ 1053] is an old man with gray hair, a beard a longer than St. Nicholas, the schema on his head, and in his hands a [miniature] church.

29

The [translation of the relics in 530 or 637 of the] holy hieromartyr **Ignatius** the God-bearer *S. 202* is an old man with gray hair, a beard longer like St. Blaise, a cross patterned cloak, the omophorion and Gospel.

And our holy father **Lawrence** the Recluse [twelfth century] of the Pecherska Lavra, is an old man with gray hair, a smaller beard than St. Sergius and separated at the end.

30

The holy hieromartyr **Hippolytus** [+ 269] *S. 202,* the pope of Rome, has long hair down to the collar of his tunic, a brown beard like St. John Chrysostom, in the cap and saccos. And [with him] the holy martyr **Chryse** resembles St. Euphemia.

And our fathers among the saints the three bishops: **Basil** the Great *S. 202,* **Gregory** the Theologian *S. 204* and **John** Chrysostom *S. 204* [their common feast was established in 1084].

31

The holy miracle workers and unmercenaries **Cyrus** and **John** [+ 311] *S. 204.* St. Cyrus is an old man with gray hair, a beard like St. Blaise, the mantle is higher than the belt, the hems of the mantle are tied up in the at the waist, the cassock is white. St. John is a young man with a dark gray cassock and holds his cloak from underneath like St. Euthymius. And [with them] the holy martyr **Athanasia** and her three daughters; they resemble St. Sophia and her daughters.

And the holy martyr **Tryphaenes** resembles St. Sophia.

And our father among the saints **Nikita** [+ 1108], bishop of Novgorod, miracle worker, is painted without a beard, with a wrinkled face, in a bishops' cap, and bishops' robes with an omophorion.

And our holy father **Barnabas** of Betlus has brown hair, a beard like St. Basil of Caesarea, but a little shorter and wider, monastic robes, the schema on his shoulder, in his hand is a scroll and the other is held in prayer; his appearance is remembered in this way, and it prevails upon one to trust in good faith that it is truc.

FEBRUARY

"The month of February has 28 days; but if it is a leap year, it has 29."

1

The holy great martyr **Tryphon** [+ 250] *S. 206* is a young man resembling St. George, with a scarlet cloak, a blue tunic, the upper garment is gathered up on the right shoulder, his arm is held up, and in the other hand is a white bird, but the left hand is held up in prayer, a mountain and a lake are under his feet and three white birds are above him.

And the holy martyrs **Perpetua** and **Felicitas** [+ c. 203]; both resemble Sts. Anna and Elizabeth.

And the holy fathers **Basil** [+ 830] and **Bendemianus** [+ 512], are old men with gray hair, beards like St. John the Theologian, and monastic robes.

2

THE MEETING OF OUR LORD GOD AND SAVIOR JESUS CHRIST *S. 206.* Over the Most Pure [Mother of God] and over Simeon there is a green canopy with hanging edges, Simeon is an old man with gray hair, a beard longer than the Theologian, the hair on his head is like that of St. Elias, his cloak is green, his tunic is blue, he is holding Christ in his arms, and in his hand there is a scroll on which is written, "Lord, now let Your servant depart in peace according to Your word for my eyes have seen Your salvation." And the Most Pure is standing as is usual, and behind her are St. Joseph, a woman who resembles St. Parasceva, who is holding two white birds, and behind Simeon is standing the holy Prophetess Anna, who is looking at the Most Pure, the temple is white, there is one peak, and a palace, and one sees a wall behind them.

And our holy father **Benedict,** being an old man he has a beard like the Theologian and monastic robes.

"The day has 10 hours and the night 14."

3

The holy and righteous **Simeon** *S. 208* the God-receiver and **Anna** *S. 108* resembles St. Parasceva, with a crimson cloak, and a green tunic; St. Simeon is described under February 2.

4

Our holy father **Isidore** of Pelusium [+ 436] *S. 208* is an old man with gray hair, a smaller beard than St. Blaise which is forked at the end, monastic robes, the tunic is ocher with white.

And our holy father **Nicholas** [+ 868] *S. 208,* the abbot of the Studion, has curly hair, a beard like St. Nicholas, shorter than St. Sergius, monastic robes, and the tunic is greenish brown.

And the murder of the holy Orthodox Prince **George** [+ 1238], the miracle worker of Vladimir, has a straight black beard, longer than St. Joachim, and he wears a princely fur coat.

And our holy father **Cyril** [+ 1532], the miracle worker of New Lake, which is 30 *"versts"* [almost 20 miles] away from St. Cyril of White Lake, is very old and gray, has a smaller beard than St. Basil of Caesarea, and a small mantle.

5

The holy martyr **Agatha** [+ 251] *S. 210* has an ocher with white cloak and a scarlet tunic.

And the holy martyr **Theodula** [+ under Diocletian] is similar.

And the holy hieromartyr **Abraham** of the Pecherska Lavra, bishop of Ruthin, has a beard like St. Blaise, bishops' vestments, in his hand a scroll on which is written, "O my God, Jesus Christ, help Your servant!"

On the same day **Abraham** of V'luvidsk, is an old man with gray hair, a beard like St. Sergius the miracle worker, and monastic robes.

6

Our father among the saints **Buculus** [disciple of St. John the Theologian] *S. 210,* bishop of Smyrna, has brown hair, more hair than St. Demetrius of Thessalonica, a low forehead, a curly or long beard, a blue cloak, an ocher with white tunic, with the omophorion and Gospel.

And our holy father **Theodosius** of Antioch is an old man with gray hair, a beard like the Theologian, only in a cassock, there are irons around his neck and waist, and the graying hair of his head comes down and around him to his feet.

And the holy martyr **Fausta** [+ 305] resembles St. Elizabeth.

And the holy virgin martyrs and sisters **Martha** and **Mary.**

And the holy martyr **Licarion** the Monk is a very young child in monastic robes.

7

Our father among the saints **Parthenius** [+ fourth century] *S. 210,* bishop of the city of Lampsacus, is an old man with balding gray hair, a beard like St. Gregory the Theologian, a cross patterned vestment, in the omophorion, his tunic is ocher with white; but in the "Kievan pages" is printed, "a curly beard."

And St. **Mastridia** is a young nun.

And the holy martyr **Julian** is a young man like St. Demetrius; being a doctor he healed the sick in the name of Christ.

8

The holy martyr **Theodore** Stratelates [+ 319] *S. 210* has brown hair like St. George, a beard like St. Nikita the martyr, in a breastplate, a scarlet with white cloak, a white short tunic, in his left hand is a shield, dark purple leggings with scarlet highlights, and in his hand a cross.

And the holy prophet **Zachariah** [+ c. 520 B.C.] *S. 212* the scythe-seer, is a young man like St. George, a cap on his head, a scarlet cloak, a blue tunic, in his hand is a scroll, and with the other hand he is pointing to the scroll with his finger on which is written, "I have seen the fiery scythe coming down from heaven." Others paint this prophet as follows: like St. Demetrius of Thessalonica without a cap. And in the printed *Prologue* he is described as in extreme old age, and with another scroll, "Behold, I have seen a lampstand all of gold, and seven lamps on top of the lampstand."

9

The holy martyr **Nicephorus** [third century] *S. 212* is a young man like St. Demetrius of Thessalonica, with a blue cloak and a scarlet tunic.

And the holy hieromartyr **Marcian** *S. 212,* the presbyter of Sicily, is an old man with gray hair like St. Clement, the pope of Rome, a beard like St. Blaise, priests' vestments, the shoulder piece is ocher, the tunic is blue with white, and he is holding the Gospel with both hands.

The **close of the feast** of the Meeting of the Lord.

10

The holy martyr **Charalampus** [+ 202] *S. 212* is an old man with gray hair and has dark features because of his old age, his hair comes down below his ears, a full face like St. Florus, a long beard like Zachariah the father of the Forerunner, a mustache, at the end a little shaggy, an ocher with green cloak, with a fold on his right hand, but not on the left, the middle tunic is greenish brown with bluish highlights, his tunic is blue, in his right hand is a scroll, "O Lord my God, where ever they celebrate my memory, forgive them their sins," and the left hand is in prayer. But it is written in the printed *Prologue,* "He was a bishop, but during his life he was a priest."

And our holy father **Prochorus** [+ 1107], a monk of the Pecherska Lavra, has a beard like St. Antipas.

And the holy and royal virgin martyrs **Ennatha, Valentina, Paula** and **Galena.**

And the holy woman **Bassa** of the Caves of Pskov resembles St. Parasceva.

11

The holy hieromartyr **Blaise** [+ 316] *S. 212,* bishop of Sebaste, is an old man with gray hair, a beard down to his chest, a cross patterned vestment with equal black and white crosses, a white tunic, omophorion and holding the Gospel in both hands. [Or] St. Blaise may have a scroll in his hand on which is written, "O Lord my God, if someone who comes into sorrows or misfortunes remembers my name, fulfill whatever is the desire of his heart."

And the holy **Theodora** [+ 867] *S. 214,* the empress resembles St. Helen the Empress and her robes are similar.

And **the seven holy women** with two children.

And our holy father **Demetrius** [+ 1392] *S. 214* the miracle worker of Priluki of Vologda, is an old man with gray hair, a short beard, but as wide as that of St. Sergius of Radonezh, monastic robes, with one hand he is blessing and in the other is a scroll, the tunic is reddish brown with white.

And the holy true believing great prince **Vsevolod** [+ 1138], who was named Gabriel in holy baptism, miracle worker of Novgorod, wears a fur coat and hat, has a beard like St. Basil of Caesarea, and holds a [model of a] church in his hand.

12

Our father among the saints **Meletius** [+ c. 381] *S. 214,* archbishop of Antioch, is an old man with gray hair like St. Blaise, a beard like St. Gregory the Theologian divided into two curls at the end, he has a scarlet cross patterned vestment, a blue with white tunic, an omophorion and Gospel.

And our father among the saints **Anthony** [+ 893], patriarch of Constantinople, is an old man with gray hair like St. Blaise, his beard is forked at the end, a cross patterned vestment, and a blue tunic.

And our father among the saints **Alexis** [+ 1377] *S. 216,* metropolitan of Moscow and all Russia. St. Alexis is in a coffin, standing at his feet is a bishop, who resembles St. Blaise, old and graying, he is holding a scroll, and behind him is a spiritual father in a klobuk, gray hair like St. Blaise, in white robes, between them there is another spiritual father with gray hair, but not a big beard, like St. Nicholas, and four more spiritual fathers, three with gray hair, the beards are not the same, one has a long beard, and one a wide beard, but the fourth spiritual father is a young man. And behind him is a simple palace, the tunic is ocher and green, or greenish brown with white, and a deacon is standing at the head of the Saint who resembles St. Stephen with a scarlet cloak and is incensing the Saint, and behind him is a priest with balding gray hair, a blue with white cloak, and between them one sees a head like the Theologian, and behind them there is a simple palace, a stone church with one peak. Bishop Alexis is an old man with gray hair, a parted beard like St. Blaise, there is a white klobuk on his head, he wears a saccos, an omophorion and holds the Gospel.

And our holy monastic mother **Mary** [+ 1113] resembles St. Eudokia.

13

Our holy father **Martinian** [+ fifth century] *S. 216* is an old man with curly gray hair and a beard like St. Clement, a purple mantle, and his tunic is ocher with white.

And our holy father **Simeon** [+ 1200] of Serbia has a beard like St. Blaise, monastic robes and the schema.

And our holy father **Artemius** of Palestine.

14

Our holy father **Auxentius** [+ 470] *S. 218* is an old man with balding gray hair, a smaller beard then St. Blaise, he is blessing with one hand, and in the other is a scroll, the tunic is ocher with white.

And our father among the saints **Cyril** [+ 869] *S. 218,* archbishop of Catania, the

117

teacher of the Slavs and Bulgarians, who translated Russian literature from the Greek, and baptized the Slavs and Bulgarians, is an old man with a beard like St. Basil of Caesarea and parted at the end, graying hair, a cross patterned vestment, an omophorion, Gospel, and a greenish brown tunic.

And the holy father **Eulogius** [+ 607] *S. 218* of Alexandria is an old man with gray hair, curly hair and beard like St. Clement, a cross patterned vestment, he is holding the Gospel with both hands, an omophorion, and a blue with white tunic.

And our holy father **Simeon** [+ 1200] of Serbia is an old man with gray hair, a beard shorter than St. Zachariah, the father of the Forerunner, a purple cross patterned vestment, a white omophorion and a Gospel, his tunic is green with white.

And the **translation of the venerable relics [in 1572] of the holy true believing Prince Michael** [+ 1244] of Chernigov from Chernigov to Moscow.

And our holy father **Therapont,** the miracle worker of White Lake, is an old man with gray hair and a beard like St. Sergius and monastic robes.

15

The holy apostle **Onesimus** [first century] *S. 218* has brown hair like St. Florus, he is standing in an omophorion, an ocher with white cloak, a blue tunic, a Gospel book is in his left hand and he is blessing with the right. His feet are bare.

And the holy martyr **Anthymus** is a young man, he has long hair down to his shoulders, a scarlet cloak, a blue tunic, a cross in his right hand and the left is held in prayer.

And the holy true believing ruler, king and great prince **Theodore** Ivanovich, of Moscow and all Russia, the new miracle worker, has a curly brown beard and royal robes.

16

The holy martyrs **Pamphilius** *S. 220* and **Porphyrius** and those with them [+ 308 or 309]. St. Pamphilius is a young man, he has long hair down on his shoulders, a scarlet cloak, a blue tunic, a cross in his right hand and the left is in prayer. St. Porphyrius is a young man like St. Demetrius of Thessalonica and resembles him in every way.

And our holy father **Flavian** *S. 220* is an old man with a beard, simple hair like the Theologian, monastic robes, the tunic is greenish brown with white.

And the holy martyr **Paramon** resembles St. Demetrius of Thessalonica in everything.

17

The holy great martyr **Theodore** Tyro [+ under Maximian] *S. 220,* has curly brown hair on his head, a beard similar to St. Florus, in a breastplate, the armor is all gold checkered, the upper cloak is scarlet, the short tunic under the breastplate is blue, the leggings are black and purple, in the right hand is a cross, and in the left a spear.

On the same day the holy **Porphyrius** is an old man with hair like St. Andrew the first called, monastic robes and the schema.

And the holy martyr **Mariamna** [first century] *S. 214,* the sister of the holy apostle Philip, resembles St. Anna.

And our holy father **Herman,** the miracle worker of Solovki, resembles St. Alexander of Svir in everything, monastic robes, he has a scroll in his hand on which is written, "I appeared to the Priest Gregory and ordered him to write my troparion and draw a picture of my appearance."

18

Our father among the saints **Leo** [+ 461] *S. 220,* the pope of Rome, has brown hair, a longer beard than St. John Chrysostom, a blue cloak patterned with crosses and circles, he is holding the Gospel with both hands and the omophorion.

And the holy martyr **Maximus** *S. 222,* resembles St. Demetrius the martyr in everything.

And our holy father **Cosmas,** the abbot of Yakhromsk, resembles St. Barlaam of Khutin.

"The day has 11 hours and the night 13."
19

The holy apostle **Archippus** [first century] *S. 222* has brown hair and the features of St. Paul the Apostle, a purple cloak, an ocher with white tunic, bare knees, he is reaching down for the tunic with the right hand, in the left hand is a cross.

And our holy fathers **Alexander** and **Michael,** both are old men like St. Cyril of White Lake, monastic robes.

And the holy martyr **Mariamna** resembles St. Parasceva.

20

Our father among the saints **Leo** [eighth century] *S. 222,* bishop of Catania, is an old man with gray hair which is sticking out a little, a beard like St. Blaise, a blue cloak and a white tunic, omophorion and Gospel, he is blessing with the right hand.

And the holy martyr **Lucy** resembles St. Euphemia.

And the holy hieromartyr **Sadoc** [+ 342 or 343], bishop of Salim and 128 clergymen with him. St. Sadoc is an old man with gray hair, a beard like St. Sergius, bishops' vestments, and with him is a crowd of presbyters, deacons and readers of all different appearances.

And our holy father **John,** bishop of Constantinople.

21

Our holy father **Timothy** [ninth century] *S. 222,* who was in Symbola, has brown hair, a plain beard a little smaller than St. Blaise, a cross patterned cloak and a white tunic.

22

The **finding of the venerable relics of the holy martyrs in Eugene** *S. 224.* The saints are lying naked in coffins before the church; the church has one peak, behind them are a middle aged priest with a beard like St. Cosmas, a young deacon, and two noblemen, who resemble Sts. Boris and Gleb, two palaces, one green and the other purple with white, and of the saints one see only the head of one. There are old men, then two young men with brown hair, and they are closing the coffins, the cover is bluish, and behind them there are yellow stripes, and of the heads of the others one sees five of them behind them.

And our holy father **Euphrosinus,** the cook, has brown hair, like St. Cosmas, the right hand is in prayer and in the left is a branch on which are the three apples from paradise.

23

The holy hieromartyr **Polycarp** [a disciple of St. John the Theologian] *S. 224,* bishop of Smyrna, is an old man with straight gray hair, a beard like St. Blaise, which is parted at the end, a cross patterned cloak, his tunic is greenish brown.

And our holy father **Polycarp,** the miracle worker of Briansk, has a beard like St. Sergius the miracle worker.

And the holy hieromartyr **Nestor** [+1492 or 1499], bishop of Pamphylia, is an old man with the features and beard similar to St. John the Theologian, a cross patterned cloak, and a blue tunic.

24

The first and second findings of the venerable head of the holy and glorious prophet **John** the Baptist, the forerunner of the Lord. The first finding was by two monks in the house of Herod, which was then brought to the town of Emesa. The second finding *S. 226* was many centuries after the first in the reign of Marcian. The head is in a container, over it is a cave, two spiritual fathers, one is digging with a spade and the other is taking the head, one is young, only in a cassock, the second has brown hair, the beard starting to become gray, the tunic is green with white, and the second has a greenish brown with ocher cassock.

And our holy father **Erasmus** [twelfth century] of the Pecherska Lavra, is an old man with gray hair, a beard like St. Nicholas, monastic robes and in the schema.

25

Our father among the saints **Tarasius** [+ 806] *S. 226,* patriarch of Constantinople, has a beard like St. Gregory the Theologian, curly hair, a purple vestment, a white tunic, omophorion and Gospel which he is holding with both hands, by his whole body and features he resembles St. Gregory the Theologian, but he is not so old and gray.

26

Our father among the saints **Porphyrius** [+ 421] *S. 228,* bishop of Gaza, is an old man with balding gray hair, a beard like St. Blaise, which at the end is narrower and parted, in the omophorion, a cross patterned cloak, and white tunic.

27

Our father among the saints **Procopius** [eighth century] *S. 228* of Decapolis has brown hair like St. Cosmas, his beard is a little gray, monastic robes, the tunic is greenish brown, he is blessing with one hand and there is a scroll in the other.

28

Our holy father **Basil** the Confessor [eighth century] *S. 228,* the co-faster with St. Procopius, has brown hair and is similar to St. Procopius the Decapolite, monastic robes, the tunic is ocher with white.

And the holy hieromartyr **Proterius** [+ 457], archbishop of Alexandria, is an old man with gray hair like St. Gregory the Theologian, has a cross patterned cloak, a white tunic, an omophorion and Gospel.

And the holy martyr **Nestor** [+ under Decius] *S. 230* has a beard like St. Blaise, the robes are similar.

And the holy mother **Domna** resembles St. Eudokia in everything.

And our holy father **Leo** the Monk the simple and **Paisius** the desert dweller.

29

Our holy father **Cassian** the Roman [+ 435] *S. 230* is an old man with straight gray hair, a low forehead, a plain beard like St. Blaise, divided at the end, bishops' vestments, the tunic is greenish brown with white; but in the "Kievan pages" he is described with monastic robes.

MARCH

"The month of March has 31 days."

1

The holy monastic martyr **Eudokia** [+ 152] *S. 232,* is in a round blue schema, has a cross in her right hand, and her left hand in prayer, her cassock is greenish brown with white; but some paint her with a cross in the left hand and the right hand in prayer.

And the holy martyrs **Antonida** and **Domnina** [+ 450] the new resemble either St. Elizabeth or St. Parasceva.

2

The holy hieromartyr **Theodotus** [+ 320] *S. 232,* bishop of Cyrenia, has gray hair, a longer beard than St. Nicholas, like St. Blaise, a scarlet cloak with a cross pattern, a reddish brown tunic, an omophorion and Gospel.

And our father among the saints **Arsenius** [+ 1409], bishop of Tver, the miracle worker, has gray hair, a beard like St. Sergius, in the schema, a mantle with fountains; he is blessing with the right hand and holds the Gospel in the left.

3

The holy martyrs **Eutropius** and **Cleonicus** and **Basilisk** [+ c. 308] *S. 232.* St. Eutropius has brown hair like Moses the God-seer, an ocher with white cloak, a blue tunic, a cross in the right hand, and a sword in a scabbard in the left. St. Cleonicus has gray hair, a beard like the Theologian, a green cloak, and an ocher tunic. St. Basilisk is a young man, he has a towel on his shoulder, he stands in the middle, his hair is like St. Nikita the martyr, only a scarlet cloak; but in the "Kievan printed pages" Cleonicus is young like St. George, and Basilisk has a beard like St. Cosmas.

Saint **Theodorit** has brown hair, a beard like St. Cosmas, and priests' vestments.

And our holy father **Paul,** the simpleton and sufferer, is an old man with gray hair like St. Nicholas, a plain beard, and monastic robes.

4

Our holy father **Gerasimus** [+ 475] *S. 234,* who lived at the Jordan River, has gray hair, a longer beard then St. Blaise, parted at the end, monastic robes, the tunic is greenish brown with white, there is an ocher colored lion at his feet, with one hand he is blessing and in the left there is a scroll, and the scroll says, "A wild animal has obedience in the name of the Lord." Others write, "Behold the obedience the wild animals had to Adam."

And the holy martyrs **Paul** and **Juliana** his sister [+ 273]. St. Paul is a young man; St. Juliana is a young maiden like St. Eudokia.

On the same day the passing of our holy father **Gerasimus** [+ 1178], the founder of the Holy Trinity Monastery in Vologda, who is an old man with gray hair, a beard like St. Basil of Caesarea, and monastic robes.

And the holy true believing and monastic prince **Daniel** [son of] Alexander [Nevsky +1303], miracle worker of Moscow, in the schema, has a smaller beard than St. Blaise but blunt, and monastic robes.

5

The holy martyr **Conon** the Gardener [third century] S. 234 has gray hair, a beard like St. John the Theologian, hair which comes past his ears on the left side, a greenish brown and green cloak down to the knees, his right hand holds a branch, and the left hand is in prayer, the fingers are pointing up, his knees are bare. Some others paint him as follows: Conon torments the demon like the martyr Nikita.

And the holy fathers **Mark** and **Michael** [fifth century] are old men without beards, but have monastic robes.

6

The holy **forty-two** martyrs at Ammoria [+ 847] S. 236. The name of the first martyr is "Theodore," who is standing, he has brown hair like St. Cosmas, a green cloak, a scarlet tunic. And the martyr next him named "George" resembles St. Constantine, is looking toward Theodore, has a scarlet cloak, an ocher short tunic and a blue tunic. Between them is a man with brown hair named "Theophilus" who resembles St. Florus, with a green cloak, ocher on the shoulder, and "Callistus" who looks like St. John the Theologian, and "Basil" resembles St. Nicholas, and another resembles St. Andrew the apostle, and the others are old and young.

On the same day the finding of the precious and Life-giving **Cross** of the Lord, when it was discovered by the blessed Empress Helen in Jerusalem. First there is the holy mountain, and on it stands the Jew Judah, who has a longer beard than St. Zachariah, a white klobuk on his head, a scarlet cloak, a blue tunic, and with him are two young men with brown hair who are standing before him, and before Empress Helen. There is a crowd of people with her, but Judah is pointing with his right hand to a cave in which the crosses can be seen laying there, the soldiers were digging out three crosses, and were carrying the three crosses to the city, to the gates of the city, there is a valley lower than the mountain. And coming out of the city is a bishop like St. Blaise, he takes the crosses and they carry them into the city but they do not know which is the Cross of Christ, and they were carrying a dead girl, the bishop, the emperor and the empress commanded they make the sign of the cross with the three crosses on the dead girl, and so they were protected by the Cross of Christ, and the dead girl rose from the dead and preached Christ, and the people bowed down to the Cross before the city, and the Emperor Constantine and Empress Helen are going into the city, and the bishop and the priests, and all the people are bowing down to the Cross of Christ, which they placed high on a mountain, and the spear and the reed and the sponge. Some paint scrolls in the hands of the emperor and empress, and on the scrolls is written, "Behold, seeking one we have found three, and having found and not knowing which [is the True Cross], the dead girl has shown us."

"The day has 12 hours and the night 12 hours."

7

The holy hieromartyrs who were bishops in Cherson: **Basil, Ephraim, Eugene, Capitonus, Eleutherius**, and the others [+ c. 300]. St. Basil *S. 236* has brown hair like St. Basil of Caesarea, his beard is parted at the end; St. Ephraim *S. 238* is an old man with gray hair and a beard like St. Athanasius; St. Eleutherius has gray hair, the beard is longer than St. Nicholas, at the end it is divided into two; St. Capitonus has a beard like St. John the Theologian; and all of them have cross patterned vestments.

8

Our father among the saints **Theophylact** [+ 845] *S. 238,* archbishop of Nicomedia, has gray hair, a beard like St. Sergius, on the end there are five curls, and a cross patterned vestment.

On the same day of our holy father **Philip,** who lived on the river at Irapa, the new miracle worker, is similar to St. Cyril of White Lake in everything.

9

The holy great **Forty martyrs at Sebaste, Dometian, Cyril, Eutychius, Nicholas, Alexander, Leontius, John,** etc. [in Armenia under Emperor Licinius] *S. 240.* There is a palace, before it are three judges; the first has brown balding hair, a beard like St. Cosmas, a scarlet cloak, a blue tunic; next to him is a man with brown hair, a longer beard than the first, a green cloak, an ocher tunic; the third is a young man, with the arm turned away from the saints, with two fingers he is pointing to his face; all three are sitting on one throne. And behind them stands a black demon, who is catching the judges with a hook, and he holds a snake in his right hand, the snake is whispering into the ear of the judges sitting there, from one to all, and before them stand the forty martyrs. The first martyr has balding gray hair, a beard like St. Athanasius, an ocher cloak, a green tunic, his hands are in prayer; behind him stands a young man like St. George, a blue cloak, a scarlet tunic, with his hands he is holding his cloak from underneath; behind him stands a man with brown hair, and a very old man with gray hair like St. Cosmas, and their cloaks are crimson, their tunics are ocher; and behind them one can see the heads of the others standing there, young men and old men and men with brown hair. The judges are sitting facing the saints, and the saints are standing before them, pointing to them with their hands, and others are making the sign of the cross with their hands, and behind the judges is a round lake, and the judges are commanding them to get into the lake, those who are to suffer for Christ, and removing their garments they are entering the lake, and others are hanging their garments on the trees and running, and they are singing a hymn with one voice, "For the crown of light we weep and wail, and for the paradise of light we suffer a little, so that for the ages we will reign with Christ the God and Savior of our souls." But one of them is not able to endure the terrible cold and jumps into the bathhouse and melts like wax. The guard of the bath is a young man whose name is "Capiclarius," and lifting his arm to heaven, and with his right hand he removes his clothes, and runs into the lake. He sees the crowns of all thirty-nine revealed, but one crown is lacking then, but he sees it in heaven, and runs into the lake, and receives the crown for his suffering. And the bathhouse stands at the end of the lake, before the saints and before the judges, and where the saints jumped in, and from here the lake flows as a flood, from the judges and from the middle of the lake and where the bathhouse stands, near the bathhouse there is a second lake, the flood out of it goes from the bathhouse a little way near the lake, and a certain youth conveys on an ox and on horses the bodies of the holy martyrs onto a fire, and before the ox there is a wood fire. And a certain woman is going out as if from the bathhouse, and carries her son on her shoulder, and his head is hanging down, and she holds him by the feet, and takes her son Militon, who is a young man in age, to the cart, and puts him with the saints, where the saints are lying in a reliquary on the cart. The woman's cloak is blue, her tunic is scarlet, and of the woman an inscription says, "The Christ-loving mother carries on her shoulder her son, and carrying him there places him on top of the forty holy martyrs, Militon by name." And the one who is conveying the saints, has a scarlet cloak. A bishop is coming with a deacon to gather the bones of the saints, the holy relics, and carries them out of the bathhouse from the other side with their tunics on top, and the bishop gathers the bones, the holy relics, and places them on a four wheeled cart, and the people are leading the ox, and the judges are looking out of the bathhouse, as through a little porch and the bishop, who resembles St. Blaise, goes behind the saints, the deacon is a young man, in the middle is a deacon with incense, and a man with brown hair behind the bishop. And some young men, who are dressed only in loincloths, are gathering the bones of the saints in the lake, and the bishop is going to the city, and they are conveying the relics to the city as well, and the city stands on a white corner, and in it there is a church with one dome, and a palace. The inscription says, "The forty martyrs in the time of Licinius the emperor: the saints stood before the governors, confessing themselves to be Christians, saying, 'Now there are three who are fighting us: Satan, the commander and the governor.'" This inscription is over the saints and over the judges. On a cloud the Savior is blessing with both hands, and over Him there is an inscription, "Indeed there are Three over them." Bishop Peter discovered the saints because the relics of the saints were shining in the water; their relics are precious, some are gold, some silver, and so he gathered them and placed them in a silver container, and covered them with a velvet cover, ocher with gold circles, and marked with scarlet lines and a black cross on the cover and decorated with white dots like pearls and gem stones.

10

The holy martyr **Condratus** [or Quadratus], and those with him [+ 258] *S. 234.* St. Condratus is a young man like St. Demetrius; his hair sticks out from his ears; he has a blue cloak, a scarlet tunic, a cross in his right hand, the left hand is in prayer; over him is a small cloud, and under the cloud there is an inscription which says, "You were led out by a cloud."

And the holy martyr **Abraham** of Vladimir, the new miracle worker, whose venerable relics were taken from the country of Bulgaria to the city of Vladimir. Four men are carrying him, but the coffin is covered; people, priests and deacons with censers are greeting him.

And our holy father **Anastasius,** patriarch of Alexandria, the eunuch, wears only a cassock, bare feet, in his hands is a scroll on which is written, "Lord, into your hand I commend my spirit."

And our holy mother **Anastasia** [+ 567] is like St. Eudokia; there is a scroll in her hand, "Lord, into your hand I commend my spirit."

And the holy martyrs **Dionysius** and **Cyprian** resemble Sts. Demetrius and Cosmas.

11

Our father among the saints **Sophronius** the Wise [+ 644] *S. 242,* patriarch of

Jerusalem, has a curly beard like St. Sergius, a vestment patterned with many crosses, omophorion and Gospel.

And our father among the saints **Euthymius** [+ 1458], archbishop of Novgorod, miracle worker, has bishops' vestments, a white klobuk on his head, a beard like St. John the Theologian, but longer and wavy.

12

Our holy father **Theophanes** [+ 818] *S. 242,* the confessor of Sigriane, is an old man with gray hair like St. Sergius, in monastic robes, the tunic is green white reddish brown; he holds a scroll in his hands on which is written, "He who testifies to Me before men, I will testify for him before God's angels."

And our father among the saints **Gregory** [+ 604] *S. 242,* pope of Rome, who composed the Presanctified Liturgy, has gray hair like St. Blaise, wears a blue cross patterned saccos with an omophorion and Gospel.

13

The translation of the venerable relics of our father among the saints **Nicephorus** [+ 846] *S. 244,* patriarch of Constantinople, who is an old man with gray hair resembling St. Blaise; he is lying in a coffin, two deacons are carrying him, one has gray hair with a beard like St. Nicholas, and the other is young, and there are other young deacons, around the middle of the coffin and old men, and one is holding [an icon of] the Most Pure with the [Christ] Child, and others crosses, at the head of the Saint is Bishop Methodius, a very old man with a longer beard than St. Nicholas, and he wears a saccos with crosses in circles, and behind him is a mountain colored ocher with white, and before them a city, the emperor, who is greeting the Saint, has brown hair like King David, a blue cloak, a scarlet tunic, his right hand is in prayer held to his chest and in his left hand there is a towel; the city is green, and in it one can see a church and palaces.

14

Our holy father **Benedict** [+ 543] *S. 246,* archimandrite of Rome, has balding gray hair, there are locks of hair on his shoulders, he has a beard like St. Blaise, not pointed at the end, monastic robes, the tunic is ocher with white, he is holding a scroll with both hands.

And our father among the saints **Theognost** [+ 1353], metropolitan of Moscow, miracle worker, has gray hair, has a beard smaller and narrower at the end than St. Alexis the metropolitan, in a blue saccos, in a klobuk, omophorion and Gospel.

15

The holy martyr **Agapitus** [or Agapius, + 303] *S. 246,* and those with him, is a young man like St. Demetrius of Thessalonica, has small curls, small curly locks are sticking out from his ears, but one can see his ears as [in an icon of] St. Demetrius, a scarlet cloak, a green tunic, the left hand is in prayer, and a cross is in the right.

And the holy martyr **Timolaus;** others paint Viculus⁷¹ as a young man resembling St. Demetrius; in the "Kievan printed pages" he is the same; a blue cloak, an ocher with reddish brown tunic, in the right hand a cross, the left hand in prayer as is customary.

And our holy father **Serapion** has a beard like St. Sergius and the same robes; the tunic is reddish brown with white.

16

The holy martyr **Sabinus** [+ 287] *S. 246* has a beard like St. Cosmas, brown hair, an ocher with scarlet cloak, a blue tunic.

And the passing of our father among the saints **Serapion** [+ 1516], archbishop of Novgorod, miracle worker, has gray hair like St. Sergius of Radonezh, and the same beard, the hair does not go past his ears; he has a reddish brown with white tunic, and a mantle with fountains.

And the holy martyr **Vitalius** is a young man like St. Demetrius, wearing a blue cloak, an ocher with reddish brown tunic; he has a cross in his right hand and the left in prayer.

And the memory of the holy and righteous sufferer for Christ **Basil,** the child on the Turukhani on the Togo River, miracle worker of the north, is young with martyrs' robes.

17

The holy and righteous **Alexis** the man of God [+ 411] *S. 248;* his features, beard and hair resemble St. John the Forerunner, he has a green with reddish brown cloak, he is holding his hands to his heart, but there can be a small scroll on which some write, "Behold, I have left father and mother, wife, family and friends, lands and possessions."

And the passing of our holy father **Macarius** [+ 1483] *S. 248,* abbot of Kalyazin, has gray hair, a smaller beard than St. Blaise, not parted, monastic robes, the cassock is green with white.

And the memory of our holy father **Adrian** [or Andreanus], who dwelt in the desert, the miracle worker of Vologda, is a very old man with a beard longer than St. Cosmas, in the schema, monastic robes.

18

Our father among the saints **Cyril** [+ 389] *S. 248,* archbishop of Jerusalem, is an old man with gray hair, a smaller beard than the Theologian, a cross patterned cloak, omophorion and Gospel; but in the printed *Prologue* about him is written, "he has a humble appearance, white hair, a handsome face, straight black eyebrows, the beard on his jaw is white and thick and parted." But others paint him with gray hair, and a beard like St. Cyril of White Lake.

On the same day the memory of our holy father **Cyril,** the abbot of Holy Trinity Monastery, miracle worker of Astrakhan, has gray hair, somewhat yellowish, a beard down to the waist blunt at the end, and monastic robes.

19

The holy martyrs **Chrysanthus** *S. 248* and **Daria** *S. 250* [+ 283]. He is a young man like St. Demetrius, his hair sticks out a little from his ears, he has a purple cloak with reddish brown lights, a reddish brown tunic, a cross in his right hand, the left hand is in prayer; he is looking at St. Daria, and the martyr Daria has a white cloth [on her head], a blue cloak, an ocher tunic, a cross in her right hand and the left is in prayer.

And our father among the saints **Thomas,** the archbishop of Constantinople, has gray hair, he resembles St. Gregory the Theologian but he is not balding, he has a saccos vestment like St. Gregory, the omophorion and Gospel.

And the holy martyr **Pancharius** [+ 302], who was physically big and handsome, is a young man like St. George, in his hand is a scroll on which is written, "Have mercy on me, O Lord Almighty, and do not be ashamed of Your servant before angels and men, but have mercy on me according to Your great mercy."

And the holy true believing princess **Mary** resembles St. Olga.

And the holy martyr **Claudius** and his wife **Tricunaria Laria,** with two sons Assonus and Maurus. St. Claudius resembles St. Boris the prince, St. Laria is like St. Helen, Sts. Assonus and Maurus resemble Sts. David and Constantine the princes.

On the same day the passing of our holy father **Innocent** [+ 1521], the abbot of the

Monastery of the Forerunner, miracle worker of Vologda, has a shorter beard then St. Blaise, and not parted, black starting to go gray, and monastic robes.

20

Our holy **fathers** killed by the Saracens in the monastery of St. Sabbas [+ 796] *S. 250.* The first father is standing with hair lower than his ears, a beard like St. Sergius, it is curly at the end; the second father has a longer beard, is balding, a big beard, bigger than St. Blaise, parted; the third father has gray hair, a beard like St. Blaise; between the first and the middle fathers there is a man with brown hair like St. Barlaam of Khutin; behind them fathers are standing in klobuks, and others in the schema, some with gray hair and some with brown; the first has a scroll which says, "Come to Me all you who labor and are heavy burdened and I will give you rest."

And the holy martyr **Photina** [or Svyetlana, the Samaritan woman at the well in St. John's Gospel] S. 228, and her five sisters **Anapholiathota, Aphodita, Parasceva, Kiriakia,** and **Domnina** who is royal like St. Catherine.

And the seven holy women martyrs who were from Amisus: **Alexandra, Claudia, Euphrasia, Matrona, Juliana, Euphemia, and Theodosia;** all resemble Sts. Anna and Elizabeth.

And the holy forefather **Abel** [In Genesis], who is a young man in a fur garment and has a scroll in his hand.

21

Our holy father among the saints **James** [+ 750] *S. 252,* bishop and confessor, is an old man with gray hair, a beard like St. Blaise, on the end there are two curls, he has a scarlet cross patterned cloak, the omophorion and Gospel.

And our father among the saints **Cyril** [disciple of St. Peter], the bishop of Catania, resembles St. Blaise.

And the holy bishop **Gregory** of Mastidi.

22

The holy hieromartyr **Basil** [+ 363] *S. 252,* presbyter of the church in Ancyra, is a very old man, with a beard like St. Blaise and parted at the end, priests' robes, the shoulder piece is ocher, the cloak is scarlet with white, under it is blue damask, the highest quality brocade.

131

And the holy royal martyr **Drosida** resembles St. Catherine in everything.

And the five holy women ascetics and rulers, **Polynaria, Taisia, Daria, Maurusa, Aglaida, Atikia, Arsaida** resemble St. Eudokia.

"The day has 13 hours and the night 11 hours."

23

Our holy father **Nikon,** and his 199 disciples [+ 250] *S. 254.* St. Nikon is an old man with gray hair, a longer beard than St. Blaise, parted at the end, in the left hand is a scroll and on the scroll it says, "Come, children, listen to me, for I will teach you the fear of the Lord," the right hand is in prayer; and before him is a spiritual father with brown hair, in a klobuk, a beard like St. Cosmas, who is looking toward Nikon, and behind him is another spiritual father who resembles St. George, and before him is a second spiritual father who is a young man in a klobuk, and Nikon wears a green tunic, reddish brown with white, and next to him is a spiritual father who resembles St. Nicholas, and there are other old men and men with brown hair, and before them is a green church with white, and at the church Nikon has his face toward it and all of the spiritual fathers are looking at him.

And the holy blessed **Philitas** the Senator [+ under Hadrian], who is a young man like St. Demetrius with a cross in his right hand.

On the same day the passing of our holy father **Herman,** the miracle worker of Solovki, who has gray hair, a beard like St. Alexander of Svir, and monastic robes.

24

Our father among the saints **Artemon** [disciple of St. Paul] *S. 256,* bishop of Thessalonica, is an old man with balding gray hair, a beard like St. Athanasius, parted at the end, a scarlet cross patterned cloak, omophorion and Gospel.

And our father Saint **James** the presbyter *S. 246* (who is named "Zachariah" in the "Kievan printed pages") is an extremely old man with much hair which goes past his ears, a beard somewhat darker than St. Blaise, and parted at the end, a purple with reddish brown brocade cloak, under it blue, with a green priests' shoulder piece.

And the holy martyr **Izah** the deacon *S. 256,* but in the "Kievan printed pages" he is named "Isaac the Deacon," the cloak on his shoulder is purple, and in his right hand is incense, and he himself is young like St. George.

25

THE ANNUNCIATION OF OUR MOST HOLY LADY AND MOTHER OF

GOD, THE EVER VIRGIN MARY *S.258*. Archangel Gabriel comes and stands before the palaces, in the palace his upper cloak is bright purple, his tunic is blue; the Theotokos is standing or sitting, and on top is [the Lord] Sabaoth from Whom is descending the Holy Spirit on the Theotokos. Others paint: the Theotokos stands at the well in the mountains, and there are palaces beyond, and at that time the angel comes and flying down from above he announces to the Theotokos, and she looks behind her. There is an "Annunciation" [icon] where Gabriel wears a cloak colored reddish brown, a blue tunic, the palaces are ocher, the Theotokos has red silk in her right hand, and a spindle in her left, between the palaces there is a scarlet city, the archangel has a staff.

26

The **Synaxis of the holy archangel Gabriel** *S. 260*. St. Michael wears a scarlet cloak, a blue short tunic and a red tunic, cherry-red purple; St. Gabriel wears a green cloak, a scarlet short tunic, a blue tunic, he is holding the Savior in a cloud, the Savior [as a] Child is on three cherubim, around the Savior are angels.

27

The holy martyr **Matrona** of Thessalonica *S. 260* has a white cloth on her head, a green cloak, a scarlet tunic, her right hand holds a cross and the left hand is in prayer.

And the holy martyr **Mamontes** of Maugis, is a young man like St. Demetrius of Thessalonica, has a blue cloak, a purple with reddish brown tunic, his hands are held in prayer; but in the "Kievan pages" it says that the one on this day resembles St. Philip.

28

Our holy father **Hilarion** the New [+ 754] *S. 262*, has brown hair, a beard like St. Cosmas, in the schema, a scroll in his hand, monastic robes, a green with reddish brown tunic; but in the "Kievan pages" it is written he had a beard like St. Blaise.

And St. **Stephen** [+ ninth century] *S. 262*, the miracle worker, has a beard like St. Sergius, narrower at the end, his hair comes below his ears, monastic robes, an ocher tunic with white, in his hand is a scroll on which is written, "We suffer a little that we might reign forever."

And the holy true believing great princesses **Basilissa** and **Anna** of Nizhegorod and Kashin, nuns.

On the same day our holy father **Faust,** miracle worker of Vologda, has gray hair, a beard narrower than St. Demetrius of Priluki, balding, and monastic robes.

29

Our holy father **Mark** [+ under Julian the Apostate] *S. 264,* bishop of Arethusa, is an old man with gray hair, a longer beard than St. Blaise, parted at the end, a cross patterned cloak, the omophorion and Gospel. [Together with] the holy martyr **Cyril** the Deacon *S. 262,* resembles St. George, a scarlet cloak on the right shoulder, and incense in the left hand; but according to the "Kievan [printed pages"] he has incense in the right hand and he is pointing down with the left hand.

And our holy father **John** the "well-keeper" [fourth century], is a young monk with monastic robes.

And the memory of our holy father **Irinarch,** the new miracle worker of Solovki, has gray hair, a beard like St. Cyril of White Lake, in a klobuk and monastic robes.

30

Our holy father **John** [+ 563] *S. 264,* author of "The Ladder," is an old man with gray hair, a beard longer than St. Blaise, he stands before a church, with monastic robes, in the schema, in his hand is a scroll on which is written, "See, brothers, how narrow the path that leads to the expanse of paradise, and how wide the path to hell." And before him stands a spiritual father with gray hair, a beard like St. Blaise, in a klobuk; a second old man with a beard like St. Athanasius, with curls at the end, and other old men and young men and some with brown hair, and they are looking at a ladder, and the ladder leads up to heaven, and two spiritual fathers are climbing up on it, angels are holding them, one spiritual father resembles St. Blaise, the second spiritual father is young, and Christ is giving them crowns, and with the right hand He is blessing, before Christ on a cloud is the Jerusalem on high, in which a choir of saints are in its palaces, and they resemble all the saints, and they are sitting at tables, and on the tables are different branches of paradise, and another spiritual father is falling from the ladder, and the demons are snaring him with their hooks into hell, and beneath the ladder is a mountain, and in the mountain a ravine and in the ravine hell, and some [monks] are standing at the ladder, and a demon spreads nets over them, [it looks like] he holds a receptacle, strewing something out of it like ashes. The ladder has thirty steps leading up to heaven: 1 forsaking the world, 2 about detachment, 3 about being a foreigner, 4 about obedience, 5 about repentance, 6 about the remembrance of death, 7 about weeping, 8 about angerlessness, 9 about the remembrance of wrongs, 10 about slander, 11 about talkativeness, 12 about lies, 13 about despair, 14 about the stomach or eating, 15 about purity, 16 about the love of money, 17 about not possessing things, 18 about not being sensitive, 19 about sleep, 20 about prayer, 21 about keeping vigil, 22 about fearfulness, 23 about meekness, 24 about faith, 25 about humility, 26 about judging, 27 about silence, 28 about mercifulness, 29 about passions, 30 about love. St. John is pointing to heaven with his hand, the crucifixion of Christ.

On the same day the passing of our father among the saints **Jonah,** metropolitan of Moscow and all Russia, miracle worker, has gray hair, a beard shorter than St Blaise, a little wavy at the end, a bishops' cap on his head, and he is wearing a green saccos with a cross pattern, omophorion and Gospel.

And our holy father **John** the Silent [+ 557], who was in the Lavra of St. Sabbas, who was previously a bishop, and became a great elder, with white hair, having a curly beard, of small stature, monastic robes; or bishops' robes since he left the episcopacy voluntarily.

31

Our holy father **Hypatius** [+ 326] *S. 266,* the bishop, miracle worker, who was of Gangra, is an old man with gray hair, a wide beard, longer than St. Blaise, parted at the end, the hair on his head comes a little beyond his ears, a purple cloak with light reddish brown, with his right hand he is holding an icon of the most holy Theotokos with the Child Jesus Christ from underneath, in a green lightened with white tunic with the omophorion, in his left hand is a scroll on which is written, "If someone does not venerate the icon of the Holy Theotokos with the glorious Child Jesus Christ, let him be anathema." At the seventh council he spoke thus, and he humiliated the heretics with this saying.

And our holy father another **Hypatius** [+ 446], the abbot of Rufinus, is an old man and the hair of his head and beard is as white as snow.

APRIL

"The month of April has 30 days."

1

Our holy mother **Mary** of Egypt [521] *S. 268.* [In the first field] she is standing naked, [otherwise] her left shoulder and side are bare, she has short brown hair, with a little gray or white; and St. Zosimas gives her a mantle, he is looking backward. In the second field Zosimas is giving her Communion of the Holy Mysteries, and they are both standing at the Jordan River; there is a little ocher mountain over the Jordan and there are trees around them.

And the passing of our holy father **Euthymius** [+ 1405], miracle worker of Suzhdal, who is an old man with a wider beard than St. Blaise, but similar robes, the omophorion and Gospel; but others paint him in monastic robes and schema with curls showing.

And the holy martyr **Abram** [+ 1229], miracle worker of Vladimir [in fact, his relics were transferred here from Bulgaria], is an old man with a beard like St. Nicholas the miracle worker, wearing princes' robes and he has a cross in his right hand.

2

Our holy father **Titus** [his life time and place are unknown] *S. 270,* miracle worker, is an old man with gray hair resembling St. Blaise, his beard is parted at the end, he wears a blue and white cross patterned cloak, and a reddish brown tunic.

The monastic St. **Theodosia,** the virgin resembles St. Eudokia.

3

Our holy father **Nikita** [+ 824] *S. 270,* abbot of Medikion, is an old man like St. Sergius, his beard is narrow at the end, he wears monastic robes, he has a scroll in his hand on which is written, "And whoever confesses Me before men, him will I confess before My Father who is in heaven."

And the holy martyrs **Agapia, Irene**, and **Chionia** of Thessalonica resemble Sts. Euphemia and Theodosia.

4

Our holy and God-bearing father **Joseph** the hymn writer and composer of canons [+ 883] *S. 270* is an old man with gray hair, a beard like St. Nicholas, but

136

narrow at the end, monastic robes, the tunic is ocher with white, he holds a book in his left hand, and with the fingers of his right hand he is pointing to heaven; but some paint him with a scroll in his hand on which is written, "[O God,] hasten to be generous and as the merciful One hurry to our aid, which You can do if You wish!"

And our holy father **George** [+ fourth century] *S. 270,* who was in Maleon; but in the "Kievan [printed pages" his name is] "Gregory." He has a curly brown beard, shorter than St. Nicholas, and monastic robes.

And the holy virgin martyrs **Pherbutha** and her sister and a servant girl [+ in Persia 341 or 343, sister of St. Simeon of April 17], both virgins [no description].

And our holy father **Zosimas** of Palestine [+ between 518 and 526], who buried the body of St. Mary of Egypt [April 1], is an old man with a beard like St. Sergius and monastic robes.

5

And the holy martyrs **Theodulus, Agathapodes** the deacon [+ 303] *S. 270,* and those with them. St. Theodulus has brown hair, a beard like the Apostle Paul; but the printed *Prologue* writes, "Theodulus was an [ordained] reader and not old, at the end his beard is curly, a blue cloak, purple red with white, and a cross in his hand. St. Agathapodes the deacon is an old man with gray hair resembling St. John the Theologian, a blue cloak, incense in his hand, a white tunic, that is the top sticharion, and everything as a deacon."

And the holy virgin martyr **Theodora** [+ 879] of Thessalonica resembles St. Eudokia.

And our holy father **Plato** [+ 814], bishop of Studion, has brown hair, a beard like the Apostle Paul, his hair comes below his ears, blue bishops' robes and a crimson tunic.

6

Our father among the saints **Eutychius** [+ 582] *S. 272,* patriarch of Constantinople, his beard and vestments resemble St. John Chrysostom.

Our holy father **Daniel** [+ 1540], abbot of Pereyaslavl the miracle worker, has gray hair, a beard pointed at the end like St. Nikon, the schema, monastic robes, he is blessing with his right hand and holding a scroll in his left.

7

Our father among the saints **George** [+ 816] *S. 272,* the bishop of Mitylene: but in the "Kievan [printed pages" named] "Sergius," is painted with gray hair, a beard like St. Blaise, a cross patterned bishops' cloak, his beard is a little wavy, his hair is wavy and comes down below his ears.

And the holy virgin martyr **Theodora** resembles the passion bearer, in armor and with a helmet on her head.

And the holy martyr **Didimus** is a young man like St. Demetrius the martyr.

And the holy martyr [**Aquilina** + c. 310, together with St. Rufinus, the deacon martyr] resembles St. Anna, and ten of her disciples.

8

The holy apostles **Herodion, Agabus,** and **Rufus, Asyncritus,** and **Hermes,** and those with them [first century]. St. Herodion *S. 274* has brown hair, a beard like St. Florus, his upper cloak is purple, his tunic is blue, he has the omophorion on his shoulders, in his hand is a book but he is pointing with the second finger. St. Agabus *S. 274* has brown hair and resembles the first apostle, but in the "Kievan [printed] pages" Agabus is a young man like St. George whom he resembles, a blue cloak and in the omophorion. St. Rufus *S. 274* resembles Herodion and stands between them and behind them, he has a purple with white cloak, a scarlet tunic, and he also wears the omophorion; they all have crosses in their left hands and are blessing with their right.

And our father among the saints **Niphont** [+ 1156], archbishop of Novgorod the miracle worker, has balding gray hair, a longer beard than St. John the Theologian, wearing a bishop's' cap, vestments, omophorion and Gospel.

9

The holy martyr **Eupsychius** [+ 362] *S. 274* is a young man who resembles St. George in everything, wears a breastplate, has a sword in his [right] hand and a scabbard in the left.

10

The holy martyrs **Terence** and **Pompeius** [+ under Decius] *S. 276* and those with them. St. Terence is middle aged, the hair on his head flows down over his shoulders, he has a beard like St. Cosmas, he is in a breastplate and armed like St. Demetrius of

138

Thessalonica, in his right hand he is holding a cross up on high and in the left a sword in its scabbard. St. Pompeius has brown hair, a beard like Sts. Florus and Laurus, his beard is a little curly, and the other thirty-six martyrs are standing behind and between Sts. Terence and Pompeius. They are a large group of men of various descriptions.

And the memory of our holy father **Tikhon,** the founder of the monastery of the Holy Mother of God in Kaluga, is a very old man with a beard like St. Blaise, wearing the schema and monastic robes.

11

The holy hieromartyr **Antipas** [disciple of St. John the Theologian in Revelation 2:13] *S. 276,* bishop of Pergamus, who has the grace from God to cure a toothache, has a scroll in his hand, "O Lord Master, save all those who hope in You." He is an old man with curly gray hair on his head, a beard like St. Blaise, and a scarlet and white cross patterned cloak, the omophorion and the Gospel.

12

The holy hieromartyr **Basil** [eighth century] *S. 276,* bishop of Parium, is an old man with curly, yellowish to gray hair, a beard like St. Euthymius, or like St. Blaise, divided at the end, a black and white cross patterned cloak, the omophorion and Gospel.

And our holy mother **Anthusa** [+ 811] resembles St. Eudokia and in her hand is a scroll on which is written, "Sing my sisters, sing to God and praise Him always, that He will be merciful toward your sins."

And the holy mother **Athanasia** [+ 860] the abbess resembles St. Eudokia.

13

The holy hieromartyr **Artemon** [+ 303] *S. 278,* is an old man starting to turn gray, he has a dark green priests' cloak, a beard like St. Blaise, narrower but not divided at the end.

St. **Simeon** is an old man with a beard like St. Gregory the Theologian, a bishops' cloak, the omophorion and Gospel.

And the holy virgin martyr **Axetria.**

And the holy true believing Emperor **Theodosius** the Younger is a young man with a crown like St. Demetrius the crown prince.

14

Our father among the saints **Martin** [+ 655] *S. 278,* the confessor, pope of Rome, is an old man with balding gray hair, a beard like St. Nicholas, a vestment like St. John Chrysostom, and in his hand a scroll.

And the holy new martyrs **Anthony, John,** and **Eustathius** who suffered in Lithuania [+ 1357] *S. 278.* St. Anthony is a prince resembling St. Boris in a fur coat, scarlet light blue; St. John is a prince like St. Gleb, an ocher cloak, crimson in the fur coat; St. Eustathius resembles St. Vladimir the prince, blue green, in a fur coat. They hold crosses in their hands and swords in scabbards in the left, they have hats on their heads, the brims are black.

And the holy blessed father **Timothy** has a beard like St. Blaise, in the saccos, omophorion and Gospel.

And the holy martyr **Thomais** of Alexandria [+ 476] resembles St. Parasceva, she has a scroll in her hand on which is written, "I permitted myself to be killed by my father-in-law to preserve the chastity of my husband's bed."

15

The holy apostles **Aristarchus, Pudens,** and **Trophimus** [first century] *S. 280.* St. Aristarchus has gray hair, he resembles St. Nicholas, an ocher with white cloak; St. Pudens has much straight gray hair, his beard is smaller than St. Blaise, a scarlet cloak, a greenish brown with white tunic; St. Trophimus resembles St. George, an ocher cloak, a green tunic; all three are standing in an omophorion and holding a cross in their hand.

And the holy martyr **Sabbas** the Goth [+ 372] resembles Sts. Cosmas or Damian.

And the holy martyrs **Basilissa** and **Anastasia** [+ under Nero] resemble St. Euphemia.

16

The holy virgin martyrs **Irene, Agape** and **Chionia** [+ 304] *S. 282.* On the first saint the shoulder is green, a purple with white cloak, a blue tunic; on the second saint the cloak is scarlet, the tunic is ocher with white, there are crosses in their [right] hands, and their left hands are held in prayer; and a second holy martyr Irene resembles St. Anna.

And our holy father **Joannicius** of Melitene is an old man with gray hair, a divided beard like St. Blaise.

And the holy martyr **Andreanus** [or **Hadrian** or **Adrian** + 251] *S. 284* is a young man with hair coming down over his shoulders on both sides, a green cloak and a scarlet tunic.

And our holy father **James,** the presbyter of Salim.

17

The holy hieromartyr **Simeon** of Persia [+ 341 or 344] *S. 284*, is an old man with a big divided beard down to his waist, monastic robes, the tunic is greenish brown with white; but in the "Kievan printed pages" he has a beard like St. Blaise.

And our holy father **Acacius** [+ 435] *S. 284,* bishop of Melitene, is an old man with gray hair, a forked beard like St. Blaise, and bishops' robes.

And our holy father **Agapitus** [+ 356] *S. 286,* pope of Rome, is an old man with balding gray hair, a forked beard like St. Blaise, a deep crimson cross patterned cloak, a reddish brown with white tunic, the omophorion and Gospel.

And the passing of our holy father **Zosimas** [+ 1478] *S. 284,* miracle worker and abbot of Solovki, who is a very old man with a beard like St. Blaise but not forked, monastic robes, in his hand is a scroll, "Do not be disturbed, brothers, but understand the example in this way, if my deeds will be pleasing before God, then our monastery will never be in want."

And holy mother **Anthusa,** the daughter of Constantine Cabasilas, resembles St. Eudokia.

And the holy martyr **John** the new, who was from the city of Alphanil, resembles a young man like St. Panteleimon.

And the holy martyr **Zakhaza** of Constantinople.

18

Our holy father **John** [+ c. 820] S. 286, the disciple of St. Gregory of the Decapolis, has gray hair, a curly beard smaller then St. John the Theologian, monastic robes, the tunic is ocher with white.

And the holy father **Cosmas** [+ ninth century] S. 286, bishop of Chalcedon, is very old, has a beard like St. Theodore of Pergium, monastic robes, and the hair on his head is thick.

And the monastic father **St. Sabbas,** has a beard like St. Antipas, and monastic robes.

And the holy mother **Athanasia** the abbess resembles St. Eudokia; there is a scroll in her left hand on which says, "Sing to God, my sisters, sing and praise Him, so that He will be merciful."

19

Our holy father **John** [+ eighth century] *S. 286,* of the Ancient Caves, has gray hair, a beard down to his waist, narrow but not forked, monastic robes, the tunic is reddish brown, in his hand is a scroll on which is written, "Brothers, suffer terrible troubles!" The hair on his head is curly.

And our holy father **Nicephorus,** the abbot of the Katabad Monastery, is starting to gray with a beard like St. Nicholas the miracle worker and monastic robes.

20

Our holy father **Theodore** Trichinas, called the "hair shirt wearer" [eighth century] *S. 288* is an old man like the holy prophet Elias, has a straight beard not forked, longer than St. Blaise, he is holding his hands to his heart, in a hair shirt, bare knees; but in the "Kievan [printed] pages" he resembles St. Blaise both in appearance and robes.

And the passing of our holy father **Alexander,** the abbot of Oshevensk, the miracle worker, which is in Cargopolis, has a black beard, a little smaller than Nicodemus of Hide Lake, is very old, and the hair on his heard is black, monastic robes, in the schema, he holds his hands up in prayer to the Savior in a cloud at the top [of the icon]. And his mother **Philippisia** resembles St. Parasceva.

And our holy father **Anastasius** is an old man with a beard like St. Antipas, and monastic robes.

21

The holy hieromartyr **Januarius** [+ 305] *S. 288* and those with him, has gray hair, is old, has a beard like St. Blaise, hair like the Apostle Andrew, bishops' robes, omophorion and Gospel; but in the "Kievan [printed] pages" he resembles St. Theodore the "Hair Shirt Wearer."

And the holy great martyr **Theodore** of Persia [second century] in the reign of Antoninus, was a land owner in the territory of Pamphilia, who for the sake of Christ was beaten terribly and thrown into a fiery furnace, who was hung up for three days and died, is a young man like St. George or St. Demetrius; but some paint him as an old and gray bishop like St. Blaise, his beard is wide at the end, a cross patterned cloak, a greenish brown with white tunic, omophorion and Gospel; and in the "Kievan [printed] pages" he is described in the same way, we [presumably the Priest John] know neither why, nor from where they [the copyists] got such a description, since they [the descriptions] do not agree in [the details of] his martyrdom; and in the printed *Prologue* it is written, "Who was a young land owner, neither a bishop nor old." And his mother the holy martyr **Philippa** resembles St. Anna.

On the same day the memory of our holy father **Philip,** who lived on the river at Irapa, the new miracle worker, is an old man with a beard like St. Cyril of White Lake and resembles him in everything and with monastic robes.

22
Our holy father **Theodore** the Sykeote [+ 613] *S. 290* is an old man with gray hair, a straight beard like St. Blaise and forked at the end, monastic robes, the tunic is ocher, he holds a rolled up scroll in his hand.

And our holy father **Maximus** [+ 434], archbishop of Constantinople, has brown hair with little curls, a straight beard
bigger than St. Athanasius, starting to get gray, divided, and bishops' robes.

And the holy martyr **Pancratius** *S. 290* is an old man with a graying beard like St. Barlaam of Khutin, a blue cloak, [his gray hair] comes down over both shoulders, a scarlet tunic, and a cross in his hands.

And the holy martyr **Alexandra** the Empress resembles St. Catherine and has the same features.

On the same day the holy blessed fool for Christ's sake **George** who lived on the Paga, the new miracle worker, is an old man with a beard like the Apostle Peter, the upper cloak is ocher with dark crimson neck and shoulder piece, his tunic is light blue, with gray hair, bare knees, and holds his hands in prayer.

23
The holy and glorious great martyr and victory bearer **George** [+ 303] *S. 290* has curly hair, is a young man in a breastplate, with a scarlet cloak, his armor has gold feather pattern, a blue tunic, at his heart a round mirror [or glass] is shining, in his right hand is a spear, and in the left a sword in its scabbard, his helmet (on which there is a cross) is behind his right shoulder, one can see his shield on the left side, a little from the right of his torso is a bow and a quiver with arrows, purple leggings,

gold with ocher boots, a club by his leg is gold and ocher, and St. George has a scroll in his hand, "Blessed are You, O Lord my God, that you did not allow me to remain in sin, which I committed in my ignorance, but You forgave them in their recognition and [You forgave them] in Your love, so that I may receive Your portion in Your kingdom. Remember, Master, those who call upon Your holy name." And some write on St. George's scroll, "Remember, Master, those who call upon Your holy name, for blessed are You for ever. Amen."

On the same day the memory of the holy blessed fool for Christ's sake **George,** the miracle worker of Novgorod, has brown hair like St. Cosmas and wears a garment like St. John of Ustyuzh.

"The day has 15 hours and the night 9."
24

The holy martyr **Sabbas** Stratelates [+ 272] *S. 290* is an old man with curly gray hair, a simple beard like St. Nicholas, in a breastplate, a blue cloak, his armor has a feather pattern, a scarlet tunic, in his right hand is a spear, and in the other hand is a sword in a scabbard, and purple leggings.

And the holy martyrs **Pasicrates** and **Valentine** [+ 228]. St. Pasicrates is a young man like St. Demetrius and St. Valentine has brown hair and a beard like St. Cosmas.

And the holy mother **Elizabeth** [lived between sixth and ninth centuries] *S. 292* the miracle worker, has bare feet, wears a single garment, and has plain hair.

And the memory of our holy father **Sabbatius** the desert dweller of Tver, the new miracle worker, is an old man with a beard like the Theologian, in the schema, and monastic robes.

25

The holy and all praised apostle and evangelist **Mark** [first century] *S. 292* is a middle aged man with brown hair, a beard like St. Cosmas, a blue cloak, a scarlet tunic, he is blessing with his hand and in the other is the Gospel, bare feet; in the printed *Prologue* is written, "flowering in old age, thick hair, but not long, and not a little surrounding the face, prominent eyelashes, and a thick black beard, plain features and ruddy," in the Gospel in Mark's [hand], "The beginning of the Gospel of our Lord Jesus Christ the Son of God as it was written in the Prophets."

26

The holy hieromartyr **Basil** [+ 322] *S. 292,* the bishop of Amasea, is an old man like

St. Blaise, with a cross patterned cloak, a blue tunic lightened with white and light gray, the omophorion and Gospel.

And the memory of our father among the saints **Stephen** [+ 1396] *S. 294,* the bishop of Perm, who is an old man, with a beard some what like St. Blaise, or shorter than St. Barlaam of Novgorod, but narrower, lies in a coffin before a church with one dome, at his head stand three spiritual fathers, one has gray hair, a beard shorter than St. Blaise, with his left arm he is lifting [the coffin] from underneath, and is holding the Saint over his head with the right, behind him is a spiritual father and a young man, and behind them one sees two heads, one has brown hair, a small beard, and the other is a young man, at the feet [of the Saint] stands a bishop with gray hair, a beard like St. Blaise, balding, reading a book, on which is written, "In the name of the Father and of the Son and of the Holy Spirit I forgive you of this." And behind him is a young deacon, holding a censer and a bowl, behind the bishop and the deacon is a priest with brown hair, and behind them a palace, and behind the spiritual fathers also, and behind the palaces one can see the walls of the city of Moscow, and the vestments on the Saint are white, the crosses are purple, the tunic is blue, the omophorion and Gospel, and he lies in Moscow, in the Church of the Savior at the Royal Palace, in the church on the right hand side by the side of the table, but in the "Kievan [printed] pages" it says he is standing.

27

The holy hieromartyr **Simeon** [first century] *S. 294,* the bishop of Jerusalem, a relative of the Lord according to the flesh, has gray hair, a shorter beard then St. Blaise, or the same beard, a cloak, a greenish brown with white tunic, omophorion and Gospel.

And the passing of our holy father **Stephen,** abbot on the lake at Kubensk, miracle worker of Vologda, is an old man with a graying beard like St. Dionysius of Glushetsk, monastic robes and the schema on his shoulders.

28

The holy apostles **Jason** and **Sosipater** [+ first century] *S. 296.* St. Jason is an old man, his hair comes down a little below his ears, a beard like St. Nicholas, an ocher with white cloak, a purple with white tunic, the omophorion on his shoulders, in his hand a scroll of the law, bare feet. St. Sosipater is an old man with a beard like St. Blaise, and curly at the end, the hair in his head is thick, a blue cloak, a scarlet tunic lightened with white, an omophorion on his shoulders; both are blessing with their right hands, but he is holding a scroll in his left hand, apostles' robes, and bare feet.

And the holy martyr **Cercyra** [first century] is royalty like St. Catherine.

And the holy martyrs **Maximus, Dada** and **Quinctilian** [+ 286]. Sts. Maximus and Dada are like Sts. Cosmas and Damian; St. Quinctilian resembles St. Andrew Stratelates, an old man.

29

The nine holy martyrs in **Cyzicus** [+ under Diocletian] *S. 296 and 298,* whose names are **Theognes, Rufus, Antipater, Theostichus, Artemas, Magnus, Theodotus, Thaumasius, Philimon,** who came from different countries and suffered various tortures and were decapitated by the sword. The first martyr is standing, and is an old man with gray hair, a divided beard like St. Sabbas the Sanctified, the cloak on his shoulder is green, the tunic is ocher, in his right hand is a feather [that is, a quill pen] and in the left a container. The second martyr has hair and a beard like St. Basil of Caesarea, an ocher cloak, a green tunic, in his hand is a cross, his second garment is yellow. The third martyr is an old man with gray hair, a beard and hair like St. Blaise, a blue cloak, an ocher tunic, and he holds a cross in his hands. The fourth martyr is an old man, with hair and a beard like the St. Menas the martyr, a scarlet cloak, a green tunic, in his [left] hand a is container and with the right hand he is pointing with a finger to the container. The fifth martyr has a beard like St. Cosmas, a scarlet cloak comes down from his shoulders like St. Cosmas, two tunics, his cloak is scarlet, the upper tunic is green, the lower one is ocher, in his hand is a container with many little compartments, in the right hand a book. The sixth martyr resembles St. Damian, a green cloak, an ocher with reddish brown tunic, in his hand a cross, he is girded with a towel, the lower tunic is bright ocher. The seventh martyr is an old man, he has a beard and balding hair like St. John the Theologian, his cloak is green with reddish brown and is coming down from his shoulders, two tunics, the upper one is ocher with white then [decorated with] bright red [Slavonic *"sourik"*], the lower one is ocher, the container has four corners, and with the right hand he is pointing with the finger. The eighth martyr is middle aged, has a beard like St. Cosmas, a bright green cloak, the tunic is ocher with scarlet, in his hand a container with little compartments, with the right hand he is pointing with a finger, the lower tunic is ocher. The ninth martyr is an old man resembling St. Nicholas by his hair and beard, his cloak is ocher with reddish brown, the tunic is dark green, he is girded with a white towel, the ends are hanging down, in his hand is a container with four corners, and with the right he is pointing with a finger, the lower tunic is ocher; all the martyrs wear boots.

And our holy father **Memnon** [time unknown] *S. 298* is an old man with a longer beard than St. Blaise, but forked, omophorion and Gospel, and otherwise monastic robes.

30

The holy and all praised apostle **James** [first century] *S. 298,* the brother of St. John the Theologian, has brown hair, a longer beard than St. Cosmas, a reddish brown cloak, bare feet, [or] in sandals.

And the uncovering of the venerable relics of our father among the saints **Nikita** [+ 1108, the same saint as on January 31], bishop of Novgorod the miracle worker, he has a brocade cloak like St. Leontius of Rostov, no beard, looks like an old man, omophorion and Gospel, and a bishops' cap on his head.

MAY

"The month of May has 31 days."

1

The holy prophet **Jeremiah** [sixth century B.C.] *S. 300* is an old man with a beard like St. John the Theologian, gray hair like St. Elias the prophet, an ocher cloak with white, a blue tunic, in his hand is a scroll on which is written, "Thus says the Lord, 'Heaven and earth will pass by, but My word will not pass away.'" Others write, "Judge righteously before the Lord of powers."

And our holy father **Paphnutius** [+ 1478] *S. 300*, abbot of Borovsk, is an old man with gray hair, a forked beard a little smaller than the Theologian, the schema, and monastic robes.

And our holy father **Mark** of Phoenix, of Mount Thrace, resembles St. Macarius the desert dweller, and is an old man with hair all over his body, a long beard down to his feet, he has a branch in his left hand covering his privates.

And the passing of our holy father **Gerasimus** [+ 1554], abbot of Boldinsk, the new miracle worker, is an old man in the schema, a beard like St. John the Theologian, monastic robes, and sometimes [he is painted as] an old man starting to gray.

2

Our father among the saints **Athanasius** the Great [+ 373] *S. 300*, archbishop of Alexandria, is an old man, his beard is a little shorter than Gregory the Theologian, his saccos has a cross pattern, the omophorion and Gospel.

And the holy martyr **Hesperas** and his wide Izoa and their children **Cyriak** and **Theodulus** [+ under Hadrian]. St. Hesperas resembles St. Eustathius, and his wife St. Izoa resembles St. Theopista, Cyriak and Theodulus resemble Sts. Agapius and Theopistus. St. Hesperas has a scroll in his hand, "We will be made free by the blood of our Lord Christ."

And the translation [in 1072] of the venerable relics of the holy princes and Russian martyrs, two brothers according to the flesh, **Boris** *S. 300* and **Gleb** *S. 302*, renamed in Holy Baptism **Roman** and **David**. St. Boris is middle aged, has a beard like St. Cosmas, a hat on his head which has a black [fur] trim, a velvet coat with purple in circles, a blue tunic, a cross in his hand, the left hand is putting a sword in its scabbard. St. Gleb is a young man with thin locks of hair down to his shoulders, a hat

148

on his head with black [fur] trim, a green brocade fur coat with an intertwining pattern, a purple tunic with white, a cross in his hand, and a putting a sword in its scabbard with the other.

3

The holy martyrs **Timothy** and **Maura** [+ 286] S. 302. St. Timothy is a young man in apostles' robes, greenish brown with reddish brown, the tunic is blue. St. Maura, who is looking towards Timothy, is similar to St. Parasceva; she has a crimson cloak, an ocher tunic, a scarf on her head, and a cross in her hand.

And the passing of our holy father **Theodosius** the abbot [+ 1074] *S. 304,* the founder of the community life of the venerable Monastery of the Caves [Pecherska Lavra] in Kiev, is an old man with gray hair, a longer beard than St. Blaise, at the end it is forked and has little curls, in two thin strands, he is lying in a coffin, his robe is dark purple, in the schema, the tunic is ocher, a bishop is standing at his feet, who has a longer beard than St. Blaise, next to him is a young deacon who is incensing the Saint, behind him are two spiritual fathers, one is an old man like St. Sergius with an ocher tunic, the other is an old man like St. Nicholas, the middle one has either brown or gray hair. There are spiritual fathers standing at the head of the Saint; one is an old man balding with a beard like St. John the Theologian, a light purple mantle, a reddish brown tunic with green, the next behind him has gray hair, a short curly beard, an ocher tunic, and between them others can be seen. There is a light green church, flanking the church are palaces. Some paint St. Theodosius standing with a scroll in his hand, "Behold, I promise you, brothers and fathers, each of you in my monastery, that if a sin should be committed, I will have to answer for it before God."

4

The holy martyr **Pelagia** [+ 287] *S. 304* has a green cloak, a crimson tunic, and a cross in her hand.

And the holy martyr and king **John** Moavin with three children, St. John is a young man.

On the same day the passing of our holy father **Micheas** [+ 1385], miracle worker of Radonezh, who is an old man with gray hair, a beard like St. Blaise, in a black klobuk, and resembles St. Sergius, with brown hair, a beard like St. Cosmas, and monastic robes.

5

The holy great martyr and queen **Irene** [first century] *S. 306,* has a royal crown on her head, a scarlet cloak, a blue tunic, a cross in her hand, and a scroll in her left.

And the holy hieromartyr **Selivan**. St. Selivan is a bishop with gray hair, a beard like St. Sergius, curly hair, omophorion and Gospel.

And the passion of the holy martyr **Drosidas,** the daughter of the Roman emperor Trajan, looks like a simple maiden, in her hands is a container of myrrh [ointment].

And our holy father **James,** who was at the Iron School, miracle worker of Kostrom, has gray hair, in the schema, a beard like St. Blaise, and monastic robes.

6

The holy and righteous **Job** [lived between 2000 and 1500 B.C.] *S. 306* has gray hair and a beard like St. Nicholas, a hat on his head, his hands are in prayer, a royal [purple] robe, his tunic has a gold border, in his hands is a scroll on which is written, "If we have received some good from the hand of the Lord, but we do not endure the evil from this I have been touched, and if we have endured, then we will have received that which is better." Another tradition portrays Job sitting on a dung heap in front of a mountain, and before him are three friends; the first friend is Eliphas the king of the Temanites, a curly beard, a royal robe; the second friend Bildad the Shuhite, the tormentor, with a brown beard, and princes' robes; the third friend Zophar the Naamathite, the king, is a young man in kings' robes, and behind him is his wife pointing down with one hand and in the other is a scroll, and on the scroll is written, "She who has Job as her husband."

The holy martyr **Barbarus** [+ 362], who was a robber, is nude, the hair on his head goes down on his shoulders, brown, a beard like St. Cosmas, in individual wisps; but others paint him as an old man with gray hair, a beard like St. John the Theologian, martyrs' robes, in his right hand is a big cross, and in the left a scroll, on which is written, "Remember us, O Lord, when You come into Your kingdom."

And our holy father **Andronicus** and his consort **Athanasia.** St. Andronicus resembles St. Sergius; St. Athanasia resembles St. Eudokia.

And our holy father **Anthony** *S. 306* of the Caves [Pecherska Lavra], in the schema, around his face are little curls, gray hair, a beard like St. John the Theologian, monastic robes, the tunic is greenish brown, with one hand he is blessing and in the other is a scroll on which is written, "Behold I have left fleeing and dwelt in the desert."

On the same day the passing of our father among the saints **Gerontius,** metropolitan of Moscow, the miracle worker, is an old man with gray hair, a wider beard than St. Blaise, forked at the end, in the saccos and klobuk.

7

The remembrance of the sign which appeared in the sky of the venerable and life-giving **Cross** in the holy city of Jerusalem in the third hour of the day on the very day of Pentecost, at the time of the honorable Emperor Constantine, the son of the Emperor Constantine the Great [in the year 351]. Emperor Constantine is a young man in a hat resting on a bed, and appearing to him the Savior, and blessing him with a cross and His hand, the royal bed is ocher, a scarlet cloak, a blue tunic, the bed is covered with white velvet, at the head armed guards are standing and around the tent, over the emperor is a cross, which appears from the stars, [formed] from seven stars, under this there is a field where the emperor is sitting, in his left hand he is holding a cross, and the right hand is held in prayer, and he is showing the crowd the cross. And in the crowd is standing an old nobleman who resembles St. Vladimir opposite the emperor, and another resembles the prophet Zachariah, with a green cloak and behind him one like St. George, with a blue cloak, a crimson tunic, and a third is like St. Boris, with a scarlet cloak, a green tunic, and behind them is a multitude of people. They have turbans on their heads, behind them is a mountain, and before all the emperor is sitting on a horse, and pointing out the golden cross to the people, which appears like stars strewn on the sky, and one sees the emperor's army behind him, and behind them a multitude of people surrounded, and others are not surrounded, Emperor Constantine is chasing with his army across the bridge on them the surrounded and is battling against the enemies, and he has a cross on a yellow standard, the evil [or pagan] army is fleeing to the city, and are beginning to throw themselves from the bridge on their horses, and a multitude of them are drowning and others are being beaten on the bridge, and the city stands open, the bridge is of stone, the foundations are of stone, the mountain is greenish brown with white, the inscription says concerning this sign, "On the following night the Lord came and said to Constantine, 'Do this, revealing this sign to you, and you will overcome all your enemies.'" And a second inscription says, "He revealed to him on the field going out with his army and at noon the image of the cross formed of light." On it was this inscription, "With this you will conquer enemies," and over the city an inscription says, "On this holy day during the days of Holy Pentecost on New Sunday of Pascha, at the third hour of the day, a great cross of light was formed in the sky, the top appeared to stretch from the holy Mount Golgotha to the Mount of Olives."

And our holy father **Neil** Sorsky, the miracle worker, has a beard like St. Cyril of White Like, curly, and monastic robes.

And our father among the saints **Arsenius,** bishop of Suzhdal, miracle worker, has brown hair, a longer beard than St. Nicholas, in a klobuk, bishops' vestments, with the omophorion and Gospel.

8

The holy glorious and all praised apostle and evangelist **John** the Theologian [first century] *S. 308* is an old man with gray hair, balding, a beard down to his chest, a little wavy, a green cloak, a blue tunic. St. John has on the Gospel book, "In the beginning was the Word, and the Word was with God, and the Word was God."

And our holy father **Arsenius** the Great [+ 450] *S. 308* is an old man with gray hair, a beard longer and wider than St. Sergius, monastic robes, the tunic is ocher with white, in his hand is a scroll, "Arsenius, flee men, be still, endure, keep silence and you will be saved."

And the holy prophet **Isaiah** [+ 710 B.C.] *S. 308* is an old man with gray hair like prophet Elias in his hair and beard, a scarlet cloak with white, a blue tunic, in his hand is a scroll on which is written, "Teach the truth to all those living on the earth," and others write, "Behold a virgin will conceive in her womb and will bear a son and they will call his name Immanuel, which they say is 'God with us.'"

9

The holy martyr **Christopher** [+ c. 250] *S. 310* has the head of a dog, in a breastplate, in his hand is a cross, and a sword in its scabbard in the other, a green cloak; and others portray St. Christopher as a young man like St. Demetrius of Thessalonica, a crimson cloak, a green tunic, in his hand is a scroll, "O Lord Almighty, wherever they honor my name and praise You, save him from his sins and do not condemn him."

And the holy martyred women **Callinica** and **Aquilina** resemble Sts. Anna and Elizabeth.

And the translation of the venerable relics of our father among the saints **Nicholas** *S. 308* Archbishop of Myra in Lycia, miracle worker, from Myra to the city of Bari [in 1087]. Two deacons are carrying the coffin, St. Nicholas the miracle worker is lying in the coffin, in front there is a young deacon, and a king with a bishop under the head of the Saint, the king resembles King David, he is holding and carrying the coffin with both hands, behind them are three spiritual fathers, one with brown hair, one old man, and a young man, wearing klobuks and one sees a city a little, and behind them there is a city, in the city are green palaces, and they are going to the city with the coffin, the city is white, and in it there is a church with three domes, and two palaces, and out of the city are coming a crowd of people and priests with crosses to meet it, two priests have gray hair, one resembles St. Sergius of Radonezh, the second resembles St. Blaise with books, there is a young deacon with incense, and others with candles, and two paupers are lying crawling at the feet of the people, and they are looking up at St. Nicholas, one is young, the other is middle aged, they have staffs in their hands, the inscription, "The translation of the venerable relics of the great hierarch miracle worker Nicholas."

On the same day the passing of the holy true believing great prince **Demetrius** Ivanovich Donskoy, miracle worker of Moscow, who is an old man with gray hair, a straight beard like St. Nicholas, curly hair, and princes' robes.

"The day has 16 hours and the night 8."

10

The holy apostle **Simon** the Zealot [first century] *S. 310* is middle aged and resembles the righteous Joachim, he is a little gray, he has a crimson cloak, a blue tunic, in his left hand is a scroll, he wears an omophorion and has bare feet.

On the same day the passing of our holy father **Dionysius,** the abbot of the Holy Trinity Monastery of Radonezh, the new miracle worker, He is a little older and grayer, he has a wider forked beard than St. Blaise, monastic robes; and others paint him in robes and in a hat, his hands held in prayer.

11

The founding of the city of **Constantinople** [330], which took place at the time of the First Ecumenical Council [325], when the first Christian Emperor Constantine the Great transferred the throne from Rome to Byzantium and widened the area of the seven hills with tremendous walls and extended their boundaries gloriously, and summoned to that place the three hundred eighty holy fathers gathered in the name of the Church of Constantinople and New Rome, and dedicated [the city] to the most holy Virgin Mother of God, and built many churches.

And the holy hieromartyr **Mocius** [+ under Diocletian] *S. 310,* is an old man with balding gray hair, a longer beard than St. Blaise, and forked at the end, an ocher cloak with white without an omophorion, and the tunic is purple with white.

And the holy monastic martyr **Theodosia** resembles St. Eudokia.

On the same day the memory of the holy blessed **Simeon,** the fool for Christ's sake, the new miracle worker of Yurev Povolsk, has a black beard similar to St. Nicholas, the hair on his head is short and black, wearing a tattered [Russian] shirt and bare foot.

12

Our father among the saints **Epiphanius** [+ 403] *S. 310,* archbishop of Cyprus, is an old man with gray hair, a beard like St. Blaise, a black vestment patterned with crosses, a green tunic, the omophorion and Gospel.

And holy father **Germanus** [+ 740] *S. 312,* the patriarch of Constantinople, has gray hair, a beard like St. Athanasius, a blue saccos with a gold cross pattern, the omophorion and Gospel.

On the same day our holy father **Pretorius,** who is an old man with gray hair, his beard is forked, he has two locks of thick curly hair and monastic robes.

13

The holy martyr **Glykeria** [+ 177] *S. 312* has a scarlet cloak, a dark green tunic, and a cross in her hands.

And the holy martyr **Alexander** [+ under Maximian in Rome] is a young man like St. Demetrius, has a scroll in his hand, "Lord Jesus Christ, let him who honors the day of my martyrdom receive healing and complete forgiveness."

And our holy father **Sergius** the Confessor is an old man with gray hair, a beard like St. Blaise, at the end it is not divided, but a little narrow, and monastic robes.

And the holy martyr **George** the Confessor [ninth century], is an old man with gray hair, a beard like St. Blaise, it is not forked at the end, but a little narrow, and his wife **Irene** and their children.

14

The holy martyr **Isidore** [+ 251] *S. 312* has brown hair like St. Florus, a blue cloak, a crimson short tunic, scarlet leggings, a green tunic, he is girded with a towel, and there is a cross in his hand.

And the holy blessed **Isidore** [+ 1474] *S. 312,* who was a fool for Christ's sake, the miracle worker of Rostov, has brown hair, a beard like St. Nikita the martyr, much hair, his right shoulder is bare, in his hand is a cross, he wears a single garment of greenish brown, his legs are bare, and the "Kievan [printed] pages" say that St. Isidore was young.

And the holy martyr **Magegnus** the "Bleacher" or "Whitener," has a brown beard, straight hair, martyrs' robes, and there is a stone under his feet.

15

Our holy father **Pachomius** the Great [+ 348] *S. 314* is an old man with gray hair resembling St. Blaise, with a longer beard but not forked, monastic robes, the corners of the mantle are knotted up, the tunic is light gray, and he has a scroll in his hand.

And our father among the saints **Isaiah** [+ 109] *S. 314,* bishop of Rostov, miracle worker, has brown hair, a beard like St. Blaise that flows down widely from the mustache, he has a white klobuk on his head, a light green cloak, a very whitened purple tunic, omophorion and Gospel.

And our holy father **Euphrosinus** [+ 1481], miracle worker of Pskov, has a beard like St. John Damascene, gray hair, monastic robes, and in his "Life" it is written, "he was a person of average size and ascetic body, he has a round head, arched eyebrows, a high forehead, enlightened by the grace of the Holy Spirit, deep, sunken, quiet eyes, having a beard going down to his chest and forked at the end, adorned with dark, sparkling but not thick gray hair."

And **Demetrius,** the Crown Prince of Moscow [+ 1591], is a young man, in a royal crown, in the royal [purple] robe, and hands in prayer.

16

Our holy father **Theodore** the Sanctified [+ 368] *S. 314,* disciple of St. Pachomius, is an old man with a graying beard like St. Blaise, monastic robes, and his tunic is ocher with white.

And our holy father **Ephraim** of Perekop [+ 1492], miracle worker of Novgorod, is an old man with a beard like St. Nicholas, and monastic robes in the schema.

17

The holy apostle **Andronicus** [first century] *S. 314* is an old man with a beard like St. Blaise, a greenish brown with purple cloak, a blue tunic, the omophorion on his shoulders, a scroll in his left hand, the right hand is in prayer, the fingers are pointing up, and with him his eighty-four disciples, a crowd of saints of every description, old, brown hair and young, and they all wear martyrs' robes.

And the holy equal to the apostles **Junia** [the helper of St. Andronicus above] resembles St. Thecla.

18

The holy martyr **Theodotus** [+ 303] *S. 316* of Ancyra is a young man like St.

Demetrius of Thessalonica, who has a scarlet cloak hanging down from both shoulders, his short tunic is green, his tunic is blue, in his left hand is a sword in its scabbard, but in the "Kievan printed pages" its says he resembles St. Cosmas.

And the seven holy virgin martyrs **Tecusa, Alexandra, Claudia, Phaina, Euphrasia,** and **Julia,** resemble Sts. Faith, Hope and Charity.

And the monastic martyr **Theodosia** the maiden, resembles St. Eudokia.

19

The holy hieromartyr **Patrick** [+ c. 100] *S. 316,* the bishop of Prussa and those with him, is an old man with a gray beard resembling St. Blaise, a scarlet cloak, a reddish purple tunic with white, a green omophorion with white, and the Gospel.

And our holy father the true believing prince **Ignatius** [+ 1523] of Uglich, who was the miracle worker at Priluki Vologda, is in the schema like St. Ephraim of Syria; but others paint him as an old man with a graying beard like St. Basil of Caesarea.

And our holy father **Cornelius** [+ 1537] of Komelsk and miracle worker of Vologda, has dark gray hair, the hair on his head is curly, he has a wide beard like St. Gregory the Theologian, and monastic robes.

20

The holy martyr **Thalaleus** [+ 284] *S. 318* is an old man with gray hair, a shorter beard than St. Blaise, an ocher with black cloak, a crimson tunic, a cross in the right hand, and the fingers of the left hand are held up in prayer.

And the holy martyr **Philaret** is a man with red hair on his head but his beard is white.

And the finding [in 1431 or 1438] of the venerable relics of our father among the saints **Alexis** *S. 318,* metropolitan of Moscow and all Russia, miracle worker. There is a church at the end, around the church is a stone wall, St. Alexis is in a saccos, lying in a coffin, with a white klobuk, on the saccos are crimson crosses, the coffin is purple with white, at the head of the Saint is standing an old man with much hair, a beard like St. John the Theologian, but narrower; behind him is standing a spiritual father with gray hair, a beard like St. Blaise, a greenish brown tunic, with green and white, his elbows and feet are bare. A bishop is standing at the middle of the coffin, there is a young prince like St. George, bowing to the Saint, holding his hands in prayer, a crimson cloak, a blue tunic, behind him is a second young man, and between them one can see another man like St. Demetrius, a green cloak, an ocher tunic, and four resembling the righteous Joachim but one sees only the shoulders, and a little gray hair.

And the holy martyr **Kyriaka** [Sunday] resembles St. Euphemia.

On the same day the passing of the holy true believing prince **Dovmont** [+ 1299], renamed Timothy in holy baptism, the miracle worker of Pskov, is an old man with gray hair, a beard like St. Gregory the Theologian, balding a little, a princes' fur coat, in his right hand is a cross and in the left his hat.

21

The holy and equal to the apostles Emperor **Constantine** the Great [+ 337] and his Christ loving mother **Helen** [+ 327] *S. 320*. The Emperor [St. Constantine] is middle aged, with a beard like St. Cosmas, curly hair, a hat on his head, a scarlet cloak, and a green tunic; St. Helen wears a royal crown and a white scarf which comes down to her neck, a purple cloak, a crimson or purple tunic, there is a cross in St. Helen's hand and St. Constantine has his hands held in prayer towards the cross.

And the holy true believing prince **Constantine** and his children **Michael** and **Theodore,** the miracle workers of Murom [+ 1129]. St. Constantine has very gray curly hair, a narrower beard then St. Blaise, but longer and forked, a hat on his head, and his children have brown hair and are youths in fur coats, both have princely clothes and crosses.

And the passing of our holy father **Cassian** [+ 1504] of Uglich on the Uchma River, who is a very old man with gray hair, in the schema, a narrower beard than the Theologian, and monastic robes.

22

The holy martyr **Basilisk** [+ together with Sts. Eutropius and Cleonimus on March 3] *S. 320* is a young man like St. Demetrius of Thessalonica, with a crimson cloak, a blue tunic, girded with a towel from the left shoulder to down around the right elbow, and in the right hand a cross.

And the holy forefather and king **Melchizedek** [in Genesis] is an old man with gray hair and a beard like St. John the Theologian, on his head is a royal crown, he wears a royal purple robe and the omophorion.

23

Our father among the saints and confessor **Michael** [+ 818] *S. 322,* bishop of

Sinnada, is an old man with gray hair, a beard wider than St. Blaise, a blue cloak with a cross pattern, an ocher tunic with white and scarlet, his right hand is in prayer, the fingers are pointing up, in the left hand he holds the Gospel.

And the finding [in 1164] of the venerable relics of our father among the saints **Leontius** [+ 1077] *S. 322*, bishop of Rostov, miracle worker. [The Saint] is lying in a coffin, he is wearing a white klobuk, he has brown hair, a green cloak with white, a blue tunic, the coffin is greenish brown with blue, a bishop, who is standing at the head of the Saint, resembles St. Blaise, he has a purple cross patterned cloak, his right hand is raised in prayer to the Saint, and the other hand is holding his cloak and the Gospel, on the right side of the bishop is standing a monk with gray hair, a beard longer than the bishop, but his cloak is white, and one can see a multitude of others, but only the tops of the heads of some. At the feet of the Saint is standing a prince resembling St. George and he is bowing to the Saint, his hands are in prayer, a green cloak, a blue tunic, he himself is middle aged like St. Cosmas, and there is an old nobleman with gray hair, a beard like St. Nicholas, a scarlet cloak, the cloak is white from the edge of the hem, a blue tunic, three youths resemble St. Demetrius, and one sees a little of a fourth, at the coffin of the Saint is standing a young man, holding both his hands in supplication, at the top is an iron, his elbows are bare, a purple with blue cloak, around all of them is ocher like an arch, because the wall of the church was not complete.

And the holy mother **Euphrosyne** [+ 1173], abbess of Polotsk, resembles St. Eudokia.

On the same day the holy king, the high priest **Melchizedek** [in Genesis], who is an old man with gray hair, a bigger beard than St. John the Theologian, whom he resembles, there is a scarf on his head, and a royal crown, and he wears the royal purple and a cloak on top.

24

Our holy father **Simeon** the Stylite [+ 596] *S. 324*, the miracle worker of Wonder Mountain, is an old man with gray hair like St. Menas the martyr, a beard like St. Nicholas, simple but not big, a white priest's cloak without crosses, he is blessing with his hand and holding the Gospel with the other, his tunic is light gray and dark gray; his shoulder piece, cloak and priest's stole are ocher; and in the "Kievan [printed] pages" he is a monastic saint on a column.

And the passing of our holy father **Nikita** the Stylite [+ 1186] of Pereyaslavl miracle worker, who is an old man with gray hair, a klobuk on his head, a blue cloak with crosses, a longer beard than St. Blaise, it is forked at the end, but the beard from the hand on the left is longer than St. Cosmas, but not down to the waist, monastic robes, not a big column, green but not covered, St. Nikita is sitting on it like St. Simeon.

25

The third finding [in c. 850] of the venerable head of the holy and glorious prophet and forerunner of the Lord, **John** the Baptist *S. 324.* A bishop carries the head of the Forerunner on a gold platter on his head with both hands, the bishop has gray hair like St. Blaise and behind him is a middle aged king who resembles St. Cosmas, who is holding the platter with the head with his hand, and is holding his other hand up in prayer, and they are going with it to the city, to the gates of the city, and the people are greeting them with candles and incense, a deacon in front of them is incensing, and behind him is a priest with gray hair resembling St. John Chrysostom, and behind the king are walking priests with gray hair, and brown hair and young priests and deacons, and they are carrying crosses and icons and Gospel books, and behind them is an ocher mountain, and in the mountain one sees a cave, in which one sees two spiritual fathers, one is an old man with gray hair the other is young, and behind them they are going to the city, and in the city one sees a church with one dome and a palace.

On the same day the holy and righteous **John** and his sister **Mary** of Yosyuzh the miracle workers. St. John is an old man with gray hair, not balding, a beard like St. John the Theologian, simple cloaks of scarlet and light blue tunics, and St. Mary resembles St. Julitta.

"The day has 17 hours and the night 7."
26

The holy apostle **Carpus** [first century] *S. 326* is an old man with gray hair, balding, a wider beard then St. Blaise, the omophorion on his shoulders, a green cloak, a blue tunic.

And the translation of the venerable relics [in 1521] of our holy father **Macarius** miracle worker of Kolyazynsky; they are carrying a coffin into the church and behind them are walking priests and deacons, and monks and people of every description.

And the memory of our holy father prince **Gabriel** and his sister **Anastasia** Vasilievna, miracle workers. St. Gabriel is an old man with gray hair in the schema a beard like the Theologian, monastic robes. St. Anastasia resembles St. Parasceva.

27

The holy hieromartyr **Therapont** [+ 259] *S. 326* has brown hair resembling St.

Florus, a purple cloak patterned with crosses, a blue tunic, he is holding the Gospel with both hands, and wears the omophorion.

The translation [into the newly built stone Cathedral of the Assumption in Moscow in 1472] of the venerable relics of our holy fathers among the saints the three hierarchs **Cyprian, Photius** and **Jonah,** of Kiev and all Russia, miracle workers. St. Cyprian is an old man with gray hair, a beard like the holy prophet Zachariah, a cap on his head, bishops' vestments, the omophorion and the Gospel. St. Photius has brown hair, but a little gray, a beard like St. Athanasius, a white bishops' cloak with a cross pattern, the hands are held in prayer, and wears a cap. St. Jonah is an old man with gray hair, a beard resembling St. Blaise, a cap on his head, bishops' vestments, the saccos and both wear an omophorion.

And our holy father **Therapont** [+ 1426], miracle worker of White Lake, is an old man with gray hair, a longer beard than St. Nicholas, but a little wider, and monastic robes.

And the holy martyr **Theodora** resembles St. Eudokia.

28

Our father among the saints **Nikita** [ninth century] *S. 326,* archbishop of Chalcedon, is an old man with gray hair, a wider, forked beard than St. Blaise, a blue cloak, his tunic is purple with blue, the omophorion and Gospel.

And the passing of our father among the saints **Ignatius** [+ 1288] *S. 328,* bishop of Rostov, miracle worker, is an old man with gray hair, a beard like St. Alexis the Metropolitan [of Moscow], but shorter, he has a white klobuk on his head, a blue brocade cloak with white, a purple tunic, the omophorion and Gospel.

And our holy mother **Theophilia** resembles St. Eudokia.

And the holy blessed **Andrew** [+ 940], who was a fool for Christ's sake, the miracle worker of Constantinople, is an old man with gray hair, a beard and hair like the prophet Elias, a greenish brown cloak with reddish brown and white going down to the knees, his right shoulder and side are bare down to his waist, he is holding his hands to his heart, and has bare feet.

And the holy martyr **Elikidas** resembles St. Euphemia.

29

The holy monastic martyr **Theodosia** the maiden [+ 730] *S. 328,* in the schema, her tunic is ocher with green and with purple, she is holding a scroll with both hands, or a cross in the other.

And the passing of the holy blessed **John** [+ 1492] S. 330, the fool for Christ's sake, the miracle worker of Ustiug, who is a young man with hair going to his ears, a white cloak wrapped around him and on his arms but his shoulder and his side are bare, his feet are bare, as well as his legs up to his knees, his hands are held in prayer.

And the holy true believing emperor and martyr **Constantine,** who suffered in the city of Constantinople for the faith of Christ under the Turkish Sultan Bachmet [in 1453], has brown hair and beard like St. Cosmas, in a royal crown and scarlet royal robes, his tunic is light blue.

30

Our holy father **Isaac** of Dalmatia [+383] S. 330 is an old man with gray hair, a beard like St. Blaise with curls at the end, a reddish purple mantle, an ocher tunic, in his hand is a scroll on which is written, "Evening and morning and noon I will pray, and cry aloud and He will hear my voice."

31

The holy apostle **Hermes** [first century] S. 146 or 152 has brown hair, a beard and hair like St. Florus, a purple cloak with white, a blue tunic, with one hand he is blessing and holds the Gospel in the other.

And the holy martyr **Hermes** [+ 166] S. 330 has brown hair like St. Florus, a scarlet cloak, a green tunic, he is girded with a towel and holds a cross in his right hand, and a sword in its scabbard in his left, and in the printed *Prologue* is written, "Hermes is a young man like St. Demetrius, in his left hand is a cross and his right hand is stretched out."

It is necessary for iconographers to distinguish and find out what is genuine among these accounts and other sources concerning what is true in the lives of the saints, and to ask good, skillful and knowledgeable people who are artist painters and readers of books, so that it [the iconographers' work] will be without fault, because I, the sinful priest John, discovered that the patternbooks together with the "Lives of the Saints," the *Prologue, The Monthly Reader* and the "Kievan printed pages" do not agree in many passages, and for this reason one ought to do research in them with great discretion.

JUNE

"The month of June has 30 days."

1

The holy martyr **Justin** the Philosopher [+ between 133 and 137] *S. 332* is middle aged, has brown hair, a beard like St. Cosmas, he has a cloth around of white silk, a blue cloak, a scarlet with white tunic, he is blessing with one hand and holds a scroll in his left hand.

And a second martyr **Justin** and those with him [who suffered together with the first St. Justin above].

And our monastic father **Dionysius** of Glushetsk [+ 1437] *S. 332,* miracle worker of Vologda, is middle aged with a beard like St. Barlaam, he is blessing with his hand and has a scroll in his left hand; it is written in the *Prologue,* "Dionysius had a head that was not small, arched eyebrows, a long face, sunken temples, quiet eyes, a thick beard down to his chest, light hair, brown going to gray."

And our holy father **Agapitus** [+ 1095] of the Pecherska Lavra, is an old man with gray hair, a longer beard than St. Sergius, in a klobuk, and monastic robes.

2

Our father among the saints **Nicephorus** [+ 806] *S. 332,* patriarch of Constantinople, is an old man with gray hair, a beard like St. Gregory the Theologian, but narrower, a cross patterned cloak, a blue tunic, the omophorion and Gospel; in the printed *Prologue* is written, "Nicephorus resembled Cyril of Alexandria in everything."

And the holy great martyr **John** [+ 1340] *S. 334,* the new martyr of Belgrade [White City], has brown hair, a longer beard than St. John Chrysostom, and a scarlet cloak.

And the memory of our holy father John the Candle Bearer, the miracle worker of Solovki Monastery, stunted growth, a brown beard, smaller than St. Nicholas and beginning to gray, emaciated, and monastic robes.

3

The holy martyr **Lucillian** of Tarsus and those with him, the child **Claudius,** and **Hypatius** [+ under Aurelian 270 - 275] *S. 334.* St. Lucillian resembles St. Florus, with a crimson cloak, a green tunic, a cross in his right hand, the left hand is in prayer, the fingers are pointing up; and in the *Prologue* is written, "He was exceedingly old in appearance, a white head, and his two children stand up to his waist."

And the holy [virgin] martyr **Paula,** and with her stand two children similar those with St. Lucillian [with whom she suffered], she herself resembles St. Parasceva ["Friday"].

On the same day the meeting of the miraculous [**Yugskaya** Mother of God] icon [in 1616].

And our holy father **Demetrius,** the abbot of Priluki, miracle worker of Vologda, has a smaller beard than St. Sergius, monastic robes and a scroll in his hand.

And the holy blessed **John,** the fool for Christ's sake, miracle worker of Moscow, has the appearance of an old man, who has not a very big beard, but appears hardly little either, balding brown hair, wrinkled, his hair flows down behind his head, a green [garment] buttoned half way down [or up], a crutch and a hat are in his left hand.

4
Our father among the saints **Metrophanes** [+ 325] *S. 334,* patriarch of Constantinople, is an old man with gray hair, a beard like St. Blaise, a blue saccos, with a light blue cross pattern, omophorion and Gospel.

5
The holy hieromartyr **Dorotheus** [+ 362] *S. 334,* bishop of Tyre, has brown hair like St. John Chrysostom, a purple cloak with a cross pattern, he is holding the Gospel book from underneath with both hands.

And the holy martyr **Marcian** [+ under Diocletian] is a young man like St. George, he wears a scarlet cloak with white, a blue tunic, and in the "Kievan [printed pages" he is called] "Martinian."

6
Our holy father **Hilarion** the New [+ 845] *S. 336,* abbot of the Dalmatian Monastery, is an old man with gray hair, a smaller beard than St. Blaise, there are curls at the ends, and monastic robes.

And our holy father **Bessarion** [fifth century] *S. 336* is an old man with gray hair, in a blue schema, a straight beard longer than St. Nicholas, and monastic robes.

And the holy martyrs **Lucian** *S. 336* and Alexander. St. Alexander has brown hair like St. Cosmas, a scarlet cloak and a green tunic. St. Lucian is a young man like St. George.

And the holy great princess **Eudokia,** Euphrosyne in monasticism, resembles St. Eudokia the miracle worker of Moscow.

And the memory of our holy father **Paisius** [+ 1504], the abbot of miracle worker of Uglich, is an old man with balding gray hair, a rounded oblong beard like St. Sabbas of Zvenigorod, and monastic robes.

7

The holy hieromartyr **Theodotus** *S. 336* has brown hair like St. Florus, a blue cloak, and a crimson tunic.

And the holy women martyrs **Cyriaka, Caleria** and **Mary** [fourth century] resemble Sts. Anna and Elizabeth.

8

The holy great martyr **Theodore** Stratelates [the translation of his relics in 319] *S. 338* has curly hair, not a very large shaggy beard, he is graying, in armor, a scarlet cloak, in his right hand is a lance and in the left a shield, a green tunic, and purple leggings.

And the finding of the venerable relics of the true believing princes **Basil** and **Constantine** miracle workers of Yaroslavl. Prince Basil is very old, he has a beard like St. Basil of Caesarea, a hat with a black [fur] trim, a purple fur coat, with white circles, in the left hand he is holding a [miniature] city in which there is a church, the right hand is in prayer, a blue tunic. Prince Constantine is middle aged with gray hair, a beard like St. Vladimir the grand prince, but a little narrower, he has a hat on his head with black [fur] trim, a blackish velvet fur coat with yellow circles with an ermine collar, in the right hand he holds a cross up, and is looking towards Prince Basil, in the left hand is a sword in its scabbard, a green tunic, and ocher boots.

Our father among the saints **Theodore** [+ 1023], the bishop of Suzhdal, miracle worker, has a beard like St. Basil of Caesarea, gray hair, bishops' vestments, and a white klobuk.

9

Our father among the saints **Cyril** [+ 444] *S. 338*, archbishop of Alexandria, is middle aged, has a cross patterned cloak, a blue tunic, omophorion and Gospel.

And the passing of our holy father **Cyril** [+ 1427] *S. 340,* abbot of White Lake, miracle worker, is an old man with gray hair, a longer and wider beard than St. Sergius, an ocher tunic with white, he is holding a scroll with both hands, on which is written, "Do not be troubled, brothers, rather on account of this understand, if my works will be pleasing to [God] then this place will never diminish."

And our holy father **Theodore** of Edessa resembles St. Blaise.

And the five holy virgin martyrs **Thecla, Mariam, Martha, Maria,** and **Naomi** [+ 346 in Persia] resemble St. Parasceva ["Friday"].

10

The holy hieromartyr **Timothy** [+ under Julian the Apostate] *S. 340,* bishop of Prussa, is an old man with gray hair, a beard longer than St. Basil, and forked at the end, a purple cross patterned cloak, an ocher with white tunic, the omophorion and Gospel.

And the holy hieromartyr **Erasmus** the bishop, in his hand is a scroll, "Lord Jesus Christ, only begotten Son of God, let anyone who asks of me for anything in Your name, let them receive their reward from You."

And the holy martyr **Alexander** [+ 313] *S. 340* has brown hair like St. Cosmas, a scarlet cloak, a green tunic, in his hand a cross, and the left hand is held in prayer with the fingers pointed up, and in the *Prologue* he is a young man. [And with him the holy virgin martyr] **Antonina** resembles St. Parasceva or St. Eudokia.

And our holy father **Alexander** [+ 1439] *S. 338,* miracle worker of Kushta Vologda, is an old man with a graying beard like St. Cyril of White Lake, monastic robes, and of middle stature, his body is emaciated, having an medium size head, a round face, quiet eyes, his full and curly beard goes down to his chest, and his dark brown hair is starting to turn gray.

11

The holy apostles **Bartholomew** *S. 340* and **Barnabas** *S. 342* [first century]. St. Bartholomew has brown hair, a beard like St. Cosmas, a green cloak, a blue tunic, and in the omophorion with a scroll. St. Barnabas has brown hair like St. Joachim the forefather of the Lord, a crimson cloak, a blue tunic, in the omophorion and with a scroll.

And our holy father **Ephraim,** the miracle worker of Novotorzhsk, resembles St.

Nicholas but wears the schema on his head and holds a [model] church in his hands.

12

Our holy father **Onuphrius** the Great [fourth century] *S. 342* is an old man, with hair like the holy prophet Elias, a long narrow beard, very white going down to his feet, he is girded about with leaves, one hand is held in prayer and the other holds a scroll, "If some one brings a *prosphora* [a small loaf of bread offered by the faithful for the Liturgy] or incense or a candle and remembers my name, the Lord will honor him in the first hour of the thousand years.

And our holy father **Peter** of Athos [+ 734] *S. 342* is nude, has gray hair, a beard that goes a little below his waist, he is girded with purplish leaves, he is looking toward St. Onuphrius, with two locks of curly hair.

And our holy father **John,** miracle worker of Moscow, called "the big hat," is a young man wearing a poncho.

"From today the sun turns from summer to winter."

13

The holy martyr **Aquilina** [+ 239] *S. 342* has a scarlet cloak, a blue tunic, in the hand a cross and the left is in prayer.

And the holy father **Triphillius** [+ 370] *S. 344,* bishop of Leucosia, has brown hair, a longer beard then St. Florus, his hair comes down past his ears, a cross patterned cloak, a white tunic, the omophorion and Gospel.

And the holy martyr **Antonida** resembles St. Euphemia.

And our holy father **Andronicus,** the abbot of the Yausa River, miracle worker of Moscow, has a gray beard like St. Nicholas, his hands are in prayer, and monastic robes.

14

The holy prophet **Elisha** [ninth century B.C.] *S 344,* is balding, has a beard like the holy prophet Moses, a purple cloak, a blue tunic, the right hand is in prayer the left hand has a scroll on which is written, "Elisha said, 'For whom are you searching? Follow me.'" [Or one may write] on Elisha's scroll, "Thus says the Lord, 'Be healed with this water: death and barrenness will not result from it.'"

And our father among the saints **Methodius** [+ 846] *S. 344,* the patriarch of

Constantinople, has brown hair like St. John Chrysostom, a cross patterned saccos, omophorion and Gospel.

And our holy father Methodius, the new miracle worker who lived on the Pesnosh, is an old man with gray hair, a smaller beard than St. Nicholas, and monastic robes.

15

The holy prophet **Amos** [eighth century B.C.] *S. 344* is an old man with gray hair like St. John the Theologian, a green cloak, a blue tunic, in his hands is a scroll and on the scroll is written, "In the last days there will be signs in sun and in the moon and in the stars." And in the printed *Prologue* is written, "Amos the prophet appears old, he had a thick beard resembling St. John the Theologian."

And the holy martyrs [+ under Diocletian], **Modestus** was an old man and **Crescentia** was a young woman.

And the holy fathers **Gregory** and **Cassian,** miracle workers of Nozomsk and Vologda [+ 1392]. St. Gregory is very old, with a straight beard like St. Nicholas, thick hair, and monastic robes. [And again] St. Gregory is very old and has a beard like St. Demetrius of Priluki.

And the holy true believing Prince **Lazarus** [+ 1389], king and autocrat of the Serbs, is an old man with gray hair, a beard like St. Nicholas, he has a hat on his head, and princes' robes.

16

Our father among the saints **Tikhon** [+ 425] *S. 346,* miracle worker, bishop of Amathus, has brown hair starting to gray, a beard like St. John Chrysostom, a black cross patterned cloak, with both hands he is holding the Gospel from underneath his vestment, and a white tunic.

And our holy father **Theodore** Sykeote is an old man with a graying beard shorter than St. Blaise, and monastic robes.

And our holy father **Tikhon,** miracle worker of Dukhovsk, wears the schema, has a longer beard than St. Barlaam, is very old, and wears monastic robes.

And our holy monastic mother **Anna.**

And our holy father **Eupatius** is an old man with gray hair, a beard like St. Alexander of Svir, in his hands he is holding an icon of the most holy Mother of God with the Pre-eternal Child.

17

The holy martyrs **Manuel, Sabel** and **Ismael** [+ 362 in Persia] *S. 346.* St. Manuel is a young man and is clean shaven like St. Demetrius of Thessalonica, and the hair on his head is curly, he is wearing three robes, blue purple scarlet, in his hand is a cross and the other hand is in prayer, he has a hat on his head with a white brim similar to the holy prophet Daniel. St. Sabel has a scarlet cloak, a green purple with white, on his head a hat. St. Ismael wears a crimson cloak with white, a blue tunic reddish brown, in his hands is a cross. All three are young.

On the same day our father among the saints **Simeon,** archbishop and miracle worker of Novgorod, is an old man in a white klobuk, a beard like St. Peter the metropolitan, in bishops' vestments, with an omophorion and Gospel.

18

The holy martyr **Leontius** [+ 73] *S. 348* has brown hair like St. Cosmas, a blue cloak, a scarlet tunic, in his hand a cross and the left is in prayer the fingers are pointing up, and in the "Kievan [printed pages"] in the right hand is a cross and the left hand is in prayer.

And our holy father **Nikita** of Chalcedon is an old man with gray hair, in the schema, a beard like St. John Damascene, monastic robes and a scroll in his hand.

19

The holy apostle **Jude** [+ first century] *S. 348,* the brother of the Lord according to the flesh, is an old man with a graying beard like St. Barlaam of Khutin, a purple cloak, a blue tunic, in the omophorion, in his hands is a scroll which he is holding with both hands and in the "Kievan [printed pages"] "in the right hand and in the left a book."

And our holy father **Paisius** the Great [fifth century] in his hand is a scroll, "For we have been given a gift by God for whosoever's sin you pray for, that sinner will be forgiven."

And the holy martyr and true believing Prince **Roman** Olgovich of Ryazan, who suffered in Orda for Christ under King Mengutemir, and whose torture was similar to St. James the Persian, has brown hair and in everything is similar to the prince St. Boris, and others say he is young in a hat, the right hand is in prayer and in the left he is holding a [model] of a town in which there is a church.

20

The holy hieromartyr **Methodius** [+ 312] *S. 348* bishop of Patra, is an old man with gray hair, has a beard like St. Athanasius, a cross patterned cloak, an ocher tunic with white, the omophorion and Gospel.

And the holy hieromartyr **Aristocleus** the Presbyter [+ under Diocletian] *S. 350,* called "Aristoclian" in the "Kievan pages," has a beard longer than St. Nicholas, but not balding, has priests' vestments, in the left hand is the Gospel, and with the right hand he is supporting his head.

On the same day our holy father **Barlaam,** the founder of the Theologian's Monastery which is on the Vagnv River, the miracle worker, is an old man with a shorter graying beard than St. Zosimas of Solovki and monastic robes.

21

The holy martyr **Julian** of Tarsus [+ under Diocletian] *S. 350* is a young man like St. George, with a blue cloak, a reddish purple tunic with white, in his hand is a cross and in the left a scroll.

And the holy martyr **Basilissa** and her son the child Celisi.

And the holy father **Basilianus,** bishop of Syria, is an old man with gray hair, a blunt beard like St. Blaise, bishops' vestments, the omophorion and Gospel.

22

The holy hieromartyr **Eusebius** [+ under Julian the Apostate] *S. 350,* bishop of Samosota, is an old man with gray hair and a beard like St. Blaise, a green cloak, a white tunic, the omophorion and Gospel.

And the finding of the venerable relics of the holy blessed **Michael** of Klops, miracle worker of Novgorod, is an old man with a graying beard like St. Barlaam of Khutin, in the schema and monastic robes.

And holy father **Sisiniuas** the Bishop, is an old man with gray hair resembling St. Blaise.

23

The holy martyr **Agrippina** [+ 275] *S. 350* resembles St. Parasceva in everything; but some paint her thus: a blue cloak, a scarlet tunic with white.

And the holy hieromartyr **Elespherias** has hair and a beard like St. Andrew the First called, priests' vestments, and holds the Gospel in both hands.

And the holy true believing prince **Roman,** miracle worker of Uglich, has the appearance of a middle aged man resembling St. Barlaam of Khutin, and has a princes' hat on.

And the meeting of the miraculous **Vladimir** Icon of our Lady, the most holy Mother of God and ever-virgin Mary [in 1480].

And the three holy youths **Probius, Molius, Urban,** being young men they wear martyrs' robes.

24

THE BIRTH OF THE HONORABLE AND GLORIUS PROPHET, FORERUNNER OF THE LORD, JOHN THE BAPTIST S. 352. St. Elizabeth is lying on a bed, the bed is as usual, a scarlet cloak, a green tunic, Zachariah the prophet is sitting at the head and he is writing in a tablet, "Let his name be John." He is sitting on a royal stool and to which there are three steps; a midwife is holding the infant in a basin but is looking back, and a maiden is pouring water into the basin, and two maidens are standing before St. Elizabeth with gifts and with beverages and with solar discs, and behind them are two palaces, one palace is green and the other is purple with white, from palace to palace there is a green veil, and some paint [this icon] as follows: Elizabeth is lying on a bed, her cloak is green, under her is a white sheet, the bed is dark greenish brown, at her head is sitting Zachariah, who is wearing a scarlet cloak, a blue tunic, the right hand he is holding to Elizabeth and with the other he is holding a scroll, on the scroll it says, "Blessed is the Lord God of Israel, who has visited and redeemed." And he himself is sitting on a throne, under his feet there are two steps, maidens are standing before Elizabeth, one is bowing her head, her cloak is scarlet, a second maiden is holding a bottle, standing before her [Elizabeth's] knees in the middle of the bed, under Elizabeth is sitting a midwife holding John the forerunner, to John, a green cloak on both sides, the midwife is wearing a purple with white cloak, standing before the midwife is a maiden pouring water into the basin, behind Zachariah is a green palace, on the other side from the maiden there is a purple palace with white, and with a scarlet veil.

And the holy hieromartyr **Orentius** has brown hair, is very old with very little hair, has a beard like St. Florus and Laurus, has green priests' vestments without the omophorion, the shoulder piece is ocher with white, he is holding the Gospel with his right hand and with the left he is holding his white tunic.

And the memory of the holy righteous **John,** the new miracle worker of Yarensk, has hair and a beard resembling St. John the Forerunner, a crimson cloak like St. Alexis the man of God, the Yarenta River is at the Solovki Inlet.

25

The holy monastic martyr **Febronia** [+ 310] *S. 352* of Alexandria is similar to St. Eudokia. Some paint her with a klobuk and mantle, her cassock is ocher with white.

And the holy monastic women in Rienia, **Hieria** and **Thomaida** and others: **Leonis, Eutropia**, all nuns [+ 310].

And the holy miracle workers of Murom, the true believing Prince **Peter,** named **David** in monasticism, the true believing Princess **Febronia,** named **Euphrosyne** in monasticism [+ 1228] *S. 354.* St. Peter is an old man with gray hair, in the schema, a beard like St. Demetrius of Priluki, monastic robes, and a scroll in his hand. St. Febronia is in the schema, similar to St. Eudokia in her appearance and robes, and her hands are held towards St. Peter in prayer.

26

Our holy father **David** of Thessalonica [+ 540] *S. 354* is an old man with gray hair, a beard like St. Euthymius the Great, or St. Blaise, he is sitting in a tree, on a big oak in the branches, on a board on top, monastic robes, under the tree is a mountain and a small lake, and there is a grove around the oak, and from the oak is hanging a jug on a rope, there are three birds sitting on the tree; and some others say that he has a beard like St. Demetrius of Priluki.

And our holy father **Demetrius** [+ 1385], bishop of Suzhdal the miracle worker, is an old man with gray hair, a longer beard than St. Sergius, crimson bishops' vestments, in a cap, omophorion and Gospel.

27

Our holy father **Samson** [+ 530] *S. 354*, the receiver of strangers, has brown hair, resembles St. Cosmas, in priests' vestments, a green shoulder piece, a white tunic, with not uncovered [hands] he is holding the Gospel with both hands.

And the holy true believing Prince **Nicholas** Kochanov, the miracle worker of Novgorod, who was a fool for Christ's sake, is an old man with gray hair, a beard going down to his waist, it is narrow and forked at the end, balding, he has a scarlet coat, with a white lining, the tunic is blue, he is girded about with a cloth, he has a cross in his hand and the other is held in prayer.

28

The recovery of the venerable relics [in 413] of the holy miracle workers and unmercenaries **Cyrus** and **John** *S. 356*. St. Cyrus is an old man with gray hair, a longer beard then St. Blaise, in his right hand he is holding a quill pen [a feather], and in the left hand is a container, monastic robes, the tunic is ocher with white. St. John has brown hair like St. Cosmas, a scarlet cloak, a blue tunic, and similarly he is holding a quill pen in one hand and a container in the other. The "Kievan [printed pages]" say they are both holding crosses and books.

29

The holy glorious and all praised apostles **Peter** and **Paul** are looking at each other, the Savior is in a cloud [first century] *S. 360*. St. Peter is an old man with gray hair, a beard like St. Nicholas, a blue tunic, his cloak is ocher with white; St. Paul is balding, has a big nose, a corner, the hair on his head comes down a little from the back of his head, he has a slightly smaller beard similar to St. John the forerunner, divided into five curls, he has bright eyes, a reddish purple cloak, a green tunic, his right hand is held in prayer. St. Peter is holding a key, and the Apostle Paul has bare feet; and others describe them thus: he is holding the Gospel, above them is the most honorable and Pre-eternal [Christ] Child in a cloud, surrounded and joined by garlands. The Apostle Peter has a scroll, "I will hasten, and will always have you, after my departure, for which things to keep memory." The Apostle Paul has a scroll, "I will never cease giving thanks for you and will always remember you in my prayers."

And the murder of the holy true believing Prince **Andrew** Bogolyubsky, miracle worker of Vladimir, resembles St. Boris the Prince, he is very old with a beard like the Theologian.

And the monastic saint **Peter** [+ 1290], the crown prince of Rostov, is very old with a sharper beard then St. Nicholas, in the schema, and monastic robes.

30

The Synaxis of the holy glorious and all praised Twelve Apostles [first century] *S. 362*. Around them is braided a garland of branches, the Savior is sitting over them on top, He is blessing with both hands towards both sides, on one side is the Most Pure [Mother of God] and on the other is St. John the Forerunner. Looking to the right side is St. **Peter,** opposite him is St. **Paul,** both looking towards each other. Behind Peter is St. **John** the Theologian holding a Gospel, a purple cloak with white, a blue tunic; behind Paul is St. **Matthew** holding a Gospel, a green cloak and blue tunic. Under John is sitting the Apostle **Andrew** with gray hair, a beard like the Theologian, a green cloak, a blue tunic; and opposite him is the Apostle

James with brown hair, a beard like St. Cosmas, a purple cloak with white and a blue tunic; behind Andrew is sitting St. **Bartholomew,** with brown hair, very old, a beard like St. Joachim the forefather of the Lord, wearing a blue cloak, a purple tunic; behind James is St. **Luke** holding a Gospel, with curly brown hair, a beard like St. Cosmas, a scarlet cloak, a blue tunic. Under Bartholomew is St. **Mark,** with brown hair, a beard like Sts. Cosmas and Damian, holding the Gospel, a purple cloak with white, a blue tunic: opposite him is St. **Simon,** who is starting to gray, a beard like St. Nicholas, a scarlet cloak with white, a blue tunic; behind Mark is St. **Philip,** who is a young man like St. Demetrius, with a scarlet cloak, a blue tunic; behind Simon is St. **Thomas,** who is a young man similar to the Apostle Philip, has a purple cloak with white, a blue tunic. Each is looking towards each other on the other side; separated from each other are Luke and Mark, and, John and Matthew. They all have scrolls in their hands, and even Peter and Paul have scrolls, and all ten [should be twelve] are in prayer, one after the other, and the inscription for all of them is, "You mounted a horse, Your apostles, O Lord, [You have taken their reins in Your hands, and Your ride became salvation truly we sing: glory to Your power, O Lord!]" the whole Irmos to the end [*Meneion,* June 29, "Another Canon to St. Paul," Tone 8, Ode 4].

JULY

"The month of July has 31 days."

1

The holy miracle workers and unmercenaries **Cosmas** and **Damian** [+ 284] *S. 364*, who suffered martyrdom in Rome. St. Cosmas is a young man like St. Demetrius of Thessalonica, wears a purple apostles' cloak, a blue tunic, he has a brush in one hand and a container in the other, and bare feet. St. Damian is a young man like St. George the martyr, with curly hair, a purple cloak with white, he is girded underneath with a cord [literally with a "margin" or "edge"], a green tunic, an ocher hem, a brush in one hand and a container in the other, his feet are in boots. In the "Kievan [printed pages"] both are identical.

2

The placing of the venerable **robe of our Lady**, the most holy Mother of God and ever-virgin Mary, in the church which is in Blachernes [472] *S. 366*. There is a white and green church with three domes: one of the domes is big, the other two are small. There is an icon of the Most Pure [Mother of God], [i.e.,] a portable icon, a green cross is standing before the altar, a Gospel book and a cross are on the altar, and the robe of the Mother of God is purple. A bishop, who resembles St. Blaise wearing a saccos with a purple cross pattern, is bowing and praying. He appears to be an old man with balding gray hair. Behind him are bishops in caps, some with gray hair and some with brown hair; they are holding their hands in prayer, and there is a young deacon with incense. There is a green palace, and in it there is a king in a cap who resembles St. Vladimir or St. Constantine, with brown hair, a blue cloak, a crimson tunic, and behind the king are princes and noblemen; the first has gray hair, a longer beard than St. Nicholas, a red coat, a green tunic; the second has brown hair, one sees only his head; and one sees the head of a third, who appears to be a young man, one does not see their garments; all hold their hands in prayer. And behind them is a queen who resembles St. Helen, and many women are standing with children, and behind the bishop are two golden bishops' crosiers, and behind the church are the walls of the city and outside are light blue [*"siniy"* in Slavonic] towers with stone walls, and the king holds his hands in prayer.

And the holy martyr **Constus** is a young man resembling St. Mamantas, who was seven years old when he died for Christ.

3

The holy martyr **Hyacinth** [+ 108] *S.366* is a young man resembling St. George, a purple cloak with white, the second [short tunic] is ocher, the third [long tunic] is blue, and a cross in his hand.

And the holy true believing princes of Yaroslavl, **Basil** [+ 1249] and **Constantine** [+ 1257] Vsevolodovich. St. Basil has a beard like St. Basil of Caesarea, and St. Constantine resembles St. Vladimir.

And the passing of our holy father **Nicodemus,** the miracle worker of Hide Lake which is in Kargopol, has an oblong, but not wide, black beard, starting to gray and narrower than St. Nikon, in the schema, and monastic robes.

4

And our father among the saints **Andrew** [+ 712] *S. 368*, archbishop of Crete, is an old man with gray hair resembling St. Blaise, a cross patterned cloak, in the omophorion, an ocher tunic with white.

And our holy mother **Martha** [+ 551] *S. 368*, the mother of St. Simeon of Wonder Mountain, resembles St. Eudokia, has a green reddish brown cassock, her hands are in prayer.

And the holy children **Lucy, Aaroi, Cyprilla,** and **Theodotia** resemble Sts. Anna and Elizabeth.

And the holy martyr **Constantine** is a young man resembling St. George in a scarlet cloak and a light blue tunic.

5

Our holy father **Athanasius of Athos** [+ 1000] *S. 368*, is an old man with balding dark gray hair, a beard like St. Sergius, a purple cloak, a greenish brown tunic with white, in his hand is a scroll on which is written, "Let us hurry, and let us take the trouble that we will attain to the heavenly kingdom."

And the finding of the venerable relics of our holy and God-bearing father **Sergius** [1422], the abbot and miracle worker of Radonezh. St. Sergius is lying in a coffin, he is an old man with gray hair, with a beard like St. Athanasius, monastic robes. Spiritual fathers are bowed down over him, among the heads is a spiritual father who is an old man who resembles St. Blaise with a klobuk, and behind him is one with brown hair, and one can see less of the other heads. There is a spiritual father in bishop's vestments in the middle of the coffin, he has a smaller beard then St. Blaise, and wears a black klobuk, and he is holding his hand to his face, and the other hand holds a book. Behind him is a young deacon with incense, there are three spiritual fathers: one is an old man resembling St. Nicholas; the second has brown hair; the third has black hair; there are black klobuks. The church is white with one dome; outside there are two palaces, one green and one ocher, and behind them one can see a little of the walls.

6

Our holy father **Sisoes the Great** [+ 429] *S. 370* has a longer and narrower beard than St. Blaise, not very dark gray, a cassock reddish brown greenish brown, in his hands is a scroll.

And the holy virgin martyr **Lucy** [+ 310].

"The day has 16 hours and the night 8."
7

Our holy father **Thomas of Malea** [tenth century] *S. 370* is an old man with gray hair, a longer beard than St. Sergius, an ocher cassock.

And our holy father **Acacius** [sixth century] *S. 372,* who is mentioned in the *Ladder [of Divine Ascent],* is a young man like St. Demetrius of Thessalonica, an ocher cassock, greenish brown white, crimson reddish brown.

And the holy virgin martyr **Kiriaka** *S. 373.*

And the holy true believing prince **Gleb** Vsevolodovich, is very old with curly gray hair, a longer and narrower beard than St. Blaise, he wears a coat similar to St. Vladimir, a blue hat with a black brim on his head, a blue tunic, a cross in the right hand, and a sword in its scabbard in the left.

And the holy true believing King **Vladislav** the miracle worker of the Serbs, is an old man with curly gray hair, he wears a royal crown, he has a beard like St. Athanasius of Alexandria, in royal robes, in the right hand is a cross and there is a scroll in his left, "Let my soul magnify the Lord and my spirit rejoice."

8

The holy great martyr **Procopius** [+ 303] *S. 372* is a young man like St. Demetrius of Thessalonica, in armor, in the right hand is a cross, and a scroll, "O God, being before this age, remember Your people and heal the sick and save the suffering, give peace to Your world," and in the left hand is a shield and a spear. And the holy martyr **Theodosia,** the mother of the martyr Procopius, resembles St. Anna.

And the holy blessed **Procopius** [+ 1303] *S. 372*, who was a fool for Christ's sake, the miracle worker of Ustyuzh, is middle aged, has a beard like St. Cosmas, a purple cloak which is coming down from the right shoulder, in his hand are three crutches, he has boots on his feet but his knees are bare.

And the holy blessed **John,** who was a fool for Christ's sake, miracle worker of Ustyuzh, is a young man in a white cloak, which is wrapped around him and on his arms, but his shoulder is bare as well as his side, and his feet are bare up to his knees, and his hands are held in prayer.

On the same day we celebrate the appearance of the **"Kazan"** icon of the most holy Mother of God [in 1579] and the **"Ustyuzh"** icon of her venerable and glorious Annunciation [in 1290].

9

The holy hieromartyr **Pancratius** [+ first century] *S. 374*, bishop of Tauromeny, has a beard like St. Blaise, but is gray at the end, a cross patterned cloak, a blue tunic with white, he is holding the Gospel with both hands, and the omophorion.

And our father among the saints **Theodore** [+ 848], bishop of Edessa, is an old man with thick gray hair, a beard like St. Blaise, a scarlet with white cross patterned cloak, a reddish brown tunic, a Gospel book in his hand and an omophorion.

And the **ten thousand saints** in Scete, and in caves and in desert places who meet a bitter death by fire and smoke. St. Theophile of Alexandria.

On the same day we celebrate the icon of the most holy Mother of God which is at **Kolocha** [1413], which depicts her with the Pre-eternal Child on both arms, and which has margins: on one margin is the holy prophet Elias and on the other is the holy miracle worker Nicholas.

10

The holy **forty-five martyrs** in Nicopolis [+ 319] *S. 374*: **Leontius, Daniel, Anthony, Timonius, Balirad**, and those with them. From the end [the first martyr] resembles St. Florus with brown hair, a crimson cloak with white, a blue tunic; the second resembles St. George, a scarlet cloak; between them is one like St. Blaise with hair over his ears, a beard like St. Sergius, a single green cloak, the shoulder piece is ocher; and the others have gray hair or brown hair, and one sees others behind them.

And the holy martyr **Appolinius** [+ under Decius] resembles St. Demetrius and has

177

a scroll in his hand on which is written, "I will pray always for the faithful believers and request salvation for all."

And the holy martyr **Siluanus** [+ fourth century] is a young man and in his hand is a scroll, "Jesus will quickly hear those in poverty and in pain and in death."

And the placing of the venerable **robe of our Lord**, God and Savior, Jesus Christ [in 1625], and of [the icons of] the Most Pure [Mother of God] **"Okovyetsia," "Kolochesky," "Tikhvin," and "Pecherska."**

And the passing of our holy father **Anthony** Pecherska [Lavra + 1073]: priests and deacons, monks and princes, old men and men with brown hair, and a crowd of all different people are burying him. Our holy father Anthony of Pecherska is described on the eighth day of May.

11

The holy equal to the apostles, martyr **Euphemia** *S. 376*, the all praised, has a crimson cloak, a green tunic, a cross is in one hand and in the other is a scroll on which is written, "I believe in one God."

On the same day the finding of the venerable relics of the holy great martyr **Euphemia** [in 451], whose venerable relics were hidden in the sea on account of the persecution, and were announced to the Emperor Constantine and Empress Irene, and they joyfully ordered that they be taken out of the depths of the sea and to be placed in the church with the entire [Fourth Ecumenical] Council, and the emperor and the empress and a multitude of bishops, and a crowd of every description.

12

The holy martyrs **Proclus** *S. 376* and **Hilary** *S. 378* [+ under Trajan]. Proclus has brown hair, resembles St. Florus, a dark crimson cloak, a scarlet tunic, a cross is in his hand and a scroll in the left. Hilary resembles St. George, a green cloak, ocher on the shoulders. In the "Kievan pages" St. Proclus resembles St. George and St. Hilary resembles St. Florus. St. Proclus has a scroll on which is written, "O Master, Creator of the entire universe, hear me, grant me the gift for asking in Your name, for my sake save from fire and famine and disturbances." St. Hilary has a scroll, "Lord Jesus Christ, grant those remembering Your servants Proclus and Hilary, forgiveness of sins and every good thing."

And the holy monastic martyr **Maria** Golendukh [sixth century] *S. 378* has a white klobuk on her head, a scarlet cloak a blue tunic, in her hand is a cross and in the other is a scroll, and on the scroll is written, "I prayed to God for the salvation of the whole world." [Transferred here from elsewhere.] And St. Maria Golendukh has a scroll in her hand, "Eternal God, hear the prayer of your servant, raise the banners of noble and worthy kings, and grant them victory over their enemies, suppress the work of Satan, and save Your holy Church, and those ruling Christian cities and every city and land, that they will be called by Your name. Protect and save them from every misfortune, from wrath and want."

And our holy father **Michael** of Maleina [+ 962] *S. 378*, is an old man with gray hair, a medium beard longer than St. Nicholas, forked at the end, in his hand is a scroll, "Lord, Jesus Christ, accept my soul in peace and save it from the tax collectors of the air [the demons who test souls after death]." And in the other hand a scroll, "My lady, the most holy mistress, the Mother of God, pray to your Son, Christ our God, that He will receive my soul in peace and that it will not be given over to the ruler of the world of this age of darkness."

And our holy father **Stephen Sabbaite** [+ 794] *S. 378* is an old man with gray hair like St. Nicholas and a similar beard to his, monastic robes, the tunic is greenish brown with white, in his hand is a scroll.

And the holy martyr **Marcian** [+ 258] is a young man like St. Demetrius of Thessalonica.

13

The **Synaxis of the holy commander in chief** [of the heavenly hosts] Gabriel and the other angelic powers [feast instituted in 982] *S. 380 (blank)*. Gabriel goes and stands; some paint [this icon] similar to the Synaxis of St. Michael [on November 8], exactly the same without change.

And the falling asleep of the holy foremother **Sarah**, the wife of Abraham [in Genesis], she resembles St. Parasceva ["Friday"].

14

The holy apostle **Aquilla** [first century] *S. 380* and **Priscilla.** St. Aquilla is an old man with gray hair, a longer beard than St. Nicholas, in the omophorion, an ocher cloak with white, a blue tunic, the Gospel is in his hand. St. Priscilla is young, has a purple apostles' cloak, a green tunic, holds the Gospel in one hand and is looking at Aquilla. Some paint Priscilla like St. Barbara.

And the holy hieromartyr **Onysimus** [+ under Diocletian], is well built, handsome, has a brown beard like St. John Chrysostom, and bishops' vestments.

And our holy father **Stephen of Makhrish** [+ 1406] is an old man with gray hair, a beard like St. Demetrius Priluki but wider, and monastic robes.

15

The holy martyrs **Kirrik** and **Julitta** [+ 305] *S. 382*, who has a green cloak, a crimson tunic, a cross in her hand a and with her left hand she is keeping Kirrik next to her, a prayer is rolled up in the scroll, "I thank You, O Lord, for having called my son first, and for making him worthy to suffer for the sake of Your holy name." St. Kirrik is a child three years old, confessing the Holy Trinity, standing in a long shirt, his knees are bare, he is holding his right hand up in the form of a cross, and he has scarlet boots on his feet.

And the falling asleep of the holy true believing great prince, equal to the apostles, **Vladimir** of Kiev [+ 1015] *S. 382*, autocrator of the Russian land, called **Basil** in holy baptism, enlightener of the Russian land by holy baptism. St. Vladimir has a scroll in his hand, "O God, having created heaven and earth, look down upon Your newly illuminated people, O Lord, and grant them to know You as the True God and strengthen them in the True Faith." In appearance and in his beard he resembles St. John the Theologian, the hair on his head is curly like St. Menas, his cloak is purple brocade with gold circles, a blue brocade tunic, in one hand is a cross, in his left hand is a sword in its scabbard, and on his head is a royal crown.

And the holy martyr **Abdias** is a young man, in his hand is a scroll and on it, "Behold, I, Abdias, am a man of the God of heaven."

And the holy true believing Great Princess **Olga** [+ 969] *S. 378*, called **Helen** in holy baptism, has a royal crown on her head and a cloth under the crown similar to St. Helen the Empress, and has similar robes as she does, in her hand is a cross, and in the other a scroll on which is written, "Casting down idols I recognize the true God, Jesus Christ."

16

The holy hieromartyr **Athenogenes** [+ 311] *S. 382*, bishop of Heracleopolis and his ten disciples. He is an old man with gray hair, has a beard like St. Blaise, in the omophorion, a purple cloak, a blue tunic, in his hand is the Gospel, in the other a scroll, "O Lord, my God, grant those who keep Your memory forgiveness of sins."

And the holy martyr **Antiochus** [+ under Diocletian] has brown hair, a beard like

St. Tikhon, in his hand is a scroll, "O God, Comforter of all, hear me, Your servant, grant me [the salvation of] each [soul] I beg of You."

And the holy martyr **Paul** and those with him, the martyrs **Alevtina** and **Chionia** [+ 308], resemble St. Euphemia, and Paul resembles St. Cosmas. In his hand is a scroll, "I prayed to God for Christians, and for all the pagans that they would come to their senses."

DESCRIPTIONS OF THE SEVEN ECUMENICAL COUNCILS

The **First Holy Ecumenical Council** S. 384 of 318 holy fathers convened against the infamous Arius who blasphemed the Son of God, in the year 5724 [should be 5833; that is, 325 A.D.] in Nicea. The Savior is appearing to St. Peter of Alexandria as a child in a torn cloak standing on an altar, His shoulder is bare, His feet are bare, the altar is scarlet, over them is a four-cornered canopy, the curtain is scarlet. On the side is Peter, who is an old man with balding gray hair, a beard like St. Nicholas, he is bowing on his knees, looking at the Savior, he is holding his hands in prayer to Him. There is a church with one dome, the Emperor Constantine is an old man with gray hair, he is sitting in a throne in a purple royal robe, he holds a scepter in his hand. Two bishops are sitting on thrones at his right hand: one has a beard like St. Nicholas and wearing a cap; and behind him is a bishop who resembles St. Athanasius, an old man with gray hair. And there are three bishops sitting on his [the emperor's] left hand: the first has brown hair, a shorter beard than St. Basil of Caesarea, one sees very little of him; the second bishop resembles St. Athanasius; and the third resembles St. Peter of Alexandria. They are speaking with Arius, who is holding his hands toward the emperor. Two men, who resemble St. Gregory with gray hair, are standing behind the emperor. Arius is looking toward the Savior, his intestines are pouring out, a reddish brown cloak, an old man with gray hair, a shorter beard than St. Blaise, and behind him is a simple green palace. Many different heretics are standing there: old men, men with brown hair, and young men. They are wearing noblemen's coats, they are pointing down with their arms, and they are wearing hats on their heads. And on the right hand side of the emperor, underneath the bishops who are sitting, there is a king standing, the king resembles St. Constantine and has similar robes and he is bowing his head. Bishops are standing opposite him: the first resembles St. Nicholas, the second resembles St. Blaise, the third resembles St. Athanasius, the fourth resembles St. Cyril wearing a cap, the fifth resembles St. Menas with a beard like St. Blaise, and all are looking towards the king. And behind them is an ocher palace, a city and towers around it, and all of the bishops have haloes.

The **Second Ecumenical Council** S. 386 of the 108 holy fathers in the year 5884 [should be 5889; that is, 381 A.D.], was the council against Macedonius, the unworthy patriarch of Constantinople, and those of one mind with him, against Sabelius of Libya, and Apollinarius of Laodicea, and against their council members. There is a dark green church with one dome, Emperor Theodosius is sitting on a throne, he is an old man with gray hair, a straight beard shorter than St. Nicholas, a purple cloak, a scepter is in his hand, on his right hand are sitting a bishop resembling St. Gregory the Theologian, the second resembling St. Nicholas, with an ocher cloak with a cross pattern, the third bishop behind them has brown hair, one sees very little; and on the [emperor's] left hand are sitting a bishop with brown hair and a beard like St. Basil of Caesarea, the second bishop resembles St. Athanasius, the third bishop resembles St. Nicholas, and holds an icon of the Most Pure [Mother of God] with the [Christ] Child, and another bishop holds an icon of the "Savior on the Towel." Beneath the feet of the emperor on the left side are standing seven priests: the first priest has brown hair, the second priest resembles St. John Chrysostom, and behind him a priest resembles the holy prophet Moses, and the other priests are old men, some with brown hair and some are young men, heretics, with ocher shoulder pieces, they are pointing down with their hands. On the right side of the emperor beneath the bishops who are sitting six bishops are standing: the first bishop resembles St. Blaise and is looking behind him, the second bishop resembles St. Nicholas and is raising his arm towards him, behind them is a bishop resembling St. John the Theologian, and behind him a bishop resembling St. Athanasius, and of the other bishops one can only see their heads. There are two ocher palaces and the walls around them and the towers are green.

The **Third Ecumenical Council** *S. 392* in Ephesus two hundred holy fathers convened in the year 5734 [should be 5939; that is, 431 A.D.] under Emperor Theodosius against the infamous Nestorius, patriarch of Constantinople, and against Dioscorus and Eutychius, and against those who are of one mind with them, because those wretches did not fear to divide our Lord Jesus Christ into two persons. A young king is sitting on a throne, he wears a scarlet cloak, a scepter is in his hand, behind him is a white church with one dome, on his right hand are sitting bishops, [one bishop resembles] St. Cyril of Alexandria, and two resemble St. Blaise, and on the left hand [sits a bishop resembling] St. John the Merciful, and behind him three bishops: the first resembles St. Stephen of Surozh, the second bishop resembles St. Gregory the Theologian, and the third bishop has brown hair and resembles St. Basil of Caesarea. There is a staircase at the king's feet, and bishops are sitting on the side, and heretics are standing on the [king's] left side: one heretic is an old man with gray hair, a long beard, dressed in cloaks and is looking behind him; and next to him is a heretic resembling St. Nicholas, touching him on the ear, and all are gesturing with their hands to [the one who looks like St.] Nicholas; the second heretic is an old man with gray hair and a wide beard and with his hand he is covering his face, and other heretics are covering their garments, they are crying, and on the [king's] right side there are two bishops: one resembles St. Blaise and the other resembles St. John the Theologian; they are bowing to [the one who resembles the miracle worker St.] Nicholas and they are taking off his vestments and omophorion. And bishops are standing behind them; some are old men with gray hair, others have brown hair, some wearing the schema are amazed; they are covering themselves with their hands. There are two palaces, green and purple, and their walls and towers are ocher with white.

The **Fourth Ecumenical Council** S. 394 was in Chalcedon in the year 5745 [should be 5959; that is, 451 A.D.] under the Emperor Marcian and 630 holy fathers assembled on behalf of the Orthodox Christian Faith against Dioscorus and Eutychius the archimandrite and against those who were of one mind with them. Emperor Marcian is an old man with gray hair and has a beard like St. Vladimir, and behind him is a green church. On the right hand of the emperor are sitting three bishops: the first bishop is an old man with gray hair resembling St. Blaise, the second has brown hair and a beard like St. Athanasius, and the third has brown hair and a smaller beard than St. Athanasius. On the left hand [of the emperor] are sitting bishops: the first bishop is an old man with gray hair resembling St. Athanasius, the second resembles St. Nicholas, without a halo, his hands are held to his mouth. Saint Euphemia is lying in a coffin, three bishops are standing at her head, and they are bowing down, they are holding their hands in prayer toward her, and they are putting a scroll in her hands; the first bishop is balding and has a beard like St. Athanasius, the second is an old man with a gray hair resembling St. Nicholas, the third has brown hair and a wider beard than St. Nicholas, and behind them are bishops: one with gray hair resembling St. Athanasius, one with brown hair, one is very old and gray, and they have Gospel books in their hands. Spiritual fathers are standing at the feet of St. Euphemia who are looking into the coffin: the first is an old man with gray hair resembling St. Nicholas, and behind him is another old man resembling St. Athanasius, there is a young man; some are wearing klobuks, and others are without klobuks. There are two palaces, one green and one ocher, and one sees very little of the walls.

The **Fifth Ecumenical Council** S. 388 was in the year 6044 [should be 6061; that is, 553 A.D.] in Constantinople. 160 holy fathers convened under Emperor Justinian the Great, the "Big Beard," concerning the resurrection of the dead and the second coming of Christ against the false reasoning of the heretics, against Origin, and Bagrius, and Dydimus, and those waging war [against the True Faith] with them. The emperor is sitting on a throne, he has brown hair, he is very old, his beard goes down to his waist and is forked and is thin. Bishops are sitting at his right hand: the first is an old man with gray hair and has a straight beard resembling St. Nicholas, the second resembles St. John Chrysostom, the third resembles St. Blaise. At his [that is, the emperor's] left hand are sitting bishops: the first with brown hair resembling St. Basil of Caesarea, the second has brown hair and resembles St. Nicholas, they are looking back, the third bishop resembles St. Gregory. Bishops are standing beneath at the feet [at the right side] of the emperor: the first is an old man with balding gray hair and a beard like St. Blaise; next to him is one with brown hair, his beard is divided at the ends; there is an old man with gray hair who resembles St. Athanasius; and others resembling St. John Chrysostom among them. Heretics are standing underneath on the emperor's left side: in front of them is one resembling St. John Chrysostom, he is covering his face with his hands, he wears a scarlet cloak; next to him is an old man with gray hair resembling St. Nicholas, he has his hands in his beard, a reddish brown cloak; and the others behind them are old men and young man, and all are turning around. And between the bishops and the heretics beneath the feet of the emperor, from the choir of bishops there is a spiritual father in a klobuk, who is digging a hole and in it one sees human bones and heads, and the inscription on it, "I say the dry bones will be the resurrection of the dead and the judgment both of the righteous and of sinners." There are two palaces, one ocher with white and the other dark green; there is a church with one dome, with chambers, but there are no walls.

The **Sixth Ecumenical Council** *S. 390* was in the year 6174 [should be 6188; that is, 680-681 A.D.] under Emperor Constantine "the Big Beard" in Constantinople. 170 holy fathers gathered against the infamous Sergius, Pyrhus, Paul, Patriarch Peter, the wicked heretics and those with them. Emperor Constantine, the "Big Beard" is an old man with a gray hair and a long thin beard down to his waist, he is sitting on a throne in a palace; his cloak is reddish purple. Two bishops are sitting at the right hand of the emperor: one is an old man with gray hair resembling St. Blaise and the other resembles St. John Chrysostom; they hold their hands in prayer. Two bishops are sitting on the left side: one has brown hair and resembles St. John Chrysostom and the other has brown hair and resembles St. Nicholas, his hair comes down past his ears. Bishops are standing underneath on the right side of the emperor: the first has brown hair a beard resembling St. Basil of Caesarea, his hands are in prayer; next to him is an old man with gray hair resembling St. Athanasius; and at the end there is a bishop with brown hair and a round beard like St. Sergius; among them one can see the heads of bishops with brown hair and of old men. Monks are standing underneath at the left hand of the emperor: the first is an old man with gray hair resembling St. Sergius, the second is an old man with gray hair resembling St. Blaise; and behind them are men with brown hair and gray hair and all have klobuks, and one is young. The palace has three peaks, and the other palaces two, and one sees very little of the wall and there are two ocher towers with white.

We celebrate the **Seventh Ecumenical Council** *S. 42* of the holy fathers on October 11, on the same day as the holy apostle Philip, one of the seven deacons, and so it is painted in a row with the Apostle Philip.

This, the Seventh Ecumenical Council was the second [council] in Nicea, the gathering of 318 holy fathers under Emperor Constantine and his mother Irene against the infamous fighters against God and heretics who do not honor the holy and venerable divine icons, and so lead others astray. The emperor is young, he is sitting, resembling Solomon, wearing a crown and a scarlet cloak; Empress Irene is sitting before him on one throne and between them is an icon of "the Savior Not Made by Human Hands," and behind them is a church with three domes. Two bishops in white vestments are sitting on the right side: one is balding like St. John The Theologian and the second resembles St. Nicholas, and between them are two more, but one can see only their heads, and behind them is a column. Two bishops are sitting on the left side: one is an old man with gray hair resembling St. Blaise and the other has brown hair and a smaller beard then St. Basil of Caesarea. Four bishops are standing underneath on the emperor's right hand side: the first resembles the holy prophet Moses the God-seer; the one next to him resembles St. Athanasius; the third with brown hair resembles St. Cosmas; the fourth resembles St. Nicholas. One is holding an icon of the Most Pure [Mother of God] with the Pre-eternal Child and another is holding the Cross of Christ painted on an icon, and behind them are a multitude of holy bishops of whom only their heads can be seen. Seven priests are standing underneath on the emperor's left hand side: the first has brown hair resembling St. John Chrysostom; the second resembles Moses and is very old; the third has gray hair like St. Athanasius; the one next to him is similar [to the third] but is balding; and behind him is one resembling St. Cosmas; and at the end is a young man resembling St. George. They all have their faces turned away and are pointing down with their hands because they are not able look at the Divinity on the holy icons. The palace is ocher; there is a second palace with three peaks.

If someone is commissioned to paint the monthly *Meneion* [that is, a calendar icon], then he will paint [the first] six councils here, and he will paint the seventh council on the eleventh day of October.

17

The holy great martyr **Marina** [+ under Diocletian] *S. 396* has a green cloak, a blue tunic, a cross in her hand, in the other a scroll on which is written, "O Lord our God, grant forgiveness of sins, salvation for the sake of my suffering, and if someone honors and heeds my martyrdom, he will be saved." Some paint St. Marina similar to St. Nikita, the tormentor of demons. If someone wants to paint her decapitation, then a guard is standing on the right side, charred wood on a sword, and the head of the saint is carried by twelve angels, and there is a bright cloud over them.

And our holy father **Lazarus** *S. 76*, who fasted in the city of Gallista, is a very old man, has a shorter straight beard than St. Basil of Caesarea, and monastic robes.

On the same day our holy father abbot **Mocius,** who lived on the Ruza River, the new miracle worker of Vologda.

18

The holy martyr **Emilian** [+ 362] *S. 396* has brown hair, resembles St. Florus, a scarlet cloak, a crimson tunic, he is girded about with a towel, and has a cross in his hand.

And the holy martyr **Hyacinth** of Amastrid is young [the time he lived is unknown].

And our holy father **Pambo** the Great [fourth century] has the schema on his head, a beard like St. Simeon Stylite, he is blessing with his right hand, and in the left is a scroll on which is written, "I said I will stay on my path if I do not sin with my tongue."

And our holy father **John** of the Pecherska [Lavra, + not before 1160] is an old man like St. Menas, in his hand is a scroll, "Lord Jesus Christ, my dearest Savior, grant those who remember me during the night or during the day forgiveness of sins."

19

The holy monastic mother **Macrina** [+ 379] *S. 396*, the sister of St. Basil the Great, has a round klobuk about her head, and an ocher cassock with white.

And our holy father **Dius** [+ 430] *S. 398*, is a little gray, has a beard like St. Sergius, a greenish brown cassock with white, and in his hand a scroll.

On the same day the holy true believing and righteous Prince **Demetrius** of Priluki, is middle aged, has a longer beard than St. Cosmas, and monastic robes.

20

The holy and glorious prophet **Elias** the Thesbite [ninth century B.C.] *S. 398* is an old man with gray hair, a beard like St. John the Theologian, long hair, down over his shoulders, a dark purple cloak, the lining is goat fur, there is a towel around his waist, the tunic is green reddish brown white, in his hand is a scroll on which is written, "Striving I have been very zealous for the Lord God Almighty."

And our holy father **Abraham** of Chyukhlom has a beard like St. Cyril of White Lake, and monastic robes.

And our holy father **Sabbas,** abbot of Stromin, the Monastery of the Holy Mother of God on the River at Duvyeyaka, has a beard like St. Sergius of Radonezh, his hair does not go past his ears, and monastic robes.

21

And our holy fathers **John** and **Simeon,** who were fools for Christ's sake [+ c. 590] *S. 400.* St. John is an old man with gray hair, a straight beard longer than St. Nicholas, his cassock is greenish brown with white. St. Simeon is an old man with straight gray hair, a smaller beard than St. Nicholas, and monastic robes.

And the holy prophet **Ezekiel** [sixth century B.C.] *S. 400* is an old man with gray hair and a beard like the prophet Elias, a scarlet cloak, a green tunic, ocher with white, in his hand is a scroll on which is written, "Because I prayed for the sinful foreigners." In the printed Prologue it is written, "In appearance he was tall by a head, he had a ruddy face and a long parted beard."

And the holy prophet **Elisias** is middle aged, has a beard like St. Cosmas, a purple cloak, a blue tunic, in his hand is a scroll on which is written, "No one will enter you, the door God closed, but only God."

And our holy father **Paisius,** the abbot and miracle worker of Galich, is an old man with gray hair, a beard like St. Macarius, which is curly and forked at the end, and monastic robes.

22

The holy myrrh-bearer and equal to the apostles, **Mary Magdalene** [first century] *S. 400,* has a green cloak, an ocher tunic, she holds a white container in her hand and a cross in the left.

And the holy hieromartyr **Phocas** [see September 22, translation of relics in 403] *S. 22* is an old man with gray hair, a beard like St. Blaise, divided in two, and thick hair.

And the holy true believing princess **Anna** Kashinska resembles St. Eudokia, and monastic robes.

"The day has 9 hours and the night 15."

23

The holy martyrs **Trophimus** and **Theophilus,** and those with them [+ under

Diocletian] S. 402. St. Trophimus has brown hair, a beard like St. Cosmas, his hair comes down on one side, he has a purple cloak, a green "wild color" with ocher short tunic, a blue tunic, and a cross in his right hand.

And the holy martyr **Artemius,** the miracle worker of Grom, Verkol, and Pinezh, is a young man like St. John of Ustyuzh, in a [long Russian] shirt with blue.

And the holy hieromartyr **Apollinarius** [+ 75], the bishop of Edessa, resembles St. Blaise of Sebastia.

And our holy father **Callinicus** resembles St. Sergius of Radonezh in everything.

And our holy monastic mother **Martha** of Levkada resembles St. Eudokia.

24

The holy great martyr **Christina** [+ 300] *S. 402* wears a scarlet cloak, a white klobuk on her head, and a green with ocher tunic.

And the holy passion-bearers, the Russian princes both brothers according to the flesh, **Boris** and **Gleb,** named Roman and David in baptism [+ 1015] *S. 402, 404.* St. Boris is middle aged, he has a beard like St. Cosmas, a hat on his head with a black [fur] brim, a purple brocade coat with black [fur] lapels, a green brocade tunic, a cross in one hand and a sword in its scabbard in the other. St. Gleb is a young man, he has a little hair coming down past his ears on both sides, a hat on his head with a black [fur] brim, a scarlet brocade coat, a blue brocade tunic, he holds a cross in one hand and a sword in its scabbard in his left hand.

And the holy martyr **Phocus** resembles St. Florus in everything.

25

And the falling asleep of St. **Anna** *S. 404*, the mother of the holy Mother of God. She has a purple cloak, a blue tunic, one hand is in prayer and a cross in her right hand.

And the holy women **Olympias** and **Eupraxia** *S. 404.* St. Olympias has a blue klobuk, a green reddish brown with ocher and with white cassock, a scroll in her hand and a cross in her right hand. St. Eupraxia has a green klobuk, an ocher cassock, a scroll in her hand and a cross in her right hand.

And our holy and God-bearing father **Macarius** of Zheltov and miracle worker of Unzhensk [+ 1444], resembles St. Sergius in everything.

27

The holy hieromartyr **Hermolaus** and those with him [+ 305] *S. 406*. He is an old man with gray hair, a beard like St. Blaise, a priests' vestment, an ocher symbol of rank with decorative tracery on the shoulders, and a blue tunic.

And the holy monastic martyr **Parasceva** resembles St. Eudokia or St. Xenia.

And our holy father **Moses** of Hungary [+ 1043], the miracle worker of Pecherska, has a beard like St. John Chrysostom, brown hair, a black klobuk, a prayer rope in his right hand, the left hand is in prayer and monastic robes.

27

The holy great martyr **Panteleimon** [+ 305] *S. 406* is a young man like St. George, he has a scarlet cloak, a green short tunic and an ocher tunic, a container in his hand, and in the other a quill pen, or [he is depicted as] a soldier like St. George, and a prayer in a scroll, "Lord Jesus Christ, fulfill all my desires in this place, and grant those in the world forgiveness of sins."

And the monastic mother **Anthissa** the abbess and her twelve sisters [eighth century].

And the passing of our holy father **Diodorus** [+ 1633], the abbot of the George Hill Monastery of the Holy Trinity which is on the Vodla River of Kargopol, the new miracle worker, on November 27, in the schema, his beard is yellowish like St. Sergius, and monastic robes.

28

And the holy apostles **Prochorus** *S. 408* and **Nicinorus, Timon** and **Parmenus** [first century]. St. Prochorus is a young man wearing a purple cloak, a blue tunic, the omophorion on his shoulders and the Epistle book in his hands. St. Nicinorus is a young man wearing a blue cloak, a purple tunic, in his hand the Epistle book and omophorion. St. Timon is an old man with gray hair and a short beard like St. Blaise, like a spade, he wears a green cloak, a reddish brown with ocher tunic, the omophorion and the Gospel, and has bare feet. St. Parmenus resembles St. Florus, deacons' vestments. In the "Kievan [printed pages"] St. Prochorus is painted like Timon.

And the holy true believing prince **Andrew** Bogolyubsky resembles St. Michael of Chernigov, with a scarlet coat and a blue tunic.

And the holy martyr **Theodotia** resembles St. Parasceva.

And in Moscow they celebrate the meeting of the icon of the Holy Mother of God called **"Smolensk"** in the Novo Dyevichi Monastery.

And the holy martyr **Mercurius** of Smolensk resembles Prince St. Boris; others paint him as a young man like St. Demetrius of Thessalonica, armed and in armor, on November 24.

29

The holy martyr **Callinicus** [+ 250] *S. 408* has brown hair, resembles St. Florus, has a greenish brown with white cloak, a crimson short tunic, a scarlet tunic, a cross in his right hand and a sword in his left.

And the holy martyr **Michael** Sinovtsa, the disciple of St. Theodore of Edessa, is a young man and one can hardly see his beard.

And the holy martyr **Theodotia** and her three children [+ under Diocletian]. Theodotia resembles St. Anna.

And the holy martyr **Sophia** and her three children.

And the birth of our holy father among the saints **Nicholas,** archbishop and miracle worker of Myra in Lycia from his father Theophanes and his mother Nonna, when his mother stood him to wash and stood up a little at night.

30

The holy apostles **Silus** and **Siluanus** and those with them [first century] *S. 408.* St. Silus has brown hair and resembles St. Luke the Evangelist, has the omophorion and the Gospel, both have bare feet, a green cloak, and a blue tunic. St. Siluanus is an old man with gray hair and a beard like St. Nicholas, with the omophorion, a scarlet cloak with green, and a blue tunic.

And the holy martyr **John** the Soldier [+ fourth century] *S. 410* has brown hair, resembles St. Cosmas, has a scarlet cloak, a blue tunic, a cross in his hand and the left hand is in prayer. Others paint John in the garments of a soldier, and in the "Kievan [printed pages"] John is a young man resembling St. Demetrius, in the right hand is a cross and in the left hand a scroll.

31

The holy and righteous **Eudocimus** [829 - 842] *S. 410* has a beard like St. Cosmas, a green upper cloak, a blue tunic; some portray him like St. Florus, with an ocher cloak, a purple reddish brown short tunic, a blue tunic, a cross in one hand and the other in prayer with his fingers pointing up.

And the holy martyr **Julitta** [+ under Diocletian] resembles St. Parasceva.

And our holy and God-bearing father **Mark** of Phina *S. 410*, of Aphra Mountain where he struggled for God, is an old man with gray hair like St. Elias the prophet, a longer beard than St. Blaise down to his knees, and a little forked but straight. But he himself is [covered with] curly [hair], he is nude, his right hand is on his heart and with the left hand he is holding a branch with which he is covering his privates.

AUGUST

"The month of August has 31 days."

1

THE PROCESSION OF THE VENERABLE AND LIFE GIVING CROSS OF THE LORD [in Constantinople from the domestic chapel of the Byzantine emperor to the great church of Hagia Sophia for the blessing of water] *S.412.* And on this day we celebrate the most merciful Savior. A four cornered fountain is standing on a mound, the Savior is in a cloud over the fountain, He is blessing towards both sides. A bishop who resembles St. Blaise is standing on the right side of the fountain, and is bowing a little, and is dipping a cross into the fountain, and there are two bishops standing behind him: both are old men resembling St. Gregory the Theologian, and behind them are priests and deacons. A king, who looks like an old man with gray hair and a beard like St. Blaise, is standing a little above the priests, and with him is a queen who resembles St. Helen. Princes and noblemen, old men, men with brown hair and young men, [all of whom are] wearing coats are standing behind the queen. The Most Pure [Mother of God] is standing at the side of the Savior, then St. Basil of Caesarea; and on the left hand are St. John the Forerunner and then St. John Chrysostom. And above the bishop before the king is a priest with brown hair who is holding a big gold cross, and on the left hand side of the fountain are standing two priests who resemble Sts. Cosmas and Damian, and a third priest resembles St. Nicholas, and they are holding towards the bishop icons of the Savior and the Most Pure and the Gospel. And next to the icons stands a young deacon with incense, and on the other side of the icons stands an abbot in vestments wearing a klobuk, and behind him are spiritual fathers, the abbot is an old man with a gray hair resembling St. John the Merciful, and behind the spiritual fathers is a portable icon on high and the Cross and the [icon of our Lady "of the] Sign." Behind the elders are standing the people, men and women and children, and from the fountain is flowing a narrow stream of water, and it is covered on the side, and along the mound and the river people are sitting and laying down, and some are standing, and others are holding each other, and some are crawling, and others are carried on wagons, and all are suffering, and they are drawing water from the stream and drinking it, and some are washing and getting well, and others are bathing in the stream. At the right hand of the Savior there is a marvelous city named "Constantinople," and in it is a church with five domes and two palaces, and on the left side is a high mountain painted ocher with white.

On the same day [we celebrate] the holy and righteous **Eleazar** and the seven holy martyrs brothers according to the flesh the **Maccabees,** whose names are as follows:

Avimus, Antonius, Gurius, Eleazar, Eusebon, Achius, Marcellus, and their teacher Eleazar, and their mother [+ 166 B.C.] *S. 414*. St. Eleazar is an old man with gray hair, a beard like St. John of Damascus, on his head there is a cloth according to the first Jewish law like St. Longinus [Oct. 16] has, and there is a cross in his right hand, and in the left a book. St. **Solomonia** has a similar cloth on her head, an ocher cloak, a cross in her right hand and the left in prayer. The seven Maccabees stand with Eleazar and Solomonia up to their waists. The first is wearing green, another is wearing scarlet, another blue and all are young and they all have crosses in their hands.

2

The translation of the venerable relics of the holy protomartyr and archdeacon **Stephen** from Jerusalem to Constantinople [in 428] *S. 414*. He is a young man in deacons' vestments [See Dec. 27].

And the passing of the holy blessed **Basil** [+ 1552, feast established 1588] *S. 414*, who was a fool for Christ's sake, the miracle worker of Moscow, has curly gray hair, a not big but curly gray beard, he is entirely nude, in his left hand are a cloth and a scroll, and his right hand is in prayer raised to his chest, his hair comes past his ears.

3

Our holy fathers **Isaac** [+ 383 see May 30] *S. 416* [his successor] **Dalmatius** *S. 416*, and [Dalmatius' son] **Faustus** *S. 416*. St. Isaac has brown hair, a shorter beard than St. Nicholas, monastic robes, a reddish brown tunic. St. Dalmatius is an old man with gray hair resembling St. Blaise, dark ocher monastic robes, his tunic is dark gray. St. Faustus has brown hair, also has a beard like St. Blaise, one sees his hands in prayer and in everything.

And our holy mother **Porphyria,** named **"Pelagia,"** who previously lived as a prostitute.

4

The seven holy youths in Ephesus *S. 418*. They are all young men resembling the holy prophet Daniel. The first youth has a green robe and bare knees; the second has a scarlet cloak, and the one next to him has a scarlet cloak also. The one next to him has an ocher cloak, and the one next to him has a crimson cloak and the one next to him has a green with ocher and white cloak. On the sides there is a big cave with little trees, and the youths are laying in it, and over the cave the Savior is in a cloud, and there are containers over their heads, they [the containers] are ocher with gold writing on them. And otherwise paint the sleeper in the middle with green robes, bare knees; the second to him with the feet, a scarlet cloak, next to the second, a pur-

193

ple cloak, next to the first an ocher cloak, and next to him a crimson cloak, and the last wears green. The mountain is ocher with white, and the there are small trees by the side of the cave, the Savior as a youth is over them, He is blessing with both hands, there are things resembling containers written with gold over the cave, and in the cave at the feet of the first youth there is a small container. Their names are as follows: **Maximilian, Dionysius, Iamblichus, Martinian, Antoninus, John, Marcellus [or Exacustodianus],** who were saved in the year 372 and after their resurrection fell asleep again, the whole of their action is described on October 22.

And the holy martyr **Eleutherius** of Byzantium [+ under Maximian] *S. 418?* is middle aged, resembles St. Cosmas, has a scarlet robe, blue tunic, a cross in his hand and a scroll in the other.

And the holy monastic martyr **Eudokia** [+ c. 363 with St. Ia of Sept. 11] *S. 416,* wears a green schema, a purple mantle and an ocher tunic; she holds a scroll with both hands. And otherwise she is painted with a mantle which has trimming on the hems, the bottom is tied up in a knot, under the mantle one sees her hands, the right hand is in prayer and the left holds a scroll.

5

And the holy martyr **Eusegnius** [+ Julian the Apostate] *S. 420* is an old man with gray hair, a beard longer then St. Nicholas, a greenish brown with white cassock, a scarlet cloak coming down from the right shoulder, a purple middle tunic, a blue [long] tunic, a cross in his hand and the right hand in prayer.

6

THE HOLY DIVINELY SPLENDID TRANSFIGURATION OF OUR LORD, GOD AND SAVIOR JESUS CHRIST *S.420.* The holy prophet Elias is on a mountain, the Savior is in a cloud dressed in white clothes, He is blessing with His hand, and has a scroll in the other hand. At the left hand of the Savior one see Moses the Great, in his hands he holds a stone tablet that resembles a book, St. Peter is under the mountain laying down, St. John falls on his knees and is looking up, and St. James has his head towards the bottom and his feet towards the top, he is covering his face with his hand. St. Elias is wearing a green cloak, Moses wears purple, James wears green, Peter wears ocher, John wears scarlet, and for fuller descriptions one has to look back himself [that is, through this book for the individual descriptions of each saint.

7

The holy monastic martyr **Dometian** [+ under Julian the Apostate] *S. 422.* is an old man with gray hair, he resembles St. Sergius, he holds a scroll with both hands, and has a dark cassock.

"The day has 10 hours and the night 14."
8
Our father among the saints **Emilian,** bishop of Kizik, [+ 815] *S. 422,* has a beard like St. Athanasius, a cross patterned cloak, the omophorion and Gospel which he holds with both hands, one can see a cloth tunic.

On the same day we celebrate the miraculous icon of the most holy Mother of God "on the **Tolga.**"

And our holy fathers **Zosimas, Sabbatius** and **Herman,** miracle workers of Solovki. St. Zosimas is very old, has a beard like St. Blaise; St. Sabbatius has gray hair and a narrower beard than St. Blaise; St. Herman is an old man with gray hair and a beard like St. Alexander of Svir; and all wear monastic robes.

9
The holy and all praised apostle and evangelist **Matthias** [first century] *S. 422* is an old man with gray hair, a beard like St. John the Theologian, a purple cloak, a blue tunic, in his hand the Gospel and with the other he is blessing. [A copyist or editor confused "Matthias" with "Matthew" which is corrected here. The following does not refer to St. Matthias:] on St. Matthew's Gospel book, "The book of the birth of Jesus Christ, the Son of David, the Son of Abraham."

And the holy martyr **Maria** of Patricia resembles St. Helen.

10
The holy martyr archdeacon **Lawrence** [+ 258] *S. 422* has brown hair, a beard like St. Cosmas, a green cloak on his arm, hair is flowing down from his right ear, and deacon's vestments.

On the same day the memory of the holy blessed **Lawrence,** the fool for Christ's sake, the miracle worker of Koduzh, is an old man with gray hair, a beard like St. Blaise that is forked at the end, a cloth on his head, he is entirely nude, he has a coat on his shoulders, which is opened wide, his right hand is in prayer and there is an axe in his left hand.

11
The holy martyr **Euplus** the archdeacon [+ 304] *S. 424* has brown hair, a beard and

hair like St. Nikita the martyr, he has a censer in his hand and a bowl in the other.

And our holy fathers **Theodore** and **Basil** of the Pecherska [Lavra in the eleventh century]. St. Theodore is old with a curly graying beard somewhat larger than St. Nicholas. St. Basil is an old man with gray hair, a beard like St. Sergius. They are wearing klobuks, monastic robes and their hands are held in prayer.

12

The holy martyrs **Photius** and **Anikita** [+ under Diocletian] *S. 424.* St. Photius has brown hair, a green cloak, a scarlet tunic, a cross in his right hand and a container similar to a deacon's in the left hand, held from underneath. And St. Anikita is a young man resembling St. George, has a purple cloak, a blue tunic, a cross in his right hand and he is holding his cloak with his left. Elsewhere he is painted with purple robes which he is holding in his left hand, the tunic at the right elbow, the upper garment, and on the left shoulder the robes on top. And in the "Kievan [printed] pages" St. Anikita's face resembles St. Cosmas.

And the holy father **Athanasius** of Alexandria.

13

Our holy father **Maximus** the Confessor [translation of his relics; see Jan. 21] *S. 424* is an old man with gray hair, a longer beard than St. Blaise, but in the "Kievan [printed pages"] it is shorter, wears monastic robes, a dark ocher tunic, and he holds a scroll in his hands.

And the holy martyr **Eudokia** [+ 460] resembles St. Helen the empress.

And the closing of the feast of the Transfiguration of the Lord.

And St. **Maximus** of Urozh [also Nov. 11, + 1433; relics uncovered incorrupt on this day in 1568], miracle worker of Moscow, is an old man with gray hair, a beard like St. Nicholas, nude, he has a cloth around his waist, his hands are in prayer.

14

The holy prophet **Micah** [c. 700 B.C.] *S. 426* is an old man with gray hair, a beard like St. John the Theologian, he has a lock of hair on his shoulder like St. Elias the prophet, he is looking towards the left, he has a green reddish brown cloak, a blue tunic, in his left hand is a scroll on which is written, "You, O Bethlehem, of the land of Judah, you are not the least among the masters of the Jews, because from you will come the leader who will pasture his people of Israel."

And our holy fathers **Theodosius** of the Pecherska Lavra and St. **Sergius** of Radonezh.

15

THE FALLING ASLEEP OF OUR LADY, THE MOST HOLY MOTHER OF GOD AND EVER VIRGIN MARY *S. 426.* Over the Savior is a fiery cherub, the Savior is holding the white soul of the most pure Mother of God. The Most Pure is lying on a bed, with her hands to her heart. An old bishop with gray hair stands on the right side; he resembles St. Blaise and has a book in his hand. An old bishop with gray hair and a long beard is standing on the left side with a book in his hands, and behind him two widowed women are crying. At the head of the Most Pure is the Apostle Peter with incense, and behind him are five apostles; and at the feet stands St. Paul, he is bowing down a little, and behind him are five apostles. On one side is an ocher with white palace, and on the other side is a green palace; one sees a little of the walls which are ocher with white.

And the miraculous icon of the most pure Mother of God **"Theodorov"** which is in Kostrom, and the full Dormition of the Mother of God which is painted on boards.

16

The translation of the image of our Lord, God and Savior Jesus Christ **"Not Made By Hands,"** which is the "Towel" from Edessa to the city of Constantinople [in 944] *S. 428.* A young apostle is holding the towel on which the Savior is depicted, a king in a crown is standing before it, he is crossing himself, the king is an old man with gray hair, he resembles the Prophet David, and behind him is a bed and a couch, and behind the bed are standing princes and noblemen, two are old men, the third is a young man, and behind them is a queen resembling St. Helen. Behind the apostle is a bishop resembling St. Blaise with a book, and behind him are three priests with brown hair, the middle priest is a young man, and behind them is a city, and in the city a church and a palace, and behind the church there is a big palace with three chambers. Some paint King Abgar with a scroll on his right hand on which is written, "A divine vision, a divine miracle." And in the left hand a scroll which says, "O Christ God, those who place their hope in You will never be cast out." And otherwise an angel of the Lord is holding the "Image Not Made By Hands on the Towel;" the angel wears a crimson cloak and a blue tunic, and in the "Kievan pages" it is similar.

And the holy martyr **Diomedas** [+ under Diocletian] *S. 428* resembles St. Florus, he has brown hair, a scarlet cloak, an ocher short tunic, a green tunic, a cross in his hand and a container in the other.

17

The holy hieromartyr **Myron** [+ 251] *S. 428* is an old man with gray hair, a beard like St. Blaise or shorter, priests' vestments, and holds the Gospel.

And our holy father **Olympius** of the Pecherska [Lavra + 1114]. St. Olympius [or Alypy] is an old man with a beard like St. Sergius that is narrow at the end, his gray hair comes down below his ears, he has the schema on his shoulders, he holds in icon of the Mother of God in his right hand and wears monastic robes.

And the holy martyrs **Paul** and **Juliana** [+ 273]. St. Paul is middle aged with curly hair, he has a beard like St. Cosmas, a scarlet cloak, a blue tunic, a cross in his hand and the left hands in prayer. St. Juliana resembles St. Parasceva ["Friday"] in everything and is looking towards Paul.

18

The holy martyrs **Florus** and **Laurus** [second century] *S. 430.* St. Florus resembles St. Nikita by his beard, St. Sergius by his hair, he has a scarlet with ocher cloak, a blue tunic, a cross in the right hand and the left hand in prayer. St. Laurus is a young man like St. George, with a scarlet cloak, an ocher with white tunic, a cross in the right hand, the left in prayer, the fingers are pointing up. In the "Kievan [printed pages"] it is so, in their right hands are crosses and scrolls, "Master of life and death, if someone remembers them in his prayers, hear him quickly, forgive and have mercy on him."

On the same day our father among the saints **Anthony,** archbishop of Vologda, the miracle worker, has a brown beard, at the end it is narrower than St. Basil of Caesarea, in a cap with the omophorion and Gospel, and bishops' vestments.

19

The holy martyr **Andrew** Stratelates and the two thousand five hundred ninety-three with him [+ under Maximian] *S. 430.* He is an old man with curly gray hair, a beard like St. John the Theologian, a breastplate, a green cloak, his armor has a pattern of little boxes, a green cloak [repeated], a blue tunic, purple leggings, a cross in his right hand, a spear in the left, and a shield behind his left hand.

And the holy martyr **Thecla** [+ 304], resembles St. Eudokia.

And our holy father among the saints **Pitirim,** bishop of Vologda, has a black klobuk on his head, is starting to gray, has a beard like St. Blaise or curly, but wider, a bishops' mantle with stripes, a reddish brown tunic, in the schema, in his hands a scroll; some paint a bishops' cap on his head.

And the holy martyr **Callistratus** resembles St. Demetrius.

20

The holy prophet **Samuel** [eleventh century B.C.] *S. 430* is an old man and has gray hair like Aaron, a horn in his hand, his beard, hair and garments resemble the prophet Zachariah, he holds a horn in his left hand, and with the right hand he is pointing to it [the horn], a crimson cloak, ocher on the shoulders, a green short tunic, a blue tunic, he has a scroll, "The Lord said, 'Fill a horn with olive oil, go to Bethlehem and summon Jesse and his sons to sacrifice, for I have seen among them a king, and anoint him for Me as I told you.'"

And the holy martyrs who suffered in **Aphrinia** are standing in every different appearance.

And the passing of our holy father **Alexander** of Tver the miracle worker.

21

The holy apostle **Thaddaeus** [first century] *S. 432* is an old man with gray hair, a shorter beard than St. John the Theologian, or similar, a purple cloak, a blue tunic, a scroll in his hand and a cross in the other.

And the holy martyr **Bassia** [+ under Maximian] *S. 432* has a purple cloak, a green tunic, a cross in her right hand and the left is in prayer, and her children **Theognia** and **Agania** are young. And others paint **Lucianus** and **Alexander** and they are standing before her in [Russian] shirts.

And the holy martyr **Callinicus** is a young man like St. Demetrius of Thessalonica, he has a green cloak, a scarlet tunic, a cross in his hand and a towel in the other.

And the passing of our holy father **Abraham** [+ 1221], archimandrite of Smolensk, the miracle worker, is an old man with thick gray hair like St. Andrew the first called, a wider beard than St. Blaise, but forked, monastic robes, and in his "Life" it is written that his form and appearance are like St. Basil the Great, a similar black beard, but has a balding head.

And the monastic Saint **Ephraim** of Smolensk [+ 1238], the miracle worker is in the schema, a beard like St. Anthony the Roman of Novgorod, monastic robes, and others paint him like St. Sabbas the Sanctified.

22

The holy martyr **Agathonicus** and those with him [+ under Maximian] *S. 432.* He has brown hair, a scanty beard like St. Florus, a scarlet cloak, an ocher with white tunic, a knot on his right shoulder but not on the left, he is holding his cloak with his left hand, the short tunic is green.

And the holy martyr **Anthysa** resembles St. Anna.

23

The holy martyr **Lupus** [with St. Demetrius of Thessalonica] *S. 432* resembles St. George, he has a purple cloak, a green tunic, a cross in his hand and the left hand is in prayer; but in the "Kievan [printed pages"] Lupus resembles St. Agathonicus.

And our father among the saints **Callinicus** [+ 963], patriarch of Constantinople, is an old man with gray hair, a beard like St. Sergius, a reddish brown with white tunic, and monastic robes or bishops' vestments.

The translation of the venerable relics of the holy true believing Prince **Constantine** of Uglich.

And the close of the feast of the Falling Asleep of the Mother of God.

"The day has 10 hours and the night 14."

24

The holy hieromartyr and apostle **Eutyches,** the disciple of Saint John the Theologian [+ first century] *S. 434,* is an old man with gray hair, a shorter beard than St. Blaise, a purple cloak, a blue tunic, the omophorion on his shoulders, he is holding a book with both hands.

And the translation of the venerable relics of our father among the saints **Peter,** metropolitan of Moscow and all Russia, miracle worker [in 1479] *S. 434.* Two priests, one with brown hair resembling St. Nicholas and the second is an old man with gray hair resembling St. Peter, are carrying [the coffin] into the church of the most holy Mother of God. There is a young deacon at [the Saint's] feet; at the head [of the Saint] another deacon, who appears to be an old man, is bowing his head to the coffin. The church has five domes, the metropolitan accompanying [the coffin] has his hands in prayer, his beard is smaller than St. Peter the metropolitan [the deceased], behind the metropolitan [leading the mourners] is a prince who is an old man with gray hair, a beard like St. Nicholas, a purple brocade cloak, a blue brocade tunic, his hands are in prayer, behind him is a princess with a scarlet cloak, a big black collar, and one sees all kinds of princes and noblemen and commoners of every description.

Next to the church is a palace, and on the other side is a tower with three peaks, and beyond the church a wall.

On the same day the passing of our holy father **Arsenius** [+ 1550] the abbot of the Komelsky Monastery, miracle worker of Vologda, is an old man with gray hair, a beard like St. Blaise, monastic robes, and a green tunic.

25

The uncovering of the venerable relics of the holy apostle **Bartholomew** from the island of Cyprus to the city of Lipari [in the sixth century] *S. 436.* [The Saint] is an old man with gray hair, has a beard like St. John the Theologian, a purple cloak, a blue tunic and [has bare feet like St. Titus].

And the memory of the holy apostle **Titus** [first century] *S. 436* who resembles St. John Chrysostom in the omophorion, a purple reddish brown cloak, a blue tunic, he holds a scroll with both hands and has bare feet.

26

The holy martyrs **Adrian** and **Natalia** [fourth century] *S. 436.* St. [Adrian] has brown hair and resembles St. Florus, a scarlet cloak, ocher at the collar, a blue tunic, a cross in the right hand and his left hand is held down. *MA 355* St. Natalia has a green cloak, a crimson with white tunic, she holds a cross in one hand and the other is pointing to the cloak.

On the same day we celebrate the meeting of the miraculous icon of the most holy Mother of God "of **Vladimir**" from the invasion of the God-less Hagarians [Tatars], the pagan King Tamerlane, who is called the "Iron Foot" [in 1395] *S. 438.* Out of the city comes Bishop Cyprian in a saccos and a cap with incense, he is an old man with gray hair, a longer beard than St. Basil of Caesarea, and behind him is Great Prince Basil who has brown hair and a beard longer than St. Constantine, and behind him is a princess. The prince is wearing a purple brocade cloak, a blue brocade tunic; the princess wears a scarlet cloak, a big beaver fur collar, and all [her] regalia. Behind Metropolitan Cyprian one sees two bishops; one has brown hair, a beard longer than Metropolitan Cyprian, the other also has brown hair, a beard like St. Cosmas. A priest is preceding them, he is an old man like St. Blaise, the people are coming out of the city, and he is carrying a portable icon of the Savior, and other deacons are carrying crosses and others are carrying a portable icon of the Most Pure Hodigitria of Vladimir; one priest is an old man with gray hair like St. Blaise, the other resembles St. Nicholas, and they are carrying it high over their heads, and under the icon is a red brocade cloth cover, and behind are priests and deacons and spiritual fathers and many people, and behind them is a high mountain, ocher with white, and behind the bishops and the princes is a white city, ocher with white, and three towers and in it one sees a church with five domes, and two palaces; one green and one purple.

27

Our holy father **Pimen** the Great [+ 450] *S. 440* is an old man with balding gray hair, a beard like St. Nicholas, monastic robes, a greenish brown tunic and he holds a scroll.

28

Our holy father **Moses** the Moor [+ 400] *S. 440* is an old man with gray hair, a narrower beard then St. Sergius, monastic robes, an ocher with white tunic, the right hand is in prayer, and a scroll in the left, "Brothers, so that we may receive forgiveness of sins, let us force ourselves a little, lest we get lazy."

And our holy father **Sabbas** of Kripets [+ 1495], miracle worker of Pskov, is an old man with gray hair, a beard like St. Peter the apostle, in the schema, and monastic robes; and elsewhere he is painted with an oblong beard, very gray, and divided into many strands.

2

THE DECAPITATION OF THE VENERABLE HEAD OF ST. JOHN THE BAPTIST OF THE LORD *S. 442*. Wearing a furry green cloak, he is bowed down on his elbows without his head, and the cut off head is laying in front of him in a container, blood and water are flowing from him, a soldier is standing behind him, he is raising his sword, in his left hand is a scabbard, a scarlet cloak, the soldier is a young man, he is girded with a towel, but the long ends [of the towel] are hanging in the blood, he has blue leggings, his arms are bare up to his elbows, and behind him is an ocher mountain with white, and behind the Forerunner is a prison with one door, and there is a wall around it; and elsewhere the Forerunner is painted in a hair garment, his hands are tied, a scarlet cloak, a green tunic, an ocher mountain, the soldier is girded with a towel, who is standing near the Forerunner. There is a scroll in his [St. John's] hand, "I have seen and witnessed to Him, this is the Lamb of God, who takes away the sins of the whole world. Repent, because the kingdom of heaven is near. Behold, the axe is already laid to the root of the tree, because every tree which does not bear good fruit will be cut off and thrown into the fire."

30

Our fathers among the saints **Alexander** [+ 340] *S. 442* and **John** [+ 595, also on Sept. 2] *S. 444* and **Paul** the New [+ 784] *S. 444*, patriarchs of Constantinople. St.

Alexander has brown hair, he resembles St. Clement, the pope of Rome, in a saccos; St. John is an old man with gray hair, a bigger beard than St. Athanasius which is shaggy at the end, he has a blue saccos; St. Paul is starting to gray, with a curly beard like St. Blaise, a purple saccos; they all have an omophorion and a Gospel book.

And the passing of our holy father **Alexander** of Svir [+ 1533] *S. 444,* the miracle worker, is an old man with gray hair, his head is balding, his white beard is not very big, sparse and wide, thinner than St. Sergius, monastic robes, a reddish brown tunic, he is blessing with his hand, and in the other is a scroll on which is written, "Brothers, suffer sorrows and difficulties so that you will be saved from eternal torments."

And the holy martyr **Felix** is a young man with a face resembling the Archangel Gabriel, martyrs' robes, three garments like St. Cosmas, a cross in his hand, in the other hand a rolled up scroll, brown hair, a scarlet cloak, the tunic looks like cloth.

31

THE PLACING OF THE VENERABLE SASH OF THE MOST HOLY MOTHER OF GOD IN BLACHERENES, BEING TRANSLATED BY BISHOP ZENON TO CONSTANTINOPLE [this day honors a miracle in the tenth century] *S. 446.* There is a white church with three domes, a bishop is standing in a saccos, he is an old man with gray hair, a beard smaller than the Theologian, before the icon of the Most Pure behind the altar stands a bishop, scarlet, and on the altar stands a container with four corners, which resembles a small all gold open chest, and the bishop with his hands is placing the scarlet sash with gold brushes into the chest, and he is looking at the Most Pure, and behind him is a young deacon with incense, and a container in the other hand, and a king is standing behind him. Some paint it as follows: there is a white church with three domes, the bishop is standing before the holy portable icon of the Most Pure which is over the altar, the altar is red silk, a bishop in a saccos is praying on the step, behind him is a young deacon holding incense, in the other hand a container, behind the deacon is an old priest with gray hair, and a beard longer than St. Nicholas, behind the priest is an old man, he has a beard resembling the priest in front of him, and behind them is a crowd of different people standing, the metropolitan is praying, he is an old man with gray hair and a beard shorter than St. John the Theologian, over the icon is a blue cover.

Stroganov Pattern Book

The Stroganov Drawings included in the 1903 Bolshakov Edition would have appeared here. They are not reproduced in this volume since they have been published already by Oakwood Publications as *An Iconographer's Patternbook: The Stroganov Tradition,* translated and edited by Fr. Christopher P. Kelley, 1992, 530 pages. (ISBN: 0-9618545-3-7) The Oakwood English edition of the Stroganov was translated from the 1869 Moscow *Stroganov Patternbook* since the drawings there were more clear and detailed and the Slavonic captions were more complete.

Appendïx

1

THE LADDER OF DIVINE ASCENT

2

JUDAS TAKES THE MONEY FROM THE SANDHEDRIN

3

The Mystical Supper

4

JESUS BEFORE PILATE

5

JESUS BEFORE HEROD

6

PILATE WASHES HIS HANDS

7

SIMON OF CYRENE CARRIES CHRIST'S CROSS

8

JOSEPH ASKING FOR THE BODY OF CHRIST

1

THREE SAINTS

SCENE FROM ST. ELIAS' LIFE: THE PRIESTS OF BAAL PRAY

SCENE FROM ST. ELIAS' LIFE: ELIAS KILLS THE PRIESTS' OF BAAL

4

SCENE FROM ST. ELIAS' LIFE: ELIAS PRAYS TO GOD

EXILE TO BABYLON

6

сотворенїе света

SCENE FROM GENESIS: THE CREATION OF LIGHT

SCENE FROM GENESIS: NOAH SUMMONS THE ANIMALS

SCENE FROM GENESIS: THE ANGEL LEADS LOT AWAY FROM SODOM

Scene from Genesis: Sara sends away Hagar

SCENE FROM GENESIS: CREATION OF ANIMALS

SCENE FROM GENESIS: PARALYTIC LET DOWN THROUGH ROOF

SCENE FROM GENESIS: SARAH AND ABRAHAM PREPARE FOOD FOR THE THREE YOUNG MEN

13

SCENE FROM MATTHEW: TWO DEMONIACS AT GADARA

SCENE FROM GOSPEL: JESUS CURES CRIPPLE

SCENE FROM LUKE: THE PRODIGAL SON

SCENE FROM GENESIS: ADAM AND EVE BURY ABEL

17

SCENE FROM JOHN: JESUS HEALS THE BLIND MAN

SCENE FROM GOSPEL: JESUS HEALS THE MAN WITH PALSY

SCENE FROM LUKE: JESUS RAISES THE WIDOW'S SON

SCENE FROM JOHN: JESUS CURES THE MAN BORN BLIND

SCENE FROM JOHN: THE WEDDING AT CANA

SCENE FROM LUKE: JESUS RAISES THE DAUGHTER OF JAORIUS

JESUS CALMS THE STORM

END OF BOLSHAKOV

COMPLETE TEXT

FOOTNOTES

1 This may be another name for the text called the "Kievan printed pages" quoted throughout the text. The cathedral in Kiev at that time was the great and ancient church of St. Sophia before the building of the present St. Vladimir Cathedral in the nineteenth century.

2 This may be the *(Summary Iconographic Patternbook of the XVIII Century)* compiled by G. Filimonov, Moscow, 1874 which is quoted in popular literature about iconography.

3 A figurative, that is, illustrated icon painter's guide. See the Introduction to *An Iconographer's Patternbook: The Stroganov Tradition* translated and edited by Fr. Christopher P. Kelley, Oakwood Publications, 1992, for more details.

4 These drawings are the sets of 8 and 23 line drawings found in the "Appendix."

5 Migne, PG 120, col. 181 and following.

6 The letter "Z" is also used for the numeral "7" in the Greek language.

7 PG 144, col. 1338.

8 Quinisext, 692, canon C. The Nicene and Post-Nicene Fathers, Second Series, Vol. xiv, page 407.

9 *The Rudder,* The Sixth Ecumenical Council, Canon C, page 407: translated by D. Cummings.

10 Reprinted in Migne, PG 155, col. 112.

11 *Orthodox Life,* No. 2., 1994, page 33.

12 The "clerical rules" referred to through out this section are the Orthodox Church's rules and traditions concerning the worthiness of candidates for the clergy and the life style of the clergy. There were probably many more rules which were more strictly enforced in the seventeenth century than now. Currently, for example, a man who committed certain serious and/or canonical sins, or who has been married twice can not be ordained. Neither can he be married to a woman who was married before, nor can he remarry and continue to serve as a clergyman. The clergy may not dance, gamble, frequent taverns, race tracks, etc. Since the icon painters perform a sacred and liturgical service for the Church like the clergy do, therefore they must meet the qualifications for candidates for ordination and live the clerical life style of faith, prayer and fasting.

13 See Billington, James. *The Icon and the Axe,* New York, 1966, page 144.

14 Found in Migne, PG 78, col. 197 - 198.

15 The *Typicon* has the same opening words. See the Glossary.

16 The Indiction in the Christian Roman Empire was the first day of the fiscal and church year that begins September 1. More exactly it was the cycle of fifteen calendar years established in the year 313 A.D.

17 The reader will find a number of almanac references printed in italics throughout the book. These references are found in the *Typicon* and are not always consistent having been taken from various manuscript traditions. The references are correct according to the Julian or "old" calendar, a reckoning still followed by the majority of autocephalous and autonomous Orthodox Churches today. To determine the Gregorian or "new" calendar date, add 13 days. Thus, September 8 falls on September 21 according to the civil calendar used throughout most of the world.

18 This can be translated also as the "leave taking" of the feast.

19 St. Alexander Nevsky was portrayed as a monk until the Holy Ruling Synod of Russia resolved in June of 1724 that in painting icons of Alexander Nevsky, no one on any account is to portray this saint as a monk, but rather in the robes of a Grand Prince.

20 This discrepancy is in the original.

21 It is not clear why the name "Timolaus" changes to "Viculus." In Latin *viculus* means "hamlet" which could be the proper name "Hamlet."

THE "A LA VIEILLE RUSSIE" CALENDAR ICONS

In the Russian Orthodox Church every day of the year commemorates one or more saints or is dedicated to a Holy Day. The collective icons depicting all the saints and feast days are called *"Svyattsy"* in Russian. There are twelve panels, one for each month, painted on both sides, making twenty-four plates. The panels are small, 5" x 5", and the number of figures is large. These are truly remarkable miniatures. They are so small that it is difficult for the eye to appreciate their outstanding quality. Every saint is represented in strict, traditional garb, with his particular attributes. Even the features of the face, no larger than a nail head, are easily distinguishable, permitting one to identify each saint, despite the fact that some of the inscriptions bearing the names in red letters have disappeared. The proportions of the figures are elongated and graceful, the colors diversified. The paintings are strongly reminiscent of the Novgorod School. They have the same soberness and purity of style of that school of Russian iconography. The figures in the feast day icons are in classical attitudes; the faces have Grecian profiles.

It was determined that the panels were not painted by a Novgorod artist of the fifteenth century, but rather by a "Tsar's Icon Painter" of the period of Ivan the terrible (1533 - 1584). The warm general color scheme is typical of the Moscow group of the "Tsar's Icon Painters" who were famous and unexcelled in the art of the miniature. Most interesting is the material on which the *"Svyattsy"* are painted. Ordinarily at that time icons were painted on specially prepared wooden panels. However, wooden panels were not used for these "Calendar Icons." Each panel, if it can be called such, is merely a rectangular piece of linen hardened by the dry *"levkas"*, Russian for the priming of gypsum and glue. In view of the extreme delicacy of these tiny icons which are over three hundred years old, one wonders how the whole group, fragile as it is, came down to modern times and to this country safe and unharmed - unmolested by fires, the rapaciousness of thieves, children's carelessness, and the extremes of climate.

As far as A La Vieille Russie has been able to determine as the result of thorough research in the catalogues of museums, exhibitions and private collections, no other complete set of *"Svyattsy"* of the sixteenth century is known to exist. Extensive exhibitions of Russian religious art were held in 1913 in Moscow and St. Petersburg in commemoration of the three hundredth anniversary of the Romanov Dynasty, but there are no *"Svyattsy"* illustrated in the thick catalogues of these exhibitions.

The saints and feasts are listed from left to right and the numbers denote the day of the month. Oakwood Publications is most grateful to A La Vieille Russie, Incorporated of New York City, for permission to publish this remarkable set of icons in its entirety.

(Photographs are of a Menology Screen from the Russian Stroganov School. late 16th century. The screen actually consists of twelve two-sided panels, representing the months in the Church calendar. The panels are painted with tempera on course linen. Each panel is a true miniature, 5 by 5 inches. Individual figures are less than 2 inches tall. The individual panels are not on wood, but rather on hardened linen.)

Permission to include Menology (Menaion) Icons courtesy of A La Vieille Russie, New York. Panel Photographer: Basil Parent

DECEMBER *(Front)* **Top** 1 Nahum; Philaret the Merciful; 2 Habakkuk; 3 Sophonias; St. Theodore of Alexandria; St. John the Silent; 4 St. Barbara; St. John of Damascus; 5 St. Sabbas; 6 St. Nicholas; 7 St. Ambrose; St Anthony; **Middle** 8 St. Patapius; 9 Conception by St. Anna; 10 Sts. Menas, Eugraphus and Hermogenes; 11 St. Daniel the Stylite; 12 St. Spyridon; 13 Sts. Eustratius, Eugene, and Orestes; St Arsenius; **Bottom** 14 Sts. Thrysus, Leucius, Philemon; 15 St. Eleutherius; St. Paul of Latros; St. Stephen of Surozh; 16 Haggai; 17 Prophet Daniel; the Youths in the Fiery Furnace. Photograph courtesy of A La Vieille Russie.

241

DECEMBER *(Back)* **Top** 18 St. Sebastian; St. Timothy; 19 St. Boniface; 20 St. Ignatius; 21 St. Juliana; St. Peter of Moscow; 22 St. Anastasia; 23 (5 of) 10 Martyrs of Crete; 24 St. Eugenia; **Middle** 25 Nativity of Jesus Christ; 26 Synaxis of the Mother of God; Sts. Euthymius, Joseph, King David, James, (another) St. Euthymius; **Bottom** 27 St. Stephen; St Theodore; 28 20,000 Martyrs; 29 14,000 Martyrs; St. Marcellus; 30 St. Anysia; St. Zoticus; 31 St. Melania. Photograph courtesy of A La Vieille Russie.

BIBLIOGRAPHY

(Book of Rules of the Holy Apostles, the Holy Ecumenical and Local Councils, and the Holy Fathers) Synodal Press, Moscow, 1893, "*Titul*" reprint, St. Petersburg, Russia, 1993, [in Church Slavonic].

Bulgakov, S. V. *(Desk Reference Book for Ordained Church Ministers) ["Nastolnaya Kniga"]*, second ed., Kharkov, 1900, [in Russian].

Climacus, St. John. *The Ladder of Divine Ascent,* Holy Transfiguration Monastery, Boston, Massachusetts, 1978.

Cracraft, James. *The Church Reform of Peter the Great,* Macmillan, London, 1971.

Dyachenko, Priest Magister Gregory. *(Complete Church Slavonic Dictionary)* in two volumes, Moscow, 1899 [from Slavonic to Russian].

Fedotov, George P. *The Russian Religious Mind: Kievan Christianity,* Harvard University Press, Cambridge, Massachusetts, 1947.

_____. *The Russian Religious Mind: The Middle Ages - the Thirteenth to the Fifteenth Centuries,* (vol. ii), Harvard University Press, Cambridge Massachusetts, 1956.

Kontzevitch, I. M. *The Acquisition of the Holy Spirit in Ancient Russia* trans. Olga Koshansky, St. Herman of Alaska Brotherhood, 1988.

Minia in twelve volumes, Press of the Kievan Pecherska Lavra, 1893 - 1894, [in Church Slavonic].

Nicodemus and Agapius, Sts., *The Rudder,* trans. D. Cummings, reprint, Chicago, 1983.

Payne, Pierre Robert Stephen. *Ivan the Terrible,* Thomas Y. Crowell Co., New York, 1975.

Poselyanin, E. ed. *(The Mother of God: a Complete Illustrated Description of Her Earthly Life and the Miracle Working Icons Blessed with Her Name.)* St. Petersburg, no date, [in Russian].

Prologue - Synaxarion, in two volumes, Synodal Press in St. Petersburg, 1896, [in Church Slavonic].

St. Herman Calendar annual publication of the St. Herman of Alaska Brotherhood, Platina, CA.

Smirnitsky, Prof. A. I. *Russian-English Dictionary*, E. P. Hutton, New York, 1981.

Taisia, Nun ed. *(The Lives of the Russian Saints: 1000 Years of Russian Sanctity)* second ed. Holy Trinity Russian Orthodox Monastery, Jordanville, NY, 1983, [in Russian].

(Trinity Russian Orthodox Calendar) annual publication of Holy Trinity Monastery, Jordanville, NY, [in Russian].

(Typikon: this is the exposition of the Church Order, which is called the Rule) The Synodal Press, Moscow, 1904 [in Church Slavonic].

Velimirovic, Bishop [St.] Nikolai. *The Prologue from Ochrid: Lives of the Saints and Homilies for every day in the Year,* in four volumes, Lazarica Press, Birmingham, 1985.

See "Books from Oakwood Publications" for
An Iconographer's Patternbook: the Stroganov Tradition
The Icon: Image of the Invisible
The "Painter's Manual" of Dionysius of Fourna

Icon-Related Books from Oakwood Publications

The Image of God the Father in Orthodox Theology & Iconography & Other Essays, <u>Fr. Steven Bigham</u>, 1994. ISBN 0-879038-15-3.
The Illuminated Gospel of St. Matthew: Calligraphy and Iconographic Illuminations in the Byzantine/Slavic Style, <u>Vladislav Andrejev</u>, 1993. ISBN 1-879038-08-0.
An Iconographer's Patternbook: The Stroganov Tradition, <u>Fr. Christopher P. Kelley</u>, 1992. ISBN 0-9618545-3-7.
The Painter's Manual of Dionysius of Fourna, <u>Paul Hetherington</u>, 1990. ISBN 1-879038-01-3.
The Icon: Image of the Invisible: Elements of Theology, Aesthetics and Technique, <u>Egon Sendler</u>, 1988. ISBN 0-9618545-07-2.
The Art of the Icon: A Theology of Beauty, <u>Paul Evdokimov</u>, 1989. ISBN 0-9618545-4-5.
Dynamic Symmetry Proportional System Is Found in Some Byzantine and Russian Icons of the 14th-16th Centuries, <u>Karyl Knee</u>, 1989. ISBN 0-9618545-2-9.
Icon Collections in the United States, <u>John Barns</u>, 1992. ISBN 0-879038-06-4.
Icons & Iconpainting (Videotape), <u>Dennis Bell</u>, 1991. ISBN 0-879038-02-1.
Unknown Palekh, <u>Vera Torzhkova</u>, 1994. ISBN 1-879038-17X.
The Iconographer's Sketchbook, <u>Charles Kovacs</u>, 1995. ISBN 1-879038-10-2.
Workbook for 'The Icon: Image of the Invisible', <u>Charles Rohrbacher</u>, Future Publication. ISBN 1-879038-11-0.
Icons of the World: Types and Styles, Slide Set, <u>John Barns</u>, Future Publication. ISBN 1-879038-21-8.

Other Books by Oakwood Publications

Orthodox Fathers, Orthodox Faith (From a Trilogy for Christ), <u>Touma Al-Khoury</u>. 1994. ISBN 1-879038-20-X.
Directory of Orthodox Parishes & Institutions in North America, 1994 Edition (For <u>Orthodox People Together</u>), 1994. ISBN 1-879038-16-1.
The Ministry of Women in the Church, <u>Elisabeth Behr-Sigel</u>, 1991. ISBN 0-9618545-6-1.
The Place of the Heart: An Introduction to Orthodox Spirituality, <u>Elisabeth Behr Sigel</u>, 1992. ISBN 10879038-04-8.
The Biography of Alexander Men, <u>Yves Hamant</u>, Future Publication. 1-879038-12-9.

Index
Church Calendar Year

A

Aaroi 175
Abbacum 89
Abdias 49, 83, 180
Abdius 67
Abel 131
Abercius 69
Abibus 81
Abraham of Chyukhlom 187
Abraham of Pecherska Lavra 114
Abraham of Rostov 73
Abraham of Smolensk 199
Abraham of Vladimir 127
Abraham of V'luvidsk 114
Abraham the monastic 58, 72
Abraham the Recluse 73
Abram of Vladimir 136
Absinyania 78
Acacius in the "Ladder" 176
Acacius of Melitene 141
Acacius of Sinai 87
Acacius of the "Ladder" 88
Acacius of Tver 108
Acacius the Patriarch 65
Achius 193
Adrian 141, 201
Adrian of Vologda 130
Aeithalas 46
Aeithalas the deacon 76
Agabus 138
Agania 199
Agape 140
Agapia 55
Agapia of Thessalonica 136
Agapitus 129
Agapitus of Rome 141
Agapitus of the Pecherska Lavra 162
Agapius the child martyr 55
Agatha 114
Agathangelus 109

Agathapodes 137
Agathocleia 54
Agathonica 65
Agathonicus 199
Aggaeus 93
Aglae 95
Aglaida 132
Agnes 106, 109
Agrippina 169
Akepsimas 76
Akindynus 76
Alevtina 181
Alexander 60, 165
Alexander Nevsky 85
Alexander of Kushta 165
Alexander of Oshevensk 142
Alexander of Svir 203
Alexander of Thessalonica 79
Alexander of Tver 199
Alexander the child 199
Alexander the martyr 125, 154
Alexander the monastic 119
Alexander the Patriarch 202
Alexander Yaroslavich 57
Alexandra 78, 131, 156
Alexandra the Empress 143
Alexis of Moscow 117, 156
Alexis the Man of God 129
Alypius the Stylite 86
Alypy 198
Amisus, seven martyrs at 131
Ammon 46
Amos 167
Amphilochius 85
Amphilochius of Glushetsk 65, 85
Amplias 74
Ananias 61
Ananias the martyr 89, 90
Ananias the Youth 94
Ananius the Presbyter 88
Anapholiathota 131

Anastasia 97
Anastasia of Thessalonica 74
Anastasia the martyr 140
Anastasia the monastic 65, 127
Anastasia the Roman 73
Anastasia Vasilievna 159
Anastasius 142
Anastasius of Alexandria 127
Anatolius 84
Andreanus 141
Andreanus of Vologda 130
Andrew 88, 172
Andrew Bogolyubsky 172, 189
Andrew of Crete 175
Andrew of Crete, martyr 67
Andrew of Smolensk 72
Andrew Stratelates 198
Andrew the bishop 56
Andrew the fool 61, 62
Andrew the holy fool 160
Andronicus 64, 65, 150, 155
Andronicus of Moscow 166
Anempodistus 76
Anikita 196
Anna 84, 188
Anna, Conception by 91
Anna Kashinska 187
Anna of Nizhegorod 133
Anna the martyr 70
Anna the monastic 74, 167
Anna the Prophetess 92, 113
Anna with St. Joachim 50
Anthia 93
Anthimus 47
Anthimus the Bishop 99
Anthissa 189
Anthony 177
Anthony of Lithuania 140
Anthony of Siya 91
Anthony of the Pecherska Lavra 150, 178
Anthony of Vologda 198
Anthony the Great 107
Anthony the Patriarch 117
Anthony the Roman 107
Anthony the youth 70
Anthusa 139, 141

Anthymus 68, 118
Anthysa 200
Antiochus 180
Antipas 139
Antipater 146
Antonida 123, 166
Antonina 165
Antoninus 81, 194
Antonius 193
Anysia 100
Aphodita 131
Aphrinia, Martyrs at 199
Aphthonius 76
Apollinaria 102
Apollinarius 188
Apollonius 93
Apostles, Synaxis of Twelve 172
Apostles, the Seventy 102
Appolinius 177
Aquilina 138, 152, 166
Aquilla 179
Arcadius of Novgorod 54
Arcadius of Novotorzhesk 93
Arcadius the child 97, 111
Archippus 119
Archippus the apostle 49
Archippus the sacristan 49
Arethas 71
Arianus 93
Aristarchus 140
Aristocleus the Presbyter 169
Arsacius the Patriarch 65
Arsaida 132
Arsenius 93
Arsenius of Novgorod 50
Arsenius of Serbia 73
Arsenius of Suzhdal 151
Arsenius of Tver 123
Arsenius of Vologda 201
Arsenius the Great 152
Artemas 146
Artemius 68
Artemius of Grom 188
Artemius of Palestine 117
Artemon 132, 139
Assonus 130

Asterius 74
Asyncritus 138
Athanasia 64, 78, 112, 142, 150
Athanasia the abbess 139
Athanasius of Alexandria 196
Athanasius of Athos 175
Athanasius of the Pecherska Lavra 89
Athanasius the Great 107, 148
Athanasius the Patriarch 71
Athanasius the Persian 109
Athenodoros 91
Athenogenes 180
Atikia 132
Atticus the Patriarch 65
Augusta 84, 86
Autonomus 52
Auxentius 92, 117
Averky 69
Avimus 193
Axetria 139
Azades 84
Azarias the Youth 94

B

Babylas 48
Bacchus 63
Balirad 177
Barbara 90
Barbarus 150
Barisabos 51
Barlaam of Chutin 77
Barlaam of India 83
Barlaam of Vagnv 169
Barlaam the martyr 83
Barnabas 165
Barnabas of Betlus 112
Barsonophius 62
Bartholomew 165, 173, 201
Baruch 60
Basil 193
Basil of Amasea 144
Basil of Ancyra 131
Basil of Cherson 125
Basil of Parium 139
Basil of Pecherska Lavra 196
Basil of Turukhani 129

Basil of Yaroslavl 164
Basil the Confessor 121
Basil the Great 101, 112
Basil the martyr 101
Basil the monastic 64, 113
Basil Vsevolodovich 175
Basilianus 169
Basilisk 123, 157
Basilissa 48, 103, 169
Basilissa of Nizhegorod 133
Basilissa the martyr 140
Bassa of Pskov 116
Bassia 199
Bebaia 49
Bendemianus 113
Benedict 128
Benedict the monastic 113
Berenice 62
Bessarion 88, 163
Bibea 67
Bildad 150
Blaise 116
Boniface 95
Boris 148, 188
Buculus 114
Byacheslav 60

C

Caleria 164
Callinica 152
Callinicus 93, 188, 190, 199
Callinicus the Patriarch 200
Callisthenia 62
Callistratus 59, 199
Callistus 47
Capiclarius 126
Capitolina 72
Capitonus of Cherson 125
Carpus 65, 159
Casdoe 60
Cassian 122
Cassian of Nazomsk 167
Cassian of Uglich 157
Catherine 85
Celisi 169
Celsius 66

Cercyra 146
Chains of St. Peter 106
Charalampus 116
Charitina 63
Chariton 59
Charity 54
Chionia 140, 181
Chionia of Thessalonica 136
Christina 188
Christopher 152
Chrysanthus 130
Chryse 112
Chrysosgonus 97
Church of the Resurrection 52
Claudia 78, 131, 156
Claudius 74, 130
Claudius the child 162
Clement of Ankyra 109
Clement of Rome 86
Cleonicus 123
Cleopatra 68, 69
Condratus 127
Conon 124
Constantine 175
Constantine of Murom 157
Constantine of Smolensk 55
Constantine of Uglich 200
Constantine of Yaroslavl 164
Constantine the Great 157
Constantine the martyr 161
Constantine the youth 70
Constantine Vsevolodovich 175
Constantinople 153
Constus 174
Coprius 58
Cornelius 52, 69
Cornelius of Komelsk 156
Cornutus 52
Cosmas 141, 174
Cosmas of Aravit 67
Cosmas of Asia 76
Cosmas of Maiuma 65
Cosmas of Yakhromsk 119
Crescentia 167
Cross
   Discovery of 124

Exaltation of the 52
in the sky 151
procession of 192
Cyprian 62
Cyprian of Kiev 160
Cyprian of Moscow 53
Cyprian the martyr 127
Cyprilla 175
Cyrenia 76
Cyriacus of Jerusalem 73
Cyriak 148
Cyriaka 164
Cyril 92
Cyril, Apostle to the Slavs 117
Cyril of Alexandria 107, 164
Cyril of Astrakhan 130
Cyril of Catania 131
Cyril of Gortyna 49
Cyril of Jerusalem 130
Cyril of New Lake 114
Cyril of White Lake 165
Cyril the Deacon 134
Cyril the martyr 125
Cyrion 90
Cyrus the Unmercenary 112, 172
Cyzicus, martyrs at 146

D

Dada 146
Dadas 60
Dalmatius 193
Damian 174
Damian of Aravit 67
Damian of Asia 76
Damian the Desert Dweller 87
Daniel 94, 177
Daniel of Moscow 124
Daniel of Pereyaslav 137
Daniel the Stylite 92
Daria 130, 132
David 99
David, monastic saint 49
David of Smolensk 55
David of Thessalonica 171
Demetrius of Galich 57
Demetrius of Moscow 153

Demetrius of Priluki 116, 163, 186
Demetrius of Suzhdal 171
Demetrius of Thessalonica 72
Demetrius the Crown Prince 155
Didimus 138
Diodorus 189
Diodorus of George Hill 87
Diodorus the martyr 60
Diomedas 197
Dionysius 194
Dionysius of Glushetsk 162
Dionysius of Novgorod 62
Dionysius of Radonezh 153
Dionysius the Areopagite 62
Dionysius the martyr 127
Dionysius the youth 70
Dios 186
Dometian 62, 104, 125, 194
Dominian 63
Dominica 65
Domna 100, 122
Domnica 103
Domnina 62, 123, 131
Dorotheus 163
Dorymedon 54
Dovmont of Pskov 157
Drosida 132
Drosidas 150

E

Ecumenical Councils, Seven 181
Elasinus 107
Eleazar 192, 193
Elesbaan 71
Elespherias 170
Eleusippus 107
Eleutherius 93
Eleutherius of Byzantium 194
Eleutherius of Cherson 125
Elias the Thesbite 186
Elikidas 160
Eliphas 150
Elisha 166
Elisias 187
Elizabeth the martyr 70
Elizabeth the Miracle Worker 144

Elpidephorus 76
Emilian 186, 195
Ennatha 116
Ephraim of Cherson 125
Ephraim of Novotorzh 111
Ephraim of Novotorzhersk 165
Ephraim of Perekop 155
Ephraim of Smolensk 199
Ephraim the Syrian 111
Epicharis 59
Epimachus 74
Epiphanius of Cyprus 154
Epiphanius with Andrew the fool 61
Epistemis 77
Erasmus of Pecherska Lavra 121
Erasmus the bishop 165
Erastus 79
Eroteis 72
Euanthia 51
Eucharistus 82
Eudocimus 190
Eudokia 123, 164, 194
Eudokia the martyr 196
Eudoxius 49
Eugene 92
Eugene, holy relics in 120
Eugene of Cherson 125
Eugenia 97
Eugraphus 92
Eulampia 64
Eulampius 64
Eulogius of Alexandria 118
Eumenes 54
Eupater 82
Eupatius 167
Euphemia 131
Euphemia the all-praised 53, 178
Euphemiana 74
Euphrasia 131, 156
Euphrosinus of Pskov 155
Euphrosinus the Cook 120
Euphrosyne 78, 108
Euphrosyne of Alexandria 58
Euphrosyne of Polotsk 158
Euphrosyne of Suzhdal 58
Euplus 195

Eupraxia 188
Eupsychius 138
Eusebius 169
Eusebon 193
Eusegnius 194
Eustace 84
Eustathius 55
Eustathius of Lithuania 140
Eustolia 79
Eustratius 92
Euthymius of Archangel 108
Euthymius of Novgorod 128
Euthymius of Sardis 99
Euthymius of Suzhdal 136
Euthymius the Great 108
Euthymius the New 66
Eutropia 171
Eutropius 74, 123
Eutych 48
Eutyches 200
Eutychius 137
Eutychius the martyr 125
Evodus 47
Exacustodianus 194
Ezekiel 187

F

Faith 54
Fathers at St. Sabbas' Monastery 131
Fathers martyred at Sinai 105
Faust of Vologda 133
Fausta 114
Faustus 193
Febronia 171
Febronia of Murom 171
Felicitas 110, 113
Felix 203
Fifth Ecumenical Council 183
First Ecumenical Council 181
Flavian 118
Florus 198
Forefathers, Sunday of Holy 94, 95
Forty Virgin Martyrs 47
Forty Women Martyrs 70
Forty-five martyrs in Nicopolis 177
Forty-two Martyrs 124

Fourteen Thousand Martyrs 100
Fourth Ecumenical Council 183

G

Gabdelas 60
Gabriel the Archangel 133, 179
Gabriel the Prince 159
Gaiana 60
Galacteon 77
Galacteon of Vologda 58, 77
Galena 116
Gennadius of Kostrom 109
George 143
   Church in Kiev 86
George of Maleon 137
George of Mitylene 138
George of Novgorod 144
George of Paga 143
George of Vladimir 114
George the Chozebite 103
George the Confessor 154
Gerasimus of Boldinsk 148
Gerasimus of Perm 110
Gerasimus of the Jordan 123
Gerasimus of Vologda 124
Germanus of Constantinople 154
Germanus the martyr 81
Gerontius of Moscow 150
Gervase 66
Gleb 48, 188
Gleb Vsevolodovich 176
Glykeria 154
Glykeria the martyr 70
Gordian 52
Gordius 101
Gorgonia 110
Gregory Decapolites 83
Gregory of Agrigentum 85
Gregory of Armenia 60
Gregory of Crete 73, 103
Gregory of Lopotov 74
Gregory of Mastidi 131
Gregory of Nazomsk 167
Gregory of Nyssa 104
Gregory of Omerits 96
Gregory of Rome 128

Gregory of Suzhdal 95
Gregory of Vologda 60
Gregory Palamas 81
Gregory the holy father 53
Gregory the Miracle Worker 82
Gregory the Theologian 110, 112
Gurias 62, 81
Gurius 193

H

Habakkuk 89
Habib 82
Hadrian 141
Haggai 93
Helen the abbess 83
Herman of Kazan 78
Herman of Solovki 119, 132, 195
Herman the martyr 81
Hermeningild 76
Hermes 63, 138, 161
Hermes the martyr 161
Hermion 48
Hermione 48
Hermogenes 92
Hermolaus 189
Hermylus 105
Herodion 59, 79, 138
Hesperas 148
Hieria 171
Hieron 78
Hierotheus 62
Hilarion of Meglin 69
Hilarion the Great 69
Hilarion the New 133, 163
Hilary 178
Hippolytus 112
Hirenarchus 87, 88
Hope 54
Hosea 67
Hyacinth 174, 186
Hypatius 56, 81, 82, 135, 162

I

Ia 51
Iamblichus 194

Icon of the Theotokos
"Kazan" 70, 177
"Kolocha" 177
"Kolochesky" 178
"of the Sign" 87
"Okovyetsia" 178
"Ozurov" 47
"Pecherska" 178
"Smolensk" 190
"Theodorov" 197
"Tikhvin" 178
"Tolga" 195
"Umilenia" 46
"Ustyuzh" 177
"Vladimir" 170, 201
"Yugskaya" 163
Ignatius of Rostov 160
Ignatius of Uglich 156
Ignatius of Vologda 96
Ignatius the God-bearer 96, 112
Indiction 46
Innocent of Vologda 130
Irais 57
Irene 54, 140, 149, 154
Irene of Thessalonica 136
Irinarch of Rostov 87
Irinarch of Solovki 134
Isaac 193
Isaac (Izah) the Deacon 132
Isaac of Dalmatia 161
Isaiah 152
Isaiah of Rostov 155
Isidore 154
Isidore of Pelusium 113
Isidore of Rostov 154
Isidore the Presbyter 103
Ismael 168
Izah the deacon 132
Izoa 148

J

Jacob of Rostov 88
Jamblicius the youth 70
James 172
James Alphaeus 64
James, brother of John 147

James, brother of the Lord 70, 99
James of Borovichi 70
James of Kostrom 64, 70, 150
James of Rostov 88
James of Salim 141
James the brother of St. John 82
James the Confessor 131
James the Persian 87
James the Presbyter 132
Januarius 142
Jason 145
Jeremiah 148
Jesus Christ
    Circumcision of 101
    Icon "Not Made By Human Hands" 197
    Meeting of 113
    Nativity of 98
    robe of 178
    Savior 192
    Theophany of 102
    Transfiguration 194
Joachim with St. Anna 50
Joannicius of Melitene 140
Joannicius of Vologda 77
Joannicius the Great 77
Joasaph of India 83
Joasaph of Kamenny 51
Job 150
Joel 68
John 177
John Chrysostom 81, 111, 112
John Eukhatsky 57
John Kolovos 79
John Moavin 149
John of Belgrade 162
John of Constantinople 120
John of Damascus 90
John of Kazan 110
John of Lithuania 140
John of Moscow 163, 166
John of Novgorod 50
John of Rostov 48
John of Solovki 80, 162
John of Suzhdal 67
John of the Ancient Caves 142
John of the "Ladder" 134

John of the Pecherska Lavra 186
John of Ustiug 161
John of Ustyuzh 81
John of Yarensk 171
John of Yosyuzh 159
John Rilsky 68
John, son of Cleopatra 68
John the Baptist
    Beheading of 202
    conception of 57
    Head of 121, 159
    Nativity of 170
    Synaxis of 103
John the Child 97
John the child 111
John the Faster 47
John the fool for Christ 187
John the Hut Dweller 106
John the martyr at Sebaste 125
John the Merciful 80
John the Metropolitan 72
John the New 141
John the Patriarch 202
John, the Priest - Editor 161
John the Silent 90, 135
John the Soldier 190
John the Theologian 59, 152, 172
John the Unmercenary 112, 172
John the well-keeper 134
John the youth 70, 194
Jonah 56
Jonah of Kiev 160
Jonah of Moscow 135
Jonah of Perm 72
Jonah the archbishop 77
Jonah the presbyter 56
Joseph of Polotsk 51
Joseph of Thessalonica 111
Joseph the Betrothed 98, 99, 100
Joseph the Hymn Writer 136
Joseph the presbyter 76
Joshua 46
Jude 168
Julia 156
Julian 48, 115
Julian of Galatia 52

Julian of Tarsus 169
Julian the presbyter 52
Juliana 53, 76, 90, 96, 124, 131
Juliana of Murom 101
Juliana the martyr 198
Julitta 180, 191
Junia 155
Justin the martyr 162
Justin the Philosopher 162
Justina 62
Justinian 81

K

Karion 90
Kiriaka 176
Kiriakia 131
Kirrik 180
Kyriaka 157

L

Laria 130
Larion 90
Laurus 198
Lawrence 195
Lawrence of Koduzh 195
Lawrence the Recluse 112
Lazarus 67, 186
Lazarus of the Serbs 167
Lazarus the Faster 78
Leo of Catania 120
Leo of Rome 119
Leo the Monk 122
Leonis 171
Leontius 67, 168, 177
Leontius of Rostov 158
Leontius the martyr 125
Leucius 93
Licarion 115
Licirion 69
Longinus 67
Longinus of Yarensk 67
Lot 68
Love 54
Lucian the martyr 163
Lucian the presbyter 66
Lucianus 199

Lucillian 162
Lucy 93, 120, 175, 176
Ludmilla 54
Luke 68, 173
Luke the monastic 77
Luke the Stylite 92
Lupus 200
Lyubov 54

M

Macarius 108
Macarius of Kalyazin 129
Macarius of Kolyazynsky 159
Macarius of Zheltov 188
Maccabees 192
Macrina 186
Macrobius 52
Magegnus 154
Magnus 146
Malachias 101
Mamas 47
Mameltha 63
Mamontes of Maugis 133
Manena 81
Manuel 168
Marcellus 100, 193
Marcellus the youth 194
Marcian 71, 115, 179
Marcian the martyr 163
Marcian the Presbyter 104
Mardarius 92
Maria Golundukh 178
Maria of Patricia 195
Maria the martyr 165
Mariam the martyr 165
Mariamna 119
Mariamne the martyr 119
Marina 185
Marinus 94
Marinus the elder 68
Mark 144, 173
Mark of Arethusa 134
Mark of Athens 108
Mark of Phina 191
Mark of Phoenix 148
Mark the martyr 60, 72

Mark the monastic 124
Marobia 89
Marous 75
Martha 46, 115, 175
Martha of Levkada 188
Martha the martyr 165
Martin of Rome 140
Martin the martyr 95
Martin the Merciful 64
Martinian 117, 194
Martinian the youth 70
Martyrian of White Lake 105
Martyrius 71
Martyrius the Black Robed 107
Martyrs, 3,618 at Nicomedia 47
Mary 82, 115
Mary Magdalene 187
Mary of Egypt 136
Mary of Ethiopia 71
Mary of Yosyuzh 159
Mary the martyr 164
Mary the monastic 73, 117
Mary, the Mother of God
  Annunciation 132
  Entry into the Temple 84
  Falling Asleep of 197
  Miasena, Synaxis at 47
  Nativity of 50
  "Protection" 61
  robe of 174
  sash of 203
  Synaxis of 98
Mary the princess 130
Mary the prostitute 53
Mary the wife of St. Xenophon 111
Mastridia 86, 115
Matrona 78, 79, 131
Matrona of Thessalonica 133
Matthew 82, 172
Matthew of the Pecherska Lavra 63
Matthias 195
Maura 74, 149
Maurus 130
Maurusa 132
Maximilian 194
Maximilian the youth 70

Maximus 119
Maximus of Constantinople 143
Maximus of Moscow 80
Maximus of Urozh 196
Maximus the Confessor 109, 196
Maximus the Greek 109
Maximus the martyr 63, 73, 146
Melania 100
Melchizedek 157, 158
Meletina 54
Meletius 116
Meleusippus 107
Memnon 146
Menas 80, 92
Menodora 51
Mercurius 86, 190
Mercurius of Smolensk 86
Methodius of Constantinople 166
Methodius of Patra 169
Methodius of Penosh 167
Metrodora 51
Metrophanes 163
Mianus 48
Micah 196
Michael of Chernigov 55, 118
Michael of Klops 104, 169
Michael of Maleina 179
Michael of Murom 157
Michael of Sinnada 157
Michael of Tver 85
Michael Sinovtsa 190
Michael the Archangel 133
  miracle at Colossae 49
  Synaxis of 78
Michael the Councilman 95
Michael the monastic 119, 124
Michael the Soldier 85
Micheas 102
Micheas of Radonezh 149
Militon 126
Misael the Youth 94
Mocius 153, 186
Modestus 167
Molius 170
Moses 48
Moses of Hungary 189

Moses of Novgorod 110
Moses the Moor 202
Myron 198
Myrope 89

N

Nadezhda 54
Nahum 89
Naomi the martyr 165
Natalia 201
Nazarius 66
Nectarius the Patriarch 65
Neil Sorsky 151
Neon 60, 74
Neonilla 73, 74, 107
Neophytus 109
Neron 78
Nestor 72
Nestor of Pamphylia 121
Nestor the martyr 122
Nicander of Pskov 64
Nicephorus 81, 115, 128, 162
Nicephorus of Katabad 142
Nicholas Kochanov 171
Nicholas of Myra 90
   birth of 190
   relics of 152
Nicholas of Pskov 91
Nicholas of the Studion 114
Nicholas Svyatosh 66
Nicholas the martyr 125
Nicholas the Monk 98
Nicinorus 189
Nicodemus 175
Nicodemus of the Pecherska Lavra 74
Nikita 53
Nikita of Chalcedon 160, 168
Nikita of Medikion 136
Nikita of Novgorod 112, 147
Nikita the Stylite 158
Nikon 132
Nikon of Radonezh 82
Nikon the martyr 60
Nilus 80
Nilus of Stolbensk 91
Niphon 97

Niphont of Novgorod 138
Nirsus 66
Nonus 66
Nymphodora 51

O

Obadiah 83
Olga 180
Olympas 79
Olympia 85
Olympias 188
Olympius of Pecherska Lavra 198
Onesimus 118
Onesiphorus 79
Onuphrius the Great 166
Onysimus 179
Orentius 170
Orestes 92
Osee 67

P

Pachomius the Great 155
Paisius of Galich 187
Paisius of Uglich 164
Paisius the desert dweller 122
Paisius the Great 168
Paladius 111
Paladius the Monk 87
Palesitus 107
Pambo the Great 186
Pamphilius 118
Pamplia 64
Pancharius 130
Pancratius 143, 177
Panteleimon 189
Paphnutius of Borovsk 148
Paphnutius of Egypt 58
Papylus 65
Paramon 88, 119
Parasceva 131
Parasceva called "Friday" 73
Parasceva of Rzhevsk 66, 88
Parasceva the monastic martyr 189
Parmenus 189
Parthenius 115
Pasicrates 144

Patapius 91
Patrick 156
Patrick the martyr 68
Paul 172, 181
Paul Kornelsky 104
Paul of Galaidos 110
Paul of Thebes 106
Paul the bishop 51
Paul the confessor 77
Paul the holy fool 123
Paul the martyr 124, 198
Paul the New 202
Paula 116, 163
Pegasius 76
Pelagia 149, 193
Pelagia the martyr 63
Pelagia the monastic 63
Perpetua 113
Pesiotus 107
Peter 172
Peter of Alexandria 86
Peter of Kazan 110
Peter of Moscow 96, 200
Peter of Mt. Athos 166
Peter of Murom 171
Peter of Rostov 107, 172
Peter the martyr 105
Phaina 156
Pherbutha 137
Philaret the martyr 156
Philaret the Merciful 89
Philemon 84, 93
Philimon the martyr 146
Philip 81, 173
Philip of Irapa 125, 143
Philip of Moscow 63, 97
Philip the deacon 64
Philippa 143
Philippisia 142
Philitas the Senator 132
Philogonius 96
Philonuida 65
Philotheus the presbyter 53
Phocas 56, 187
Phocus 188
Photina 131

Photius 196
Photius of Kiev 160
Pilicia 85
Pimen the Great 202
Pitirim of Vologda 198
Plato 83
Plato of Studion 137
Polactia 78
Polycarp 120
Polycarp of Briansk 120
Polyeuctus 104
Polynaria 132
Polyxenia 57
Pompeius 138
Porphyria 193
Porphyrius 76, 79, 86, 118, 119
Porphyrius of Gaza 121
Pretorius 154
Probius 170
Probus 65
Prochor of Radonezh 50
Prochorus 189
Prochorus of Pecherska Lavra 116
Proclas 72
Proclus 178
Proclus the Patriarch 71, 83
Procopius 85, 121, 176
Procopius of Ustyuzh 177
Prosdoce 62
Protase 66
Proterius 121
Pudens 140
Pulcheria the Empress 51

Q

Quadratus 56, 127
Quartus 79
Quinctilian 146

R

Raida 54
Raisa 49
Ralius 71
Razas 71
Razumnik 92
Rebecca the monastic martyr 57

256

Rhais 49, 57
Ripsima 60
Roman of Uglich 170
Roman Olgovich 168
Roman the martyr 71
Roman the sweet singer 61
Romanus 83
Rufina 47
Rufus 138
Rufus the martyr 146

S

Sabbas 142
Sabbas of Kripets 202
Sabbas of Stromin 187
Sabbas of the Serbs 106
Sabbas of Zvenigorod 89
Sabbas Stratelates 144
Sabbas Stylite 61
Sabbas the Goth 140
Sabbas the Sanctified 90
Sabbatius 54
Sabbatius of Solovki 59, 195
Sabbatius of Tver 144
Sabel 168
Sabinus 129
Sadoc 68, 120
Sadoth 68
Salamanes the Silent 109
Samaritan Woman 131
Samonas 81
Samson 171
Samuel 199
Sarah 179
Scete, 10,000 saints 177
Sebastian 95
Sebastiana 54
Second Ecumenical Council 181
Selivan 150
Serapion 129
Serapion of Novgorod 129
Sergius of Radonezh 58, 175, 197
Sergius of Vologda 63
Sergius the Confessor 154
Sergius the martyr 63
Seven holy women 116

Seven Youths at Ephesus 69
Seventh Ecumenical Council 65, 185
Severian 50
Shemaiah 104
Siluanus 178, 190
Silus 190
Simeon of Novgorod 168
Simeon of Persia 141
Simeon of Serbia 117, 118
Simeon of Yurev 153
Simeon Stylite 46
Simeon the bishop 139
Simeon the fool for Christ 187
Simeon the God-receiver 113
Simeon the hieromartyr 54
Simeon, the Lord's relative 145
Simeon the Stylite 158
Simon 173
Simon the Zealot 153
Sisiniuas 169
Sisinius the Patriarch 65
Sisoes the Great 176
Sixth Ecumenical Council 184
Snadulia 76
Solomonia 193
Sophia 54, 190
Sophia of Suzhdal 54, 77
Sophonias 89
Sophronius the Wise 127
Sosipater 145
Sosipatra 79
Soson 49
Speusippus 107
Spyridon 92
Spyridon of the Pecherska Lavra 74
Spyridon of Vologda 90
Stachys 74
Stephanida 80, 100
Stephen 193
Stephen, King of Serbia 74
Stephen of Kazan 110
Stephen of Kubensk 145
Stephen of Makhrish 180
Stephen of Perm 145
Stephen of St. Sabbas Monastery 73
Stephen of Surozh 93

Stephen of the Jordan 105
Stephen Sabbaite 179
Stephen the Miracle Worker 133
Stephen the New Confessor 87
Stephen the Protomartyr 99
  relics of 53
Stratonicus 105
Svyetlana 131
Sylvester 101
Syncletia 71
Syncletica 102
Synesius 92

T

Taisia 63, 105, 132
Tarachus 65
Tarasius 121
Tatiana 105
Tecusa 156
Tecussa 78
Ten Martyrs of Crete 97
Terence 73, 138
Thaddaeus 199
Thalaleus 156
Thaumasius 146
Thecla 55, 57, 84, 165, 198
Theoctist 47
Theodora of Alexandria 51
Theodora of Caesarea 100
Theodora of Thessalonica 137
Theodora the Empress 93, 116
Theodora the empress 81
Theodora the Greek 100
Theodora the martyr 138, 160
Theodore Ivanovich of Moscow 118
Theodore of Alexandria 90
Theodore of Chernigov 55
Theodore of Edessa 165, 177
Theodore of Murom 157
Theodore of Pamphilia 56
Theodore of Pecherska Lavra 196
Theodore of Persia 142
Theodore of Rostov 88
Theodore of Smolensk 55
Theodore of Suzhdal 164
Theodore of the Studion 80, 111

Theodore Stratelates 115, 164
Theodore Sykeote 143
Theodore Sykeotes 167
Theodore the Branded 99
Theodore the holy fool 108
Theodore the Sanctified 155
Theodore Trichinas 142
Theodore Tyro 119
Theodore Yaroslavich 47
Theodorit 123
Theodosia 131, 136, 176
Theodosia the maiden 156
Theodosia the monastic martyr 153, 160
Theodosius 104
Theodosius of Antioch 114
Theodosius of Astrachan 61
Theodosius of the Pecherska Lavra 149, 197
Theodosius the Emperor 139
Theodota 54, 76, 97
Theodotia 175, 189, 190
Theodotia the martyr 70
Theodotus 123, 146, 155, 164
Theodula 108, 114
Theodulus 137, 148
Theognes 146
Theognia 199
Theognost of Moscow 128
Theoktista 79
Theonas 102
Theopemptus 102
Theopentus 64
Theophanes the Confessor 128
Theophanes the confessor 64
Theophile of Alexandria 177
Theophilia 160
Theophilus 187
Theophylakt 125
Theopistes 55
Theopistus the child martyr 55
Theostichus 146
Therapont 159
Therapont of Monza 92
Therapont of White Lake 118, 160
Thespesius 84
Thessalonica the martyr 78
Third Ecumenical Council 182

Thomaida 171
Thomais of Alexandria 140
Thomas 63, 173
Thomas of Constantinople 130
Thomas of Malea 176
Three Hierarchs of Moscow 63
Thrysus 93
Tikhon 167
Tikhon of Dukhovsk 167
Tikhon of Kaluga 139
Timolaus 129
Timon 189
Timonius 177
Timotheus 100
Timothy 109
Timothy of Prussa 165
Timothy of Symbola 120
Timothy the holy father 140
Timothy the martyr 95, 96, 149
Titus 201
Titus the holy father 136
Tricunaria Laria 130
Triphillius 166
Trophimus 54, 140, 187
Trophimus of Suzhdal 55
Tryphaenes 112
Tryphon 63, 113
Twenty Thousand Martyrs 99

U

Urban 170

V

Valentina 116
Valentine 144
Varisavus 51
Varlaam the martyr 83
Varus 68
Vera 54
Victor 78, 80
Viculus (?) 129
Vincent 80
Vitalius 129
Vladimir of Kiev 180

Vladislav 176
Vsevolod of Novgorod 116
Vsevolod of Pskov 87

W

Wenceslaus 60

X

Xanthippa 57
Xenia of Rome 110
Xenophon 110

Z

Zachariah (James) 132
Zachariah, father of the Forerunner 48
Zachariah the monastic 90
Zachariah the Prophet 115
Zakhaza of Constantinople 141
Zenobia 74
Zenobius 74
Zephaniah 89
Zinoida 65
Zophar 150
Zosimas 60
Zosimas of Palestine 137
Zosimas of Solovki 141, 195
Zosimas the martyr 55
Zoticus 100